Medical mishaps

Medical mishaps

Pieces of the puzzle

Edited by
Marilynn M. Rosenthal
Linda Mulcahy
Sally Lloyd-Bostock

Open University Press
Buckingham · Philadelphia

Open University Press
Celtic Court
22 Ballmoor
Buckingham
MK18 1XW

email: enquiries@openup.co.uk
world wide web: http://www.openup.co.uk

and
325 Chestnut Street
Philadelphia, PA 19106, USA

First Published 1999

A catalogue record of this book is available from the British Library

ISBN 0 335 20258 6 (pb)   0 335 20259 4 (hb)

Library of Congress Cataloging-in-Publication Data
Medical mishaps:pieces of the puzzle / edited by Marilynn M. Rosenthal,
   Linda Mulcahy, Sally Lloyd-Bostock.
      p. cm.
   Includes bibliographical references and index.
   ISBN 0–335–20259–4 hb. – ISBN 0–335–20258–6 pb
   1. Medical errors. 2. Medical errors–Great Britain.
I. Rosenthal, Marilynn M. II. Mulcahy, Linda, 1962– . III. Lloyd-
Bostock, Sally M.
   [DNLM: 1. Medical Errors. 2. Clinical Competence.
3. Malpractice. 4. Physician Impairment. 5. Risk Management.
6. Patient Satisfaction. WB 100 M48675 1998]
R729.8.M434 1998
610–dc21
DNLM/DLC
for Library of Congress   98–21881
                                                                     CIP

Typeset by Graphicraft Limited, Hong Kong
Printed in Great Britain by Biddles Ltd, Guildford and King's Lynn

Contents

List of boxes, figures
and tables

Notes on contributors

Judith Allsop is professor of health policy at De Montfort University. She has researched and written widely on aspects of health policy and complaints. She was a member of the Cabinet Office Complaints Task Force and the Wilson Committee on health service complaints.

Johan Calltorp is professor of health policy and management at the Nordic School of Public Health in Gothenburg, Sweden. His current research focus is the changing pattern of healthcare delivery and its organizational consequences in the Swedish health service. He is a member of the steering committee of the European Health Policy Research Network.

E. Jane Chapman is the clinical risk and medico-legal manager at Northwick Park and St Mark's NHS Hospital Trust. She is also chair of the Association of Litigation and Risk Managers (ALARM).

Marc Conradi studied psychology and medical sociology in The Netherlands. In 1995, he obtained his PhD with a thesis entitled 'Errors of general practitioners'. He presently works as a consultant in healthcare.

B.A.J.M. de Mol is a cardiopulmonary surgeon at the Academic Medical Centre of the University of Amsterdam and professor of safety science in healthcare at the Delft University of Technology. He is an expert in the field of risk and damage assessment, particularly in the area of healthcare.

Edward Dickinson is part of the Research Unit of the Royal College of Physicians where he is currently working on the new national clinical audits and the innovative Action on Clinical Audit project. Edward's projects focus on how care systems work and can be improved using lessons from industry.

Liam Donaldson is the Chief Medical Officer of the NHS. He was formerly regional director and director of public health for one of the eight regions of the NHS and professor of applied epidemiology at the University of Newcastle upon Tyne. He has published widely on health service, professional practice and public health issues.

Maeve Ennis is a health psychologist and lecturer in psychology applied to medicine at University College London. Her research interests focus on medical accidents and medical education and she is currently working on the development of a new curriculum for the Royal Free and University College London School of Medicine.

Lars H. Fallberg is a teacher and researcher in management, health law and European Community law at the Nordic School of Public Health in Gothenburg, Sweden. He is a member of the editorial board of the *European Journal of Health Law* and an expert on patients' rights for the World Health Organization.

Gary Fereday is a research and information officer at the Association of Community Health Councils for England and Wales, where he takes the lead on complaints work. He was previously at the Nuffield Institute for Health at the University of Leeds and was a researcher for Margaret Beckett MP when she was the shadow health secretary.

Robert Gibberd is director of the Health Services Research Group and an associate professor at the Department of Statistics, University of Newcastle, Australia. His research focuses on statistical methods to monitor the quality of healthcare, resource allocation and strategic planning models for hospitals in Australia.

John Hamilton is dean of the Faculty of Medicine and Health Services, University of Newcastle, Australia. He is a physician and chairman of the consortium for the Quality in Australian Health Care Study. He is interested in the implications of studies on the quality of healthcare for medical education.

Bernie Harrison trained as a registered nurse and midwife in the UK and is currently at Royal North Shore Hospital, Sydney, Australia. She is co-ordinator of its hospital-wide quality programme and was project manager for the Quality in Australian Health Care Study.

Raymond Hoffenberg was professor of medicine at the University of Birmingham from 1972 until 1985. From 1983 to until 1989 he served as president of the Royal College of Physicians in London. He was president of Wolfson College, Oxford from 1985 until 1993 and a visiting professor of medical ethics at the University of Queensland from 1993 until 1995.

Sir Donald Irvine CBE is president of the General Medical Council, an office he has held since September 1995. He is an active teacher and has written widely, especially on quality matters in medical practice, medical education and professional regulation.

Lucian L. Leape is a medical doctor working at the Department of Health Policy and Management, at Harvard School of Public Health. He was one of the principal investigators on the influential Harvard Medical Practice Study. His research interests centre on error in medicine and he has authored a number of publications on the topic.

Sally Lloyd-Bostock is reader in law at Birmingham University and a Fellow of the British Psychological Society. She has conducted extensive research in psychological aspects of civil disputes and legal decision-making, the regulation of health and safety and law and healthcare.

Linda Mulcahy is the Lawfords reader in law at the University of North London. For the past 11 years she has been conducting research into disputes in a medical setting. She has published widely on the operation of hospital complaints systems and has recently been commissioned by the Department of Health to evaluate its medical negligence mediation pilot scheme.

Vivienne Nathanson has been on staff of the British Medical Association since 1984 and is currently head of the Professional Resources and Research Group, whose remit includes ethics, science and health policy. She qualified in medicine at the Middlesex Hospital Medical School in 1978 and subsequently held various hospital posts in internal medicine.

Nicholas Nicol is a barrister specializing in public and social welfare law. He is currently in private practice at Staple Inn Chambers. He was formerly director of policy and research at the Public Law Project (1997) and a caseworker at the Southwark Law Centre (1988–91).

Susan Polywka received her law degree from Oxford University before qualifying as a solicitor. She is currently risk and litigation manager at the Oxford Radcliffe Hospital NHS Trust and coordinator of the NHS Mediation Pilot scheme in Anglia and Oxford regions.

James Reason is professor of psychology at the University of Manchester, whence he graduated in 1962. For the last thirty years he has been investigating how people contribute to the breakdown of complex, well-defended systems. He is a Fellow of the British Psychological Society and received the 1995 Distinguished Foreign Colleague Award from the US Human Factors and Ergonomics Society.

Jean Robinson is a visiting professor at the School of Health Sciences at the University of Ulster and a long-time campaigner on behalf of patients. She has been chair of the Patients Association, a lay member of the General Medical Council and was a cofounder of Consumers for Ethics in Research. She is currently an honorary research officer for the Association for Improvements in Maternity Services and a member of the committee of Action for Victims of Medical Accidents.

Marilynn M. Rosenthal is professor of sociology, director of the programme in health policy studies and director of the Forum on Health

Policy at the University of Michigan, Dearborn. She has published widely on issues around medical mishap and malpractice.

Arnold Simanowitz is a solicitor who was in private practice until 1982. Since then he has been the chief executive of Action for Victims of Medical Accidents. He is a member of the Department of Health Working Party on Medical Negligence. His particular concerns are the reduction of medical accidents and the accountability of the medical profession.

Charles Vincent is a senior lecturer in psychology at University College London. He has carried out research into the causes and consequences of medical mishaps for some years, recently focusing on the application of human factors methods in medical settings. He is director of the Clinical Risk Unit which carries out research and training in risk management.

Kieran Walshe joined the Health Services Management Centre (HSMC), University of Birmingham, in 1995. He has been both an NHS manager and a health services researcher, and his research, consultancy and education activities at HSMC reflect a continuing interest in both arenas.

Ross McL. Wilson is an intensive care physician and directs the hospital-wide quality programme at Royal North Shore Hospital, Sydney, Australia. He was the project director of the Quality in Australian Health Care Study, and currently is chair of the NSW Ministerial Advisory Committee on the Quality of Health Care.

Acknowledgements

The editors would like to thank all the authors in this volume for contributing to a lively debate on medical mishaps. Our thanks also go to Jennifer Spiegel who typed the manuscript and drew our attention to many inconsistencies and errors. Her professionalism is, as always, remarkable. We would also like to thank Jenny Dix for her help in organizing the conference at which the idea of a book was first discussed. Finally, we would like to thank Jacinta Evans and Joan Malherbe at Open University Press for their patience and understanding. Our thanks also go to the *Journal of the American Medical Association* which allowed us to reprint an article by Lucian Leape which appears as Chapter 2 in this collection. The editors would like to dedicate this book to Connor, Sam, Georgina, Alexandra, Madeleine, Kit and Alex, for whom we would like the world to be a better place but who have already improved it beyond measure.

Abbreviations and acronyms

ACHCEW	Association of Community Health Councils for England and Wales
ADR	alternative dispute resolution
ASRS	Air Safety Reporting System
AVMA	Action for Victims of Medical Accidents
BMA	British Medical Association
CCB	county complaints board
CHC	community health council
CME	continuing medical education
CNST	Clinical Negligence Scheme for Trusts
CTG	cardiotocograph
FAA	Federal Aviation Administration
GFT	general failure types
GMC	General Medical Council
GP	general practitioner
HDR	high dose rate
HSC	Health Service Commissioner
LMC	local medical committee
MARS	Medical Access and Results System
MRB	Medical Responsibility Board (Sweden)
NBHW	National Board of Health and Welfare (Sweden)
NBR	Medical Disciplinary Board (Sweden)
NCEPOD	National Confidential Enquiry into Perioperative Deaths
NFLIS	No Fault Liability Insurance Scheme
NHS	National Health Service
NHSE	National Health Service Executive
OECD	Organization for Economic Co-operation and Development

PA   Patients Association
PACE   Promoting Action on Clinical Effectiveness
QAHCS   Quality in Australian Health Care Study
RCGP   Royal College of General Practitioners
RCN   Royal College of Nursing
RCP   Royal College of Physicians
SPRI   National Planning and Rationalization Institute (Sweden)
UKCC   United Kingdom Central Council for Nursing, Midwifery and
          Health Visiting

Foreword

Richard Smith
Editor of the *British Medical Journal*

Five days after I started to practise as a qualified doctor, a colleague who had started with me killed a patient. I had admitted the patient: a young woman with pernicious anaemia, a treatable condition. We sat and chatted on a sunny Sunday afternoon. I liked her. She was admitted to have a sample of bone marrow taken from her breastbone, a minor procedure. When my colleague put the needle into her breastbone she collapsed and never recovered consciousness. It took quite some time for the senior doctors to diagnose that my colleague had punctured a major artery. Cardiothoracic surgeons were called from another hospital, but she died on the operating table.

My colleague seemed to 'cope', but it may be no coincidence that many years later his name was erased from the medical register for driving while disqualified and drunk. He had had severe alcohol and drug problems.

A year later I was injecting lignocaine into the arm of a small boy in order to anaesthetize his lower arm. An inflated blood pressure cuff should have stopped the drug entering the boy's body. After I injected the drug, a large dose, I realized that the cuff was not inflated. The drug went straight into his body. My blood ran cold. What would happen? Would this small boy die, killed by me in front of his mother? The way I felt then stays with me 20 years later, but nothing happened. The boy was fine and I was lucky.

A doctor friend told me a few weeks ago that the same thing had happened to him twice. His patients had both fitted. The conversation led on to other errors he had made recently. There were several, and they haunted him. He is a very experienced and highly respected doctor, but he finds it increasingly difficult to come to terms with the mistakes he makes. He talked as well of a surgeon friend, who had had two deaths in a weekend. One patient who died was the wife of a senior official in the hospital.

Every doctor who has practised medicine has made mistakes. Most have at some time made major mistakes and precipitated the death of a patient. It is 'part of being a doctor', and it leaves one feeling uncomfortable. Doctors who are close friends often talk about the mistakes they make, the mishaps that happen to them, but, as this book shows, medicine has found it difficult to accept the errors, study and discuss them, and find ways to minimize them. Why?

This book will tell readers a great deal about how many mishaps happen, why and how they happen, how doctors and patients respond, and about ways to minimize them, but I want to offer some preliminary observations from my own experience. My observations revolve around two dramatic insights that came to me in flashes.

The first occurred 20 years ago when I worked in a casualty department. I felt very unprepared for the work and would rise at 4 a.m. every day and read *The Casualty Officer's Handbook*. In retrospect, it was a poor book. Unable to admit that I was unprepared for the job (feeling that it was my fault, nobody else's) I muddled through, hoping that nothing awful would happen. Things went wrong every day, but I learnt how to survive. All the time I pretended to patients that I was in complete charge, well able to solve their every problem. That is what I thought was expected of me.

The moment of insight came when a colleague said one day as we looked at a radiograph of what might or might not be a fractured ankle: 'You know, you don't have to pretend that you know everything. Patients know you can't know everything.' I was stunned. What he said was so obviously true. How could anybody know everything and solve every problem? How, I reflected, did I ever get myself into the absurd position that I thought I was expected to know everything? But I was not alone. Somehow our medical education, or rather the process of absorbing the culture of medicine, gave us the idea that we should know everything. One result was that we learn to hide our ignorance. Yet education depends on people understanding, even celebrating, their ignorance.

Ten years later I was examined by a medical student when I was having a hernia repair. I did not tell him I was a doctor but asked if I could have the operation under a local anaesthetic. He spoke to me as to a fool and explained that it was impossible to do a hernia repair under local anaesthetic. I knew he was wrong, but he spoke with complete conviction.

Endless evidence shows that doctors are failing to absorb the most recent evidence into their practice (unsurprising when there are 20,000 disorganized medical journals), and yet many doctors, particularly hospital doctors, resent any implication that they are not practising optimally and might need any help with keeping up to date. Colleagues I work with had this confirmed at a focus group they held recently. Only junior doctors might benefit from a compilation of best evidence.

If you are taught to pretend that you know everything then it can be agonizing to admit mistakes and receive complaints.

My second startling insight came at a conference ten years after I worked in the casualty department. A representative of Marks & Spencer, one of Britain's most successful retail stores, told the conference: 'Complaints should be viewed positively because every complaint gives you an opportunity to do better.' Even though this was again stating the obvious, I was stunned. It had simply never occurred to me to see a complaint as something positive, and many doctors (and retailers) are, I think, still unfamiliar with this simple idea. Later I learned the ideas of 'continuous improvement', that 'every defect is a treasure' and that 'there are no bad people, only bad systems'. But many doctors react against the notions of 'quality improvement' and 'evidence-based medicine' because they resent any idea that what they are doing is of low quality or not evidence-based.

Now I work as the editor of a medical journal, the *British Medical Journal (BMJ)*, where we assiduously collect and analyse all complaints. We adopt a minimum definition of what constitutes a complaint. While jogging in Prague I fell in with a professor of cardiology who told me he never read the *BMJ* because we do not publish enough large randomized controlled trials. That is on our complaints database, and we have strategies to try and attract more large trials to the journal.

We even court complaints. 'The more you alienate, the more you reach', said Jerry Rubin. We like bold covers and think that we have pitched our boldness too low if nobody in our conservative audience complains. But I must not be smug. Journalism, even medical journalism, is very different from medicine. We do not deal with people's lives, minds, emotions and loved ones. Doctors do, and their pretence at infallibility is a *folie à deux*. Patients would like their doctors to be infallible, and so doctors try to oblige.

The point of these stories is to underline the central message of this book – that mishaps in medicine can be understood, approached and ultimately reduced only if considered in their cultural context. Systems engineers and statisticians cannot alone reduce mishaps in medicine. Doctors need the help of social scientists, and this book provides that help together with insights from many others, including senior doctors, managers and epidemiologists.

The book should help reduce the failure rate in medicine, which is probably at least 1 per cent – in other words, at least one in every 100 of the activities taken by doctors, nurses and others goes wrong. As the quality guru, W.E. Deming, pointed out: 'If we had to live with [a proficiency level of] 99.9 per cent [failure rate] we would have: two unsafe plane landings per day at O'Hare, 16,000 pieces of lost mail every hour, 32,000 bank checks deducted from the wrong bank account every hour.' Yet medicine has a 1 per cent failure rate. We must do better – and to do so we need the insights that this book provides.

London, February 1998

Part one | Mapping and understanding medical mishaps

Beyond blaming and perfection: a multi-dimensional approach to medical mishaps[1]

Linda Mulcahy and Marilynn M. Rosenthal

Introduction

When things go wrong with medical treatment it affects both those being treated and those responsible for the provision of care. The unveiling of medical mishaps can prompt strong reactions because it challenges the basic assumption that healthcare professionals heal or alleviate pain. Basic tenets of the relationship between patients and doctors are called into question and this can lead to a breach of trust, suspicion and anger. But despite the many incentives to avoid medical mishaps, plotting and understanding the incidence and causes of mishap is not easy. Nor is it a straightforward task to determine how the aftermath of a medical mishap should be managed. In this book we attempt to set out a range of issues which arise in response to these problems and suggest some ways forward. We try to reveal different pieces of the medical mishap puzzle, but we conclude that there are in fact many different puzzles and that the issues and priorities to be identified differ according to the perspective being adopted.

The management of medical mishaps is increasingly being seen as an issue of strategic importance by clinicians, managers academics and policymakers. Over the last decade there has been a burgeoning of initiatives aimed at identifying errors and improving medical practice. In the United Kingdom these include programmes in total quality and risk management, the use of confidential surveys and the development of risk-pooling strategies through the setting up of the Clinical Negligence Scheme for Trusts. Most recently the NHSE has launched a debate on how 'clinical governance' is achieved. Debate has also focused on the development of incident and 'near miss' reporting, evidence-based practice, safe whistleblowing, criterion based and significant event clinical audit and the publication of detailed guidance on agreed national standards (see, for example, Butler 1988; NHS Executive 1997). At the same time, management of health services has been strengthened and doctors have been encouraged to become involved in coordination and planning and not just the provision of services. More recently still, the powers of the General Medical Council (GMC) have been extended to allow wider investigations of doctors' conduct to take place, the role of medical education has been put under scrutiny and the ability of civil litigation to resolve medical negligence disputes has been reviewed (Lord Chancellor's Department 1996; see also Irvine, Chapter 14; Ennis, Chapter 12). All these projects seek to ensure that risks are avoided, adverse events rapidly detected, investigated and lessons learnt and that systems are in place to ensure continuous improvements in clinical care.

Despite these initiatives, evidence from a number of sources indicates that a substantial number of patients suffer iatrogenic injuries, a proportion of which are life-threatening or fatal. Using evidence from the Harvard Medical Practice Study (Brennan *et al.* 1991; Leape *et al.* 1991), Leape calculates that if the aviation industry had as many fatalities as the hospital sector in New York State there would be three jumbo jet crashes there every two days. Other studies reported in this volume, which adopt similar methodologies, even suggest that the Harvard figures underestimate the rate of mishaps (Leape, Chapter 2; see also Robinson, Chapter 22). They also demonstrate that medical mishaps are a universal phenomenon crossing international boundaries.

Despite the recognition that medical mishaps are a sizeable problem, the literature on them was sparse before 1990. Those studies which have been undertaken have tended to focus on the aftermath of mishaps rather than on their incidence and cause. A broader picture of mishaps is emerging, but slowly. We are only just beginning to understand the size of the problem and its ramifications. Debate is hindered by the fact that data and views about how to react to the issues come from diverse and often uncoordinated sources. In the UK audit and risk management in primary care have been especially fragmented and dissemination of results patchy. The development of primary care groups allows some scope for improvement but there are also fears that some primary care groups risk being ill-equipped for the job (Cook 1998). It is clear that we have some way to go before the shape, characteristics and implications of medical mishap puzzles are fully revealed to us. We see this as an area of complex and interlocking perspectives. The divergence of views can prompt the polarization of positions and act as a deterrent to wider debate. But conversely, appreciation of the different perspectives can enhance understanding and provide a basis for more effective action.

In this collection of essays we have aimed to bring together some of the best and most up-to-date research on medical mishaps as well as commentaries from those involved in the provision and receipt of care and the policy process. It is an important feature and strength of the collection that it presents so many voices. A number of different discourses and perspectives emerge from the collection which would not normally be considered within the confines of one publication. Some of the views expressed are controversial and many are in conflict, but all the contributors share genuine concerns about medical mishaps and all have something to learn from each other.

Debate on mishaps is not only being conducted in the UK and in medical circles. For this reason our collection reflects international and multidisciplinary perspectives. The book includes a number of cross-cultural, cutting-edge empirical studies, as well as attempts to document and prevent error within different jurisdictions. Contributors to this volume suggest a number of ways in which our approaches to medical mishaps, the management of disputes and the education of doctors must change. They also identify a programme of future work which needs to be undertaken if we are to be able adequately to address the issues raised. But the 'cutting edge' is only the beginning. The entire collection raises a new set of questions and a new set of challenges: How are the data collected on mishap to be used? How are the victims of mishaps best served? How do we deal with the realities of medical uncertainty and convey this to patients without destroying trust and hope? How do we improve data and data collection on the incidence, characteristics and causes of mishaps? How far should we extend notions of responsibility for mishaps beyond 'problem' doctors? What are the strategies and incentives for change? It is our hope that this book will act as a catalyst to further debate and in doing so begin to frame answers to some of these questions.

Mapping and understanding medical mishaps

This collection is organized into four main parts. In Part One contributors discuss the incidence and characteristics of medical mishap, and how they can be avoided. Leape makes it clear that not all iatrogenic injury is caused by error, and most errors do not lead to injury. But of the iatrogenic injuries which do come about most are due to error and therefore potentially preventable. It may not be realistic to expect that all errors can be eradicated, but they can be managed. As well as presenting the findings of various studies which demonstrate the magnitude of the problem, the chapters in Part One provide a number of practical suggestions as to how error can be avoided.

Vincent and Reason (Chapter 3) develop the discussion of the characteristics of mishaps and progress it by reviewing the underlying causes by reference to two case studies. They consider how those involved in the provision of healthcare should respond to mishaps when it is likely that they have been caused by factors other than an individual's mistake or lack of care. The focus of attention to date has been on blaming individual actors for untoward events and viewing them as the problem (see Allsop and Mulcahy, Chapter 9; Robinson, Chapter 22). Yet the cause of errors may be beyond the individuals' control and, as a consequence, systems relying on error-free performance are doomed to fail (see Leape, Chapter 2). The contributors argue that much can be learned from root-cause analysis in other high-risk industries and from human factors research and cognitive psychology about how to adopt a systemic approach to mishaps.

Efforts at error prevention have been hampered by a medical 'perfectibility model' which does not allow for fallibility and discourages a systemic approach to the understanding of mishaps. It is often assumed that if only doctors were properly trained and motivated then they would make no mistakes. When doctors err then it is blame which is used to encourage proper performance in them and others. Alternatively, the emphasis is placed on 'sick' doctors who have become addicted to drugs or alcohol and cause mishaps as a result. This goes some way towards explaining the barriers to the identification of systemic causes of medical mishap which currently hamper the efforts of managers (see Donaldson, Chapter 17). Another consequence of this approach is that complaints and claims have too often been used as a prism through which to understand, explain and react to mishaps. Part One of this volume presents a convincing case for replacing the emphasis on individual error with an emphasis on systemic failure.

An international perspective

In Part Two, researchers from the UK, USA, Sweden, The Netherlands and Australia provide accounts of how attempts have been made in these jurisdictions to identify and respond to medical mishaps. These contributors provide a set of case studies which indicate the failures and successes of managing error in different jurisdictions. A number of data sources exist which can be used to identify mishaps, including complaints, medical negligence claims, disciplinary action, claims for recompense under no-fault compensation schemes, audit programmes, incident reporting, recertification schemes, and continuous education schemes, as well as reporting of accidents and near-accidents. Some of the studies are based on survey methodologies and others on multiple research techniques. In each chapter these data sources are reviewed and appraised for the contribution they make to the identification of risk and mishaps in different countries. They help to reveal the incidence and characteristics of mishaps. They also demonstrate the methods which can be employed to reveal mishap.

Chapters 4–7 provide examples of what we suspect is an almost universal problem: lack of integrated data systems for the identification of risk and mishap. All the contributors describe multiple, overlapping and faulty mechanisms for the revelation, investigation and mitigation of error within and across countries. There is clearly considerable scope for greater collaboration, integration and coordination of data. Another common theme is the lack of organizational learning and wasted opportunities for this. It is hardly reassuring that a number of contributors conclude that the rate of mishaps in their jurisdiction is in all likelihood little better than that identified by Leape (Chapter 2). This conclusion brings its own risks. As we have reviewed these chapters we have become concerned about the extent to which such conclusions will facilitate complacency because rates of mishap appear relatively stable across jurisdictions. There is now widespread evidence of a sizeable and costly problem, but there remains much to be done to establish an effective response from policy-makers.

The escalation and mitigation of mishaps

In Part Three we focus on three main issues: first, the part complaints and claims play in the identification of medical mishaps; second, how those for whom medical care is provided may react to being the victim of mishap by making a formal complaint or legal claim; and third, how staff react to being the subject of a complaint or claim.

The link between medical mishaps and the expression of dissatisfaction is not straightforward (see Lloyd-Bostock, Chapter 8; Mulcahy, Chapter 11). As the Harvard Medical Practice Study demonstrated, the vast majority of adverse events do not form the basis of a complaint or claim. Conversely, some claims and complaints may arise where no errors or mishaps have occurred. It is clear, then, that complaints and legal claims are extremely blunt tools by which to identify and respond to mishaps and compensate victims, and that they encourage the propensity to individualize blame identified in Part One of this collection. It is only in recent years that an interest has developed in using complaints and claims data to prevent future mishaps, and integrated systems designed for this purpose, where developed, remain in their infancy.

It must not be forgotten that, unlike the other data sources outlined in earlier chapters, complaints and claims are unique in that they are patient-initiated attempts at revelation of mishaps. The civil justice system provides a financial incentive for patients and their carers to contribute to this process by bringing claims. Although this may not be the primary motivation for claimants (see Lloyd-Bostock, Chapter 8; Vincent and Reason, Chapter 3; Robinson, Chapter 22), it is clear that claims and complaints provide a unique type of external check on internal NHS management of mishap. They may not always amount to very comprehensive indicators of the cause and effect of mishaps. Patients may not always be able to identify error or may fear retribution if they make a complaint. But, where an error is revealed and compensation is due, they provide an important reminder of who is most affected by medical mishaps and the tragic consequences of some errors. They can also provide an antidote to internal complacency.

But do complaints and claims encourage the exposure of information necessary to respond effectively to broader quality issues? Incidents which are investigated in the course of responding to a grievance often receive intensive attention, but lawyers and investigators are not always interested in why the care was substandard and many facts which are pertinent to the cause may not be relevant to the presentation of a legal claim (see Vincent and Reason, Chapter 3). Most investigations remain confidential to the organizations conducting them and the majority of legal claims which are pursued are settled out of court and out of the public eye. However, it may be that elaborately reasoned court decisions have a 'ripple effect' on quality and risk management in the NHS which gives them an influence out of proportion to the small percentage of cases which reach the courts (Galanter 1983; Fiss 1984; Dingwall 1994). The same might also be said of the investigations of the Health Service Commissioner (HSC) although the House of Commons Select Committee has expressed some doubts that such a knock-on effect occurs as a result of complaints referred to the HSC. Indeed, the successive reports of the HSC have expressed dismay at the frequency with which the same examples of mismanagement of care come to be investigated and the lack of organizational learning which occurs. The chapters by Rosenthal and Allsop and Mulcahy suggest reasons why this happens.

Grievance systems attempt to perform a number of functions including redress and compensation. Their contribution to quality management is commonly seen as a hoped-for ripple effect, but their use for this purpose is akin to using a hammer to crack a nut. It may even be counterproductive. Doctors see complaints and claims, as well as management of them, as threats to their clinical autonomy and integrity. Grievance systems prompt both doctors and claimants to engage in identity building work which protects the validity of their account of what happens and seeks to undermine the arguments of the other side. While identity work of this kind is an everyday occurrence in all walks of life, it is clear that grievance systems serve to exacerbate the sense of dissatisfaction felt by patients and prompt a particular type of defensive reaction from professionals who are blamed. The result is that important data about mishap becomes hidden, ignored or clouded by the context in which it is examined.

We return to the central point that emphasis on the incompetent doctor shifts the focus away from the more fundamental questions posed by Vincent and Reason about systemic approaches to mishaps. This can give grievance systems an appearance of being unfair, of punishing individuals unjustly. Doctors are particularly concerned that generally competent and able doctors are being punished for discrete instances of sub-standard care while doctors seen to be incompetent by colleagues or system failures are not publicly exposed (Mulcahy and Selwood 1995; Rosenthal 1995). When individuals are seen as scapegoats this provides a further disincentive to effective participation in the investigation of grievances by professionals.

Dissatisfaction with grievance systems has come from a number of quarters including patient groups, policy-makers, service providers and members of the judiciary (Lord Chancellor's Department 1996). On the whole, these criticisms relate to how the aftermath of medical mishap is handled. Grievance procedures tend to encourage the polarization of positions, promote unsatisfactory settlement or abandonment rather than resolution of disputes, and result in a residue of dissatisfaction among the parties (see Allsop and Mulcahy, Chapter 9; Lloyd-Bostock, Chapter 8; Mulcahy, Chapter 11).

Can future initiatives mitigate defensive responses to medical mishap, its exposure, aftermath and management, or are these responses inevitable? In her chapter, Ennis (Chapter 12) explores the potential for education of doctors to prepare them better for the uncertainties and trauma of medical mishap and error and demonstrates the strategic importance of communication skills training. For Ennis, this is not an 'add-on' skill, but an integral part of being a competent clinician. Her literature review demonstrates how failures to communicate effectively can cause medical mishaps and reinforce once more the dangers of the perfectability model.

In her chapter on the Department of Health's mediation scheme, Mulcahy (Chapter 11) describes the piloting of a more conciliatory approach to the management of grievances. She reveals a tension between the need to pursue quality and the need for the individual parties to get effective resolution of their dispute, and suggests that an approach which encourages resolution rather than financial settlement may leave the parties less scarred. Unlike court based adjudication mediation allows for data on quality improvement and reassurances about future care to became part of a package of flexible remedies which can be offered to injured patients. Moreover, representatives from directorates of an NHS provider can attend and take part in the mediations and this in turn lessens the emphasis on individual blame while allowing claimants to present their grievances and concerns to those in authority. Given the emphasis being placed on mediation by policy-makers in the UK this is likely to be an important trend and template for the future resolution of disputes.

Views from the coalface

In Part Four we present the views of key players in the debate about medical mishaps who have everyday responsibility for protecting those in receipt of care and those who provide it. These chapters are shorter than others in the collection in order to facilitate the representation of a wide number of views. Their inclusion is an important feature of the book since dialogue between those 'at the coalface' and those who research and comment on developments in health service provision is crucial to well-informed discussion in the future.

What has become clear in our review of this part of the book is that there are three worlds, intimately dependent on each other, yet seemingly in entirely different orbits – those of the patient, the doctor and the manager. They cannot exist without each other, yet they are often filled with misconceptions, apprehensions and distrust of each other. Patients overwhelmingly want information, an apology and assurance that the mishap will not happen again to someone else. Doctors want respect and recognition that they have worked hard for the patient in an often difficult environment. They may perceive patients as ungrateful, even vindictive, when they challenge their professional expertise. The patient often sees the doctor as aloof, disinterested and inaccessible at a time when they are especially vulnerable. Managers are positioned across these worlds with loyalties to both.

The professional voice

Focusing on standards of care has been a concern of medics ever since they first emerged as a distinct professional group. Striving for competence and high standards has always been a feature of the organization of education, training and registration of doctors. Nathanson (Chapter 15) argues that the guidance produced by the British Medical Association (BMA) has consistently encouraged doctors to raise their standards of practice and urge colleagues to do the same. But recent decades have seen enormous shifts in medical mishap initiatives, and the chapter by Dickinson (Chapter 16) reflects the amount of change which has occurred. The development of medical audit, epidemiology, adverse outcome analysis, and concern about sick doctors have reflected the commitment of professional leaders to facilitate more effective performance (Royal College of General Practitioners 1985; Royal College of Physicians 1989; 1993; National Confidential Enquiry into Perioperative Deaths (NCEPOD) 1990; 1995; see also Nathanson, Chapter 15). At the same time, reforms of the NHS have been directed at promoting such initiatives and ensuring that value for public money is achieved through more intensive regulation of quality.

Disclosure of medical mishaps has also been framed in terms of the ethical obligations of doctors. Nathanson (Chapter 15) makes the point that much of the effort of ethicists has been directed at encouraging doctors to admit error without necessarily admitting liability. She argues that this reflects the absolute imperative for patients to be informed about what is happening to them. Part of the change which has occurred has been a general willingness to acknowledge that medicine has poor as well as able practitioners and that the profession has a duty to deal with the former.

Confidential enquiry reports of the kind pioneered in the UK have demonstrated that medics can and will cooperate in the collection of data on medical mishaps. Walshe (Chapter 4) suggests that these are the best and most encouraging examples of data available on adverse events and medical accidents in the UK. Although there are disadvantages to the surveys when it comes to being able to identify and react to individual instances of error and variations in the type of error reported, they are undoubtedly less threatening for the medical profession than claims and complaints and provide a way forward for the pragmatist.

But overall, the medical profession has been slow to respond to concerns about the levels of avoidable error (see Leape, Chapter 2; Walshe, Chapter 4; Rosenthal, Chapter 10) and more systematic consideration of the issue only seems to have occurred since it became compulsory to introduce medical audit systems with the 1990 reforms of the NHS. There has been a reluctance on the part of doctors to be honest about mistakes (see Nathanson, Chapter 15) although it may be misleading to generalize. Irvine (Chapter 14) reminds us that attitudes in the medical profession represent a broad spectrum of beliefs.

A number of suggestions are put forward in this volume as to why the issue of medical mishaps has not been given more attention. Leape (Chapter 2) suggests that the problem results partially from a lack of awareness of the severity of the issue. This may have come about as a result of the ways in which medical mishaps occur. The crashing of an aeroplane or the sinking of a ferry are immediately obvious in ways in which medical error is not. Medical mishaps may result from a catalogue of tiny errors, and even then an adverse outcome may not ensue. Moreover, medicine is an inexact science and those being treated are already suffering from disease or illness. It is not always easy to separate injuries caused by treatment from those caused by the condition being treated.

Many studies have documented the realities of uncertainty in clinical practice. These range from sociological studies to meta-analyses of autopsy reports (Fox 1957; Freidson 1970; Bosk 1979; Anderson *et al.* 1989; Barendregt *et al.* 1992; Rosenthal 1995). It is argued that from uncertainty comes the special ways doctors think about their work. This serves as the foundation for the special culture of medicine and the strong sense of collegiality and protection that exists among doctor colleagues. Medical students gradually learn that they are being 'trained for uncertainty' and doctors understand this in daily practice. Of course, the degrees of uncertainty will differ with the specialty, with the individual patient, as well as the circumstances and setting. Medical uncertainty derives from uncertainties in basic knowledge and technique, and uncertainties in the knowledge and techniques of the individual practitioner.

Notions of risk, therefore, are embedded in the daily practice of medicine. Risks are expected and unhappily endured as part of the nature of the work. A few may deny that these risks manifest themselves as mistakes at all (Rosenthal 1995). The very language that doctors use to talk about their work conveys this thinking. Paget (1988) documents the use of such forms as 'avoidable and unavoidable complications', 'going bad', 'the patient failed the medication', 'what are errors now weren't errors then' and 'normal mistakes'.

But a number of contributors also make reference to the culture of medicine and the part it plays in encouraging a reactive rather than a proactive approach to mishaps. In her chapter, Rosenthal (Chapter 10) draws attention to a professional culture that offers rationales, explanations and support if the doctor is integrated into a colleague network, as most are. She argues that there is ready-made sympathy and intellectual understanding that mishaps are an expected part of the job. Too often, retreating into this support network means withdrawing from patients just when their needs may be greatest.

But it has also been suggested that doctors and their educators have to take responsibility for the creation of a dominant image of the infallible practitioner (see Nathanson, Chapter 15), what Leape (Chapter 2) calls the 'perfectibility model'. Doctors may be trained for uncertainty but present certainties in their everyday work as a way of engendering confidence in patients and reinforcing their claim to expertise. Doctors are also social-ized to strive for error-free practice. As a result they may see error as a failure of character and often assume that every error is negligent. Perhaps the belief that all doctors are capable of perfection and that it is only incompetence or illness that leads to mistakes poses less of a threat than recognition that medical mishaps pervade all service provision. Leape (Chap-ter 2) argues that while the creation of high expectations is desirable, it can also create a strong pressure towards intellectual dishonesty, an incentive to cover up rather than admit. Those who are too forthcoming about mistakes make themselves vulnerable to increased surveillance, complaints, negligence claims, disciplinary action and a loss of respect among col-leagues. Donaldson (Chapter 17) sees a defensive stance as inevitable while a culture of blame exists.

This collection provides important accounts of the consequences of the 'perfectibility model' and the damage it can do (see, in particular, Allsop and Mulcahy, Chapter 9; Rosenthal, Chapter 10). It is clear that making mistakes and experience of the aftermath, such as when a complaint en-sues, can be painful and emotionally devastating (Ennis and Vincent 1994). While Leape (Chapter 2) suggests that medics become isolated by their experiences, other contributors to this volume reveal important informa-tion about the networks used by doctors in their search for support. But these networks are almost exclusively medical. Managers are rarely drawn into information and support networks. Doctors seem to be experiencing considerable unease about many of the new initiatives being introduced to deal with mishap, in particular because of fears that their clinical judge-ment and freedom is being undermined (Hurwitz 1998). There is a major barrier to be overcome here if we are to achieve a multidisciplinary and inter-organizational approach to managing medical mishaps in which doctors and managers work side by side and together.

The manager's voice

Managers occupy a position in which they are needed to bridge the worlds of patients, doctor and policy-maker, yet they are rarely the subjects of research. While they work alongside doctors in the planning and regula-tion of services, as public servants they also have an obligation to guard the public purse and respond rationally to patients' needs for healthcare services. The 1990 reforms of the NHS have altered the nature of managers' relationship with doctors quite dramatically, increasing the incentives for cost containment and for the introduction of systems which make the cost of the NHS and resources involved in service provision more visible.

The challenges facing managers are not just how to design systems for the identification and management of risk, mishaps and their consequences but also how to implement them effectively. The contributors to this book raise a number of important concerns about designing such systems and the development of methodologies for implementation. Effective risk management programmes require a considerable commitment from the key actors in healthcare organizations. Gaining the confidence of professionals is undoubtedly the greatest challenge facing managers. The most sophisticated systems will not be used unless they have the confidence of medics, whether involvement is considered compulsory or voluntary.

The patient

Finally we come to consider the needs and expectations of the most important people in the whole risk and quality management process, patients. This collection reveals how different such expectations can be from providers. Doctors are concerned that patient expectations of the healthcare system are unduly high and that as a result their demands are often unreasonable or their concerns misplaced. Here and elsewhere, mention is commonly made of the occurrence of defensive medicine, young clinicians avoiding certain specialties because of the higher risk of litigation, and the breakdown of a relationship which has traditionally been based on trust. This can culminate in an image of the 'greedy patient' (see Simanowitz, Chapter 19).

Representatives of the patient voice provide powerful reminders of the personal tragedy which can come about as a result of a mishap which leads to injury. The patient or patient's family are often distraught, frightened and angry in the face of what they experience as an unexplained mistake that could include pain, possible disability and even death. Unlike many of the other contributions, the emphasis in this part of the book is on the harm which individuals suffer rather than the organizational use which can be made of data on mishaps in the quest to provide good-quality care for a general population of patients. Few would disagree that such people must be supported in their quest for financial compensation if this can serve to alleviate the worst effects of a poor treatment outcome. Nicol (Chapter 21) complements these arguments by discussing the positive role that the law can play in the resolution of disputes, and in particular its part in enabling procedural safeguards to be put in place to ensure that the disputants are treated fairly.

Lloyd-Bostock's (Chapter 8) empirical research into complaints and claims serves to underpin many of the statements made by patients' groups. In her chapter she provides hints as to why complaints cast such a shadow over the discussion of medical mishap. Drawing on her background in social psychology, she conceptualizes the making of a complaint as breaking doctors' normative expectations of how patients should behave. She also suggests that it is the systems themselves which often exacerbate a patient's sense of grievance and that a breakdown in communication is a common cause of complaints.

In the absence of automatic reporting of injury to patients, an effective explanation of the consequences, or other systems for securing redress, complaints and claims are the only mechanisms which patients can use to force an explanation or compensation from a healthcare provider. It would appear to be significant that although a number of contributors stress the importance of openness with patients and the training of doctors in good communication skills, this rarely translates into an assertion that patients should be informed of avoidable harm caused by clinicians (but see Polywka and Chapman, Chapter 18). Yet this would seem to be an essential right of patients, especially since they are often ill-placed to discover iatrogenic injury on their own (see Nathanson, Chapter 15).

Concluding remarks

It is not our contention that providers of healthcare can ever obliterate the incidence of mishaps. The practice of medicine is an inherently uncertain enterprise and some adverse outcomes are inevitable. The same is true of error because as humans we are fallible and also because medicine is a stressful and risk-laden practice. But, as providers have increasingly recognized, mishaps can be managed. However, successful management is dependent on coordinated information systems and on data about the characteristics and size of the problem being regularly generated and reviewed.

The epidemiology of medical mishaps is underdeveloped and studies on the scale of the Harvard Medical Practice Study or the Quality in Australian Health Care Study (QAHCS) have not been reproduced elsewhere. When writers refer to a universal problem they tend to be guessing. There are many indications in this volume that much more research has to be done before we can really understand the occurrence and characteristics of medical mishaps, but we do seem to know enough to be clear that the problem is a sizeable one. Moreover, there are measures that can be taken to control and minimize mishaps. But lack of knowledge and attitudes can inhibit these positive steps. We need to understand much more about the impact of the structure of health service provision on mishaps, the reasons for variations between specialties and how medical audit operates and information is disseminated as a result of it. Understanding the features of the problems posed by medical mishaps is not an easy task, and involves an understanding of medical-scientific processes, features of treatment and specialties, and human nature.

There is no one simple or universal way to prevent mishaps, and adopting a systemic approach is complicated, expensive and requires a substantial human commitment to be made. This is largely because it requires providers to draw on diverse pieces of information. Management of mishaps involves formal internal organizational systems, such as medical and clinical audit, complaint and claims handling, adverse outcome analysis, incident reporting systems, risk management and quality assurance, epidemiological research and training and accreditation processes. A number of these initiatives are supported by formal external influences such as that exerted by the Royal Colleges and the ethical standards promoted by the BMA. Management of mishaps may also involve informal organizational or group activity such as gossip networks and the shaming and boycotting of colleagues. Finally, it also involves victim-initiated regulatory processes, most notably the making of a complaint or medical negligence claim.

A number of practical ways forward are suggested by this collection. Leape (Chapter 2) suggests that attention should be paid to each stage of the system and initiatives aimed at making it difficult for humans to err. He suggests that discovery of errors can be improved by efficient and routine identification and investigation, and that errors can be prevented by such factors as reduced reliance on memory, improved information access, error-proofing, standardization of tasks, training and identification of psychological precursors to error such as fatigue. In a similar vein, Vincent and Reason (Chapter 3) argue that account should be taken of task factors, team factors, situational factors and organizational factors. Investigatory techniques of the kind outlined are expensive, but so are the consequences of error in financial and human terms. Moreover, there is evidence from other industries that, on balance, such techniques result in overall savings.

It becomes clear in the course of reading the contributions to this volume that it is not sufficient to lay blame for medical mishaps in any one quarter. Like disease and illness, mishaps are a problem for everyone, and the consequences of, and responsibility for, them concern a wide range of people. Patients need to become stronger partners in the therapeutic relationship and to be facilitated to do this. Respect for the doctor's efforts can be combined with respectful and persistent question-asking. Encouraging and inviting openness is a two-way effort, particularly if patients convey an understanding of the risks that may be involved in their case.

Doctors have individual and collective responsibility for the care they provide. Problem and sick doctors need attention and action to remove them from practice or to limit their practice where appropriate. Allowing them to act as locums is not an acceptable solution. We also have to find ways to reduce mishaps in the practice of the ordinary, good and responsible doctors, who make up the overwhelming majority of the profession. Above all, there is a need to break away from the myth of perfectibility and to look at systemic as well as individual failure.

It is incumbent on leaders of the profession and senior doctors to guarantee better supervision of young doctors. Repeated research has documented their vulnerability to mistakes, because they are asked to work extraordinarily long hours, to do more than they are capable of and because senior doctors are not readily available to them. The public is sceptical of the attitude that says this is good training for young doctors. It is training at an awful price, both for patients and doctors.

There is undoubtedly hope for the future. The GMC has recently been granted stronger tools to weed out incompetence. Changes are also occurring in medical education (see Ennis, Chapter 12). Evidence-based medicine is gaining credibility in helping competent doctors to break out of inappropriate practices, and these initiatives are becoming powerful tools for change. As the profession builds more open relationships with patients, it needs to use its own empirical research systematically to improve diagnosis and treatment. Medical culture needs to change to incorporate a deep commitment to authentic, lifelong learning and self-scrutiny in the daily and weekly practice of medicine, using techniques that encourage learning from mistakes rather than rationalizing mistakes (Bosk 1979; 1986).

As we write, it is clear that the movement towards a centrally driven quality management programme remains firmly on the UK government's policy agenda. In its recent consultation paper, the government has given powers to a new National Institute of Clinical Excellence to provide national guidance, enforce healthcare standards and services which will be increasingly measured against evidence-based standards (NHSE 1998). In addition new clinical governance initiatives will require trusts to set up quality improvement processes and to ensure that good practice ideas and innovations are systematically disseminated through the publication of clinical guidelines, death rates after surgery are to be published for every hospital in England and Wales from October 1998. It is also expected that the government will introduce a Commission for Health Improvement to monitor the performance of trusts and, in extreme cases, allow the health secretary to sack trust boards. The Commission is expected to visit every trust every three to four years and to have special investigatory powers (Healy 1998). The NHSE's recent consultation paper on quality in the NHS sets out an ambitious agenda for charge which proposes greater manageral involvement in clinical quality and stronger central direction (NHSE, 1998; Walshe 1998). The consultation paper tightens the web of formal legal controls or quality by giving clear statutory responsibility for the issue on chief executives and NHS boards and its advice will carry semi-statutory force. Annual reports on clinical governance will be required of trusts from 1999.

Part of the impetus for these initiatives has been the enormous cost of medical mishaps. In December 1997 it was estimated by a healthcare information company that potential savings of at least £100 million could be achieved if hospitals across the UK improved their clinical performance (Chadda 1997). The case for radical reform has also been made much easier in the wake of the GMC's inquiry into the deaths of 29 children at the Bristol Royal Infirmary and the announcement of an investigation into the Kent and Canterbury cervical cancer screening investigation. These cases have given a fresh urgency to debate and raised expectations that changes will be made and that they will prevent repetition. Ironically the Bristol case provides a salutary reminder of the limited effect of formal regulation of medical work. Hunter (1998) has argued that the tragedy of the case is that sufficient evidence of what was going wrong existed for a considerable time and was known to senior clinicians and managers but not acted upon. It is clear that formal regulatory frameworks send out important messages and construct important avenues for information but that the existence of avenues does not guarantee their use.

In light of the data which are coming forward on the incidence of medical mishap, the level of concern about the issues has been woefully inadequate and the toughest issue remains using the findings to modify clinical practice. Many studies that have been replicated over the years point, over and over again, to the same patterns of error. Yet there is not strong evidence that the findings lead to improved clinical practice. The practice of medicine is hazardous, but the error rate in medicine is substantially higher than that tolerated in other risk-laden industries such as aviation or nuclear power (see Leape, Chapter 2).

It is particularly encouraging that within this volume there are new calls for an environment to be created in which doctors are able to be honest about their mistakes. There are compelling reasons for doing so which involve the basic assumption that doctors act in the patient's interest (Wu *et al.* 1997). If combined with a good relationship that conveys uncertainty without destroying hope, it can only strengthen the partnership of patient and doctor in dealing with medical problems. The energy needed to maintain this momentum is great and the efforts formidable. However, the goals are worthy and there is much at stake.

Note

1 One of the problems with bringing together a collection of this kind is having to cope with the huge variety of terms used to describe medical mishaps and related phenomena. There is no standard terminology to describe this field of study (see Donaldson, Chapter 17). Our title refers to 'mishaps' and many of the contributors also use this term, but our review of the literature revealed the use of a variety of terms including: error; negligence; incompetence; misconduct; deficient or substandard care; inadequate treatment; failure; mistake; impaired vigilance; complication; accident; adverse event; and adverse outcome. Of course, not all of the users of these terms are attempting to refer to the same phenomenon. Some of these words and phrases refer to a discrete event, others to its aftermath; some remain neutral while others attribute or imply blame. Researchers sometimes select a term which reflects the sort of study they are undertaking, or they might use the terms interchangeably.

It is inevitable that as our understanding of medical mishaps increases and matures, the language used will reflect the nuances between different sorts of mishaps. Leape (Chapter 2), for instance, makes distinctions between different types of error, including those which are skill-based (slips), those which involve rule- or knowledge-based error (mistakes) and latent errors or 'accidents waiting to happen' which involve system designs. Similarly, Conradi and de Mol (Chapter 5) describe how in The Netherlands doctors have distinguished between medical-technical errors, relational errors and carelessness errors (see also Vincent and Reason, Chapter 3). We have deliberately referred to mishaps in this opening chapter because it is less specific than many of the terms used and can serve to encompass them and broader debate.

References

Anderson, R.E., Hill, R.B. and Key, C.R. (1989) The sensitivity and specificity of clinical diagnostics during five decades: Toward an understanding of necessary fallibility, *Journal of the American Medical Association*, 261(11): 1610–17.

Barendregt, W.B., de Boer, H.H. and Kubat, K. (1992) Autopsy analysis in surgical patients: A basis for clinical audit, *British Journal of Surgery*, 79(12): 1297–9.

Bosk, C. (1979) *Forgive and Remember: Managing Medical Failure*. Chicago: University of Chicago Press.

Bosk, C. (1986) Professional responsibility and medical error, in L. Aiken and D. Mechanic (eds) *Applications of Social Science to Clinical Medicine and Health Policy*. New Brunswick, New Jersey: Rutgers University Press.

Brennan, T., Leape, L., Laird, N. *et al.* (1991) Incidence of adverse events and negligence in hospitalised patients: The results from the Harvard Medical Practice Study I, *New England Journal of Medicine*, 324: 370–6.

Butler, P. (1998) Wetting the whistle, *Health Service Journal*, 29 January: 12.

Chadda, D. (1997) Hospitals' poor clinical performance costs NHS more than £100m a year, *Health Service Journal*, 11 December: 5.

Cook, R. (1998) Picture in profile, *Health Service Journal*, 9th July, 26–27.

Dingwall, R. (1994) Litigation and the threat to medicine, in J. Gabe, D. Kellaher and G. Williams (eds) *Challenging Medicine*. London: Routledge.

Ennis, M. and Vincent, C. (1994) The effects of medical accidents and litigation on doctors and patients, *Law and Policy*, 16(2): 97–122.

Fiss, O. (1984) Against settlement, *Yale Law Journal*, April/July: 1073–90.

Fox, R. (1957) Training for uncertainty, in R. Merton, G. Reader and P. Kendall (eds) *The Student Physician: Introductory Studies in the Sociology of Medical Education*. Cambridge, MA: Harvard University Press.

Freidson, E. (1970) *Professional Dominance*. New York: Atherton Press.

Galanter, M. (1983) The radiating effects of the courts, in K. Boyum and L. Mather (eds) *Empirical Theories about Courts*. New York: Longman.

Healy, P. (1998) Ministers fall back on old pledges in wake of heart babies scandal, *Health Service Journal*, 11 June, 3.

Hunter, D. (1998) A case of under-management, *Health Service Journal*, 25 June, 18–19.

Hurwitz, B. (1998) *Clinical Guidelines and the Law – negligence, discretion and judgement*. London: Raddiffe.

Leape, L., Brennan, T., Laird, N. *et al.* (1991) Incidence of adverse events and negligence in hospitalised patients: Results of the Harvard Medical Practice Study II, *New England Journal of Medicine*, 324: 377–84.

Lord Chancellor's Department (1996) *Access to Justice*. London: HMSO.

Mulcahy, L. and Selwood, M. (1995) 'Being heard: Consultants' voices, final report', unpublished report. Oxford Regional Health Authority Clinical Complaints Project.

NCEPOD Steering Group (1990) *National Enquiry into Perioperative Deaths*. London: NCEPOD.

NCEPOD (1995) *Report of the National Confidential Enquiry into Perioperative Deaths 1992–3*. London: NCEPOD.

NHS Executive (1997) *Improving Outcomes in Colorectal Cancer*. Leeds: NHSE.

NHS Executive (1998) *A First Class Service: Quality in the new NHS*. Leeds: NHSE.

Paget, M. (1988) *The Unity of Mistakes: A Phenomenological Interpretation of Medical Work*. Philadelphia: Temple University Press.

Rosenthal, M. (1995) *The Incompetent Doctor: Behind Closed Doors*. Buckingham: Open University Press.

Royal College of General Practitioners (1985) *What Sort of Doctor? Assessing Quality of Care in General Practice*. London: RCGP.

Royal College of Physicians (1989) *Medical Audit: A First Report. What, Why and How?* London: RCP.

Royal College of Physicians (1993) *Medical Audit: A Second Report*. London: RCP.

Walshe, K. (1998) Going first class with the NHS, *Health Service Journal*, 9 July, 18.

Wu, A.W., Cavanaugh, T.A. and McPhee, S.J. (1997) To tell the truth – ethical and practical issues in disclosing medical mistakes to patients, *Journal of Internal Medicine*, 12(12): 770–5.

2 | Error in medicine[1]

Lucian L. Leape

Introduction

For years, medical and nursing students have been taught Florence Night-ingale's dictum – first, do no harm (Nightingale 1863). Yet evidence from a number of sources, reported over several decades, indicates that a sub-stantial number of patients suffer treatment-caused injuries while in the hospital (Schimmel 1964; Steel *et al.* 1981; Bedell *et al.* 1991; Brennan *et al.* 1991; Leape *et al.* 1991).

In 1964 Schimmel reported that 20 per cent of patients admitted to a university hospital medical service suffered iatrogenic injury and that 20 per cent of those injuries were serious or fatal. Steel *et al.* (1981) found that 36 per cent of patients admitted to a university medical service in a teaching hospital suffered an iatrogenic event, of which 25 per cent were serious or life-threatening. More than half of the injuries were related to use of medication (Steel *et al.* 1981). In 1991 Bedell *et al.* reported the results of an analysis of cardiac arrests at a teaching hospital. They found that 64 per cent were preventable. Again, inappropriate use of drugs was the leading cause of the cardiac arrests. Also in 1991, the Harvard Medical Practice Study reported the results of a population-based study of iatrogenic injury in patients hospitalized in New York State in 1984 (Brennan *et al.* 1991; Leape *et al.* 1991). Nearly 4 per cent of patients suffered an injury that prolonged their hospital stay or resulted in measurable disability. For New York State, this equalled 98,609 patients in 1984. Nearly 14 per cent of these injuries were fatal. If these rates are typical of the United States, then 180,000 people die each year partly as a result of iatrogenic injury, the equivalent of three jumbo-jet crashes every two days.

When the causes are investigated, it is found that most iatrogenic injuries are due to errors and are, therefore, potentially preventable (Bedell *et al.* 1991; Dubois and Brook 1988; Leape *et al.* 1993). For example, in the Harvard Medical Practice Study, 69 per cent of injuries were due to errors; the balance was unavoidable (Leape *et al.* 1993). Error may be defined as an unintended act (either of omission or commission) or one that does not achieve its intended outcome. Indeed, injuries are but the 'tip of the iceberg' of the problem of errors, since most errors do not result in patient injury. For example, medication errors occur in 2–14 per cent of patients admitted to hospitals (Lesar *et al.* 1990; Raju *et al.* 1989; Classen *et al.* 1991; Folli *et al.* 1987), but most do not result in injury (Bates *et al.* forthcoming).

Aside from studies of medication errors, the literature on medical error is sparse, in part because most studies of iatrogenesis have focused on injuries (for example, the Harvard Medical Practice Study). When errors have been specifically looked for, however, the rates reported have been distressingly high. Autopsy studies have shown high rates (35–40 per cent) of missed diagnoses causing death (Anderson *et al.* 1989; Goldman *et al.* 1983; Cameron and McGoogan 1981). One study of errors in a medical intensive care unit revealed an average of 1.7 errors per day per patient, of which 29 per cent had the potential for serious or fatal injury (Gopher *et al.* 1989). Operational errors (such as failure to treat promptly or to get a follow-up culture) were found in 52 per cent of patients in a study of children with positive urine cultures (Palmer *et al.* 1983).

Given the complex nature of medical practice and the multitude of interventions that each patient receives, a high error rate is perhaps not surprising. The patients in the intensive care unit study, for example, were the recipients of an average of 178 'activities' per day. The 1.7 errors per day thus indicate that hospital personnel were functioning at a 99 per cent level of proficiency. However, a 1 per cent failure rate is substantially higher than is tolerated in industry, particularly in hazardous fields such as aviation and nuclear power. As Deming (1987) points out, even 99.9 per cent may not be good enough: 'If we had to live with 99.9 per cent, we would have: two unsafe plane landings per day at O'Hare, 16,000 pieces of lost mail every hour, 32,000 bank checks deducted from the wrong bank account every hour.'

Why is the error rate in the practice of medicine so high?

Physicians, nurses and pharmacists are trained to be careful and to function at a high level of proficiency. Indeed, they probably are among the most careful professionals in our society. It is curious, therefore, that high error rates have not stimulated more concern and efforts at error prevention. One reason may be a lack of awareness of the severity of the problem. Hospital-acquired injuries are not reported to the newspapers like jumbo-jet crashes, for the simple reason that they occur one at a time in 5000 different locations across the USA alone. Although error rates are substantial, serious injuries due to errors are not part of the everyday experience of physicians or nurses, but are perceived as isolated and unusual events – 'outliers'. Second, most errors do not harm. Either they are intercepted or the patient's defences prevent injury. (Few children die from a single misdiagnosed or mistreated urinary infection, for example.)

But the most important reason why physicians and nurses have not developed more effective methods of error prevention is that they have a great deal of difficulty in dealing with human error when it does occur (Hilfiker 1984; Christensen *et al.* 1992; Wu *et al.* 1991). Their reasons are to be found in the culture of medical practice.

Physicians are socialized in medical school and residency to strive for error-free practice (Hilfiker 1984). There is a powerful emphasis on perfection, both in diagnosis and treatment. In everyday hospital practice, the message is equally clear: mistakes are unacceptable. Physicians are expected to function without error, an expectation that physicians translate into the need to be infallible. One result is that physicians, not unlike test pilots, come to view an error as a failure of character – you weren't careful enough, you didn't try hard enough. This kind of thinking lies behind a common reaction by physicians: 'How can there be an error without negligence?'

Cultivating a norm of high standards is, of course, highly desirable. It is the counterpart of another fundamental goal of medical education: developing the physician's sense of responsibility for the patient. If you are responsible for everything that happens to the patient, it follows that you are responsible for any errors that occur. While the logic may be sound, the conclusion is absurd, because physicians do not have the power to control all aspects of patient care (Berwick 1989b). Nonetheless, the sense of duty to perform faultlessly is strongly internalized.

Role models in medical education reinforce the concept of infallibility. The young physician's teachers are largely specialists, experts in their fields, and authorities. Authorities are not supposed to err. It has been suggested that this need to be infallible creates a strong pressure to intellectual dishonesty, to cover up mistakes rather than to admit them (McIntyre and Popper 1989). The organization of medical practice, particularly in the hospital, perpetuates these norms. Errors are rarely admitted or discussed among physicians in private practice. Physicians typically feel, not without reason, that admission of error will lead to censure or increased surveillance, or, worse, that their colleagues will regard them as incompetent or careless. Far better to conceal a mistake or, if that is impossible, to try to shift the blame on to another, even the patient.

Yet physicians are emotionally devastated by serious mistakes that harm or kill patients (Hilfiker 1984; Christensen *et al.* 1992; Wu *et al.* 1991). Almost every physician who cares for patients has had that experience, usually more than once. The emotional impact is often profound, typically a mixture of fear, guilt, anger, embarrassment and humiliation. However, as Christensen *et al.* (1992) note, physicians are typically isolated by their emotional response; seldom is there a process to evaluate the circumstances of a mistake and to provide support and emotional healing for the fallible physician. Wu *et al.* (1991) found that only half of house officers discussed their most significant mistakes with attending physicians.

Thus, although the individual may learn from a mistake and change practice patterns accordingly, the adjustment often takes place in a vacuum. Lessons learnt are shared privately, if at all, and external objective evaluation of what went wrong often does not occur. As Hilfiker (1984) points out: 'We see the horror of our own mistakes, yet we are given no permission to deal with their enormous emotional impact. . . . The medical profession simply has no place for its mistakes.' Rosenthal explores the ways in which doctors react to mistakes in more depth in Chapter 10 of this collection.

Finally, the realities of the malpractice threat provide strong incentives against disclosure or investigation of mistakes. Even a minor error can place the physician's entire career in jeopardy if it results in a serious bad outcome. It is hardly surprising that a physician might hesitate to reveal an error to either the patient or hospital authorities or to expose a colleague to similar devastation for a single mistake.

The paradox is that although the standard of medical practice is perfection – error-free patient care – all physicians recognize that mistakes are inevitable. Most would like to examine their mistakes and learn from them. From an emotional standpoint, they need the support and understanding of their colleagues and patients when they make mistakes. Yet, they are denied both insight and support by misguided concepts of infallibility and by fear: fear of embarrassment by colleagues, fear of patient reaction, and fear of litigation. Although the notion of infallibility fails the reality test, the fears are well grounded.

The medical approach to error prevention

Efforts at error prevention in medicine have characteristically followed what might be called the perfectibility model: if physicians and nurses could be properly trained and motivated, then they would make no mistakes. The methods used to achieve this goal are training and punishment. Training is directed towards teaching people to do the right thing. In nursing, rigid adherence to protocols is emphasized. In medicine, the emphasis is less on rules and more on knowledge.

Punishment is through social opprobrium or peer disapproval. The professional cultures of medicine and nursing typically use blame to encourage proper performance. Errors are regarded as someone's fault, caused by a lack of sufficient attention or, worse, lack of caring enough to make sure you are correct. Punishment for egregious (negligent) errors is primarily (and capriciously) meted out through the malpractice tort litigation system.

Students of error and human performance reject this formulation. While the proximal error leading to an accident is, in fact, usually a 'human error', the causes of that error are often well beyond the individual's control. All humans err frequently. Systems that rely on error-free performance are doomed to fail.

The medical approach to error prevention is also reactive. Errors are usually discovered only when there is an incident – an untoward effect on or injury to the patient. Corrective measures are then directed towards preventing a recurrence of a similar error, often by attempting to prevent *that* individual from making a repeat error. Seldom are underlying causes explored.

For example, if a nurse gives a medication to the wrong patient, a typical response would be exhortation or training in double-checking the identity of both patient and drug before administration. Although it might be noted that the nurse was distracted because of an unusually large case load, it is unlikely that serious attention would be given to evaluating overall work assignments or to determining if large case loads have contributed to other kinds of errors.

It is even less likely that questions would be raised about the wisdom of a system for dispensing medications in which safety is contingent on inspection by an individual at the end point of use. Reliance on inspection as a mechanism of quality control was discredited long ago in industry (Berwick 1989b; Deming 1982). A simple procedure, such as the use of bar coding like that used at supermarket counters, would probably be more effective in this situation. More imaginative solutions could easily be found – if it were recognized that both systems and individuals contribute to the problem.

It seems clear, and it is the thesis of this chapter, that if physicians nurses, pharmacists and administrators are to succeed in reducing errors in hospital care, they will need to change fundamentally the way they think about errors and why they occur. Fortunately, a great deal has been learned about error prevention in other disciplines, information that is relevant to the hospital practice of medicine.

Lessons from psychological and human factors research

The subject of human error has long fascinated psychologists and others, but both the development of theory and the pace of empirical research accelerated in response to the dramatic technological advances that occurred during and after World War II (Reason 1992). These theory development and research activities followed two parallel and intersecting paths: human factors research and cognitive psychology.

Human factor specialists, mostly engineers, have been largely concerned with the design of the man–machine interface in complex environments such as airplane cockpits and nuclear power plant control rooms. Cognitive psychologists have concentrated on developing models of human cognition that they have subjected to empirical testing. Lessons from both spheres of observation have greatly deepened our understanding of mental functioning. We now have reasonably coherent theories of why humans err, and a great deal has been learned about how to design work environments to minimize the occurrence of errors and limit their consequences.

A theory of cognition

Most errors result from aberrations in mental functioning. Thus, to understand why errors occur we must first understand normal cognition. Although many theories have been espoused, and experts disagree, a unitary framework has been proposed by Reason (1992; see also Vincent and Reason, Chapter 3) that captures the main themes of cognitive theory and is consistent with empirical observation. It goes as follows.

Much of mental functioning is automatic, rapid and effortless. A person can leave home, enter and start the car, drive to work, park, and enter the office without devoting much conscious thought to any of the hundreds of manoeuvres and decisions that this complex set of actions requires. This automatic and unconscious processing is possible because we carry a vast array of mental models, *schemata* in psychological jargon, that are 'expert' on some minute recurrent aspect of our world. These schemata operate briefly when required, processing information rapidly, in parallel and without conscious effort. Schemata are activated by conscious thought or sensory inputs; functioning thereafter is automatic.

In addition to this automatic unconscious processing, called the *schematic control mode*, cognitive activities can be conscious and controlled. This *attentional control mode* or conscious thought is used for problem-solving as well as to monitor automatic function. The attentional control mode is called into play when we confront a problem, either *de novo* or as a result of failures of the schematic control mode. In contrast to the rapid parallel processing of the schematic control mode, processing in the attentional control mode is slow, sequential, effortful and difficult to sustain.

Rasmussen and Jensen (1974) describe a model of performance based on this concept of cognition that is particularly well suited for error analysis. They classify human performance into three levels: (1) skill-based, which is patterns of thought and action that are governed by stored patterns of pre-programmed instructions (schemata) and largely unconscious; (2) rule-based, in which solutions to familiar problems are governed by stored rules of the 'if X, then Y' variety; and (3) knowledge-based, or synthetic thought, which is used for novel situations requiring conscious analytic processing and stored knowledge.

Any departure from routine – a problem – requires a rule-based or knowledge-based solution. Humans prefer pattern recognition to calculation, so they are strongly biased to search for a pre-packaged solution – a 'rule' – before resorting to more strenuous knowledge-based functioning.

Although all three levels may be used simultaneously, with increasing expertise the primary focus of control moves from knowledge-based towards skill-based functioning. Experts have a much larger repertoire of schemata and problem-solving rules than novices, and they are formulated at a more abstract level. In one sense, expertise means seldom having to resort to knowledge-based functioning (reasoning).

Mechanisms of cognitive errors

Errors have been classified by Reason (1992) and Rassmussen and Jensen (1974) at each level of the skill-, rule- and knowledge-based model. Skill-based errors are called *slips*. These are unconscious glitches in automatic activity. Slips are errors of action. Rule-based and knowledge-based errors, by contrast, are errors of conscious thought and are termed *mistakes*. The mechanisms of error vary with the level.

Slips

Skill-based activity is automatic. A slip occurs when there is a break in the routine while attention is diverted. The actor possesses the requisite routines; errors occur because of a lack of a timely attentional check. In brief, slips are monitoring failures. They are unintended acts.

A common mechanism of a slip is *capture*, in which a more frequently used schema takes over from a similar but less familiar one. For example, if the usual action sequence is ABCDE, but on this occasion the planned sequence changes to ABCFG, then conscious attention must be in force after C or the more familiar pattern DE will be executed. An everyday example is departing on a trip in which the first part of the journey is the same as a familiar commuting path and driving to work instead of to the new location.

Another type of slip is a *description error*, in which the right action is performed on the wrong object, such as pouring cream on a pancake. *Associative activation errors* result from mental associations of ideas, such as answering the phone when the doorbell rings. *Loss of activation errors* are temporary memory losses, such as entering a room and no longer remembering why you wanted to go there. Loss of activation errors are frequently caused by interruptions.

A variety of factors can divert attentional control and make slips more likely. Physiological factors include fatigue, sleep loss, alcohol, drugs and illness. Psychological factors include other activity ('busyness'), as well as emotional states such as boredom, frustration, fear, anxiety or anger. All these factors lead to preoccupations that divert attention. Psychological factors, though considered 'internal' or endogenous, may also be caused by a host of external factors, such as overwork, interpersonal relations, and many other forms of stress. Environmental factors, such as noise, heat, visual stimuli, motion and other physical phenomena, also can cause distractions that divert attention and lead to slips.

Mistakes

Rule-based errors usually occur during problem-solving when a wrong rule is chosen – either because of a misperception of the situation and, thus, the application of a wrong rule, or because of misapplication of a rule, usually one that is strong (frequently used), that seems to fit adequately. Errors result from misapplied expertise.

Knowledge-based errors are much more complex. The problem-solver confronts a novel situation for which he or she possess no preprogrammed solutions. Errors arise because of the lack of knowledge or misinterpretation of the problem. Pattern matching is preferred to calculation, but sometimes we match the wrong patterns. Certain habits of thought have been identified that alter pattern matching or calculation and lead to mistakes. These processes are incompletely understood and are seldom recognized by the actor. One such process is *biased memory*. Decisions are based on what is in our memory, but memory is biased towards overgeneralization and overregularization of the commonplace (Norman 1984). Familiar patterns are assumed to have universal applicability because they usually work. We see what we know. Paradoxically, memory is also biased towards overemphasis on the discrepant. A contradictory experience may leave an exaggerated impression far outweighing its statistical importance (for example, the exceptional case or missed diagnosis).

Another mechanism is the *availability heuristic* (Tversky and Kahneman 1981), the tendency to use the first information that comes to mind. Related are *confirmation bias*, the tendency to look for evidence that supports an early working hypothesis and to ignore data that contradict it, and *overconfidence*, the tendency to believe in the validity of the chosen course of action and to focus on evidence that favours it (Reason 1992).

Rule-based and knowledge-based functioning are affected by the same physiological, psychological and environmental influences that produce slips. A great deal of research has been devoted to the effects of stress on performance. Although it is often difficult to establish causal links between stress and specific accidents, there is little question that errors (both slips and mistakes) are increased under stress. On the other hand, stress is not all bad. It has long been known that 'a little anxiety improves performance'. Yerkes and Dodson (1908) showed that performance is best at moderate levels of arousal. Poor performance occurs at both extremes: boredom and panic (Allnutt 1987). *Coning of attention* under stress is the tendency in an emergency to concentrate on one single source of information, the 'first come, best preferred' solution (Allnutt 1987). (A classic example is the phenomenon of passengers in a crashed aircraft struggling to open a door while ignoring a large hole in the fuselage a few feet away.) *Reversion under stress* is a phenomenon in which recently learned behavioural patterns are replaced by older, more familiar ones, even if they are inappropriate in the circumstances (Allnutt 1987).

The complex nature of cognition, the vagaries of the physical world, and the inevitable shortages of information and schemata ensure that normal humans make multiple errors every day. Slips are most common, since much of our mental functioning is automatic, but the rate of error in knowledge-based processes is higher (Reason 1992).

Latent errors

In 1979, the Three Mile Island incident caused both psychologists and human factors engineers to re-examine their theories about human error. Although investigations revealed the expected operator errors, it was clear that prevention of many of these errors was beyond the capabilities of the human operators at the time. Many errors were caused by faulty interface design, others by complex interactions and breakdowns that were not discernible by the operators or their instruments. The importance of poor system design as a cause of failures in complex processes became more apparent (Perrow 1984). Subsequent disasters, notably Bhopal and Chernobyl, made it even clearer that operator errors were only part of the explanation of failures in complex systems. Disasters of this magnitude resulted from major failures of design and organization that occurred long before the accident, failures that both caused operator errors and made them impossible to reverse (Reason 1992; Perrow 1984).

Reason (1992) has called these *latent errors*, errors that have effects that are delayed, 'accidents waiting to happen', in contrast to active errors, which have effects that are felt immediately. While an operator error may be the proximal 'cause' of the accident, the root causes were often present within the system for a long time. The operator has, in a real sense, been 'set up' to fail by poor design, faulty maintenance or erroneous management decisions.

Faulty design at Three Mile Island provided gauges that gave a low pressure reading both when pressure was low and when the gauge was not working, and a control panel on which 100 warning lights flashed simultaneously. Faulty maintenance disabled a safety back-up system so the operator could not activate it when needed. Similarly, bad management decisions can result in unrealistic workloads, inadequate training and demanding production schedules that lead workers to make errors.

Accidents rarely result from a single error, latent or active (Reason 1992; Perrow 1984). System defences and the abilities of frontline operators to identify and correct errors before an accident occurs make single-error accidents highly unlikely. Rather, accidents typically result from a combination of latent and active errors and breach of defences. The precipitating event can be a relatively trivial malfunction or an external circumstance, such as the weather (as in the case of the freezing of O-rings that caused the *Challenger* disaster).

The most important result of latent errors may be the production of psychological precursors, which are pathologic situations that create working conditions that predispose to a variety of errors (Reason 1992). Inappropriate work schedules, for example, can result in high workloads and undue time pressures that induce errors. Poor training can lead to inadequate recognition of hazards or inappropriate procedures that lead to accidents. Conversely, a precursor can be the product of more than one management or training failure. For example, excessive time pressure can result from poor scheduling, but it can also be the product of inadequate training or faulty division of responsibilities. Because they can affect all cognitive processes, these precursors can cause an immense variety of errors that result in unsafe acts.

The important point is that successful accident prevention efforts must focus on root causes – system errors in design and implementation. It is futile to concentrate on developing solutions to the unsafe acts themselves. Other errors, unpredictable and infinitely varied, will soon occur if the underlying cause is uncorrected. Although correcting root causes will not eliminate all errors – individuals still bring varying abilities and work habits to the workplace – it can significantly reduce the probability of errors occurring.

Prevention of accidents

The multiplicity of mechanisms and causes of errors (internal and external, individual and systemic) dictates that there cannot be a simple or universal means of reducing errors. Creating a safe process, whether it be flying an airplane, running a hospital, or performing cardiac surgery, requires attention to methods of error reduction at each stage of system development: design, construction, maintenance, allocation of resources, training, and development of operational procedures. This type of attention to error reduction requires responsible individuals at each stage to think through the consequences of their decisions and to reason back from discovered deficiencies to redesign and reorganize the process. Systemic changes are most likely to be successful because they reduce the likelihood of a variety of types of errors at the end-user stage.

The primary objective of system design for safety is to make it difficult for individuals to err. But it is also important to recognize that errors will inevitably occur and plan for their recovery (Reason 1992). Ideally, the system will automatically correct errors when they occur. If that is impossible, mechanisms should be in place to detect errors at least in time for corrective action. Therefore, in addition to designing the work environment to minimize psychological precursors, designers should provide feedback through instruments that provide monitoring functions and build in buffers and redundancy. Buffers are design features that automatically correct for human or mechanical errors. Redundancy is duplication (sometimes triplication or quadruplication) of critical mechanisms and instruments, so that a failure does not result in loss of the function.

Another important system design feature is designing tasks to minimize errors. Norman (1984) has recommended a set of principles that have general applicability. Tasks should be *simplified* to minimize the load on the weakest aspects of cognition: short-term memory, planning, and problem-solving. The power of *constraints* should be exploited. One way to do this is with 'forcing functions', which make it impossible to act without meeting a precondition (such as the inability to release the parking gear of a car unless the brake pedal is depressed). *Standardization* of procedures, displays and layouts reduces error by reinforcing the pattern recognition that humans do well. Finally, where possible, operations should be easily *reversible* or difficult to perform when they are not reversible.

Training must include, in addition to the usual emphasis on application of knowledge and following procedures, a consideration of safety issues. These issues include understanding the rationale for procedures as well as how errors can occur at various stages, their possible consequences, and instruction in methods for avoidance of errors. Finally, it must be acknowledged that injuries can result from behavioural problems that may be seen in impaired physicians or incompetent physicians despite well-designed systems; methods for identifying and correcting egregious behaviours are also needed.

The aviation model

The practice of hospital medicine has been compared, usually unfavourably, to the aviation industry, also a highly complicated and risky enterprise but one that seems far safer. Indeed, there seem to be many similarities. As Allnutt (1987: 858) observed:

> Both pilots and doctors are carefully selected, highly trained professionals who are usually determined to maintain high standards, both externally and internally imposed, whilst performing difficult tasks in life-threatening environments. Both use high technology equipment and function as key members of a team of specialists . . . both exercise high level cognitive skills in a most complex domain about which much is known, but where much remains to be discovered.

While the comparison is apt, there are also important differences between aviation and medicine, not the least of which is a substantial measure of uncertainty due to the number and variety of disease states, as well as the unpredictability of the human organism. Nonetheless, there is much physicians and nurses could learn from aviation.

Aviation – airline travel, at least – is indeed generally safe: there are more than 10 million take-offs and landings each year, with an average of fewer than four crashes a year. But, it was not always so. The first powered flight was in 1903, the first fatality in 1908, and the first mid-air collision in 1910. By 1910, there were 2000 pilots in the world and 32 had already died (Perrow 1984). The US Air Mail Service was founded in 1918. As a result of efforts to meet delivery schedules in all kinds of weather, 31 of the first 40 Air Mail Service pilots were killed. This appalling toll led to unionization of the pilots and their insistence that local field controllers could not order pilots to fly against their judgement unless the field controllers went up for a flight around the field themselves. In 1922, there were no Air Mail Service fatalities (Perrow 1984). Since that time, a complex system of aircraft design, instrumentation, training, regulation and air traffic control has developed that is highly effective at preventing fatalities.

There are strong incentives for making flying safe. Pilots, of course, are highly motivated. Unlike physicians, their lives are on the line as well as those of their passengers. But airlines and airplane manufacturers also have strong incentives to provide safe flight. Business decreases after a large crash, and if a certain model of aircraft crashes repeatedly, the manufacturer will be discredited. The lawsuits that inevitably follow a crash can harm both reputation and profitability.

Designing for safety has led to a number of unique characteristics of aviation that could, with suitable modification, prove useful in improving hospital safety. First, in terms of system design, aircraft designers assume that errors and failures are inevitable and design systems to 'absorb' them, building in multiple buffers, automation and redundancy. As even a glance in an airliner cockpit reveals, extensive feedback is provided by means of monitoring instruments, many in duplicate or triplicate. Indeed, the multiplicity of instruments and automation have generated their own challenges to system design: sensory overload and boredom. Nonetheless, these safeguards have served the cause of aviation safety well.

Second, procedures are standardized to the maximum extent possible. Specific protocols must be followed for trip planning, operations and maintenance. Pilots go through a checklist before each take-off. Required maintenance is specified in detail and must be performed on a regular (by flight hours) basis. Third, the training, examination and certification process is highly developed and rigidly, as well as frequently, enforced. Airline pilots take proficiency examinations every six months. Much of the content of the examinations is directly concerned with procedures to enhance safety.

Pilots function well within this rigorously controlled system, although not flawlessly. For example, one study of cockpit crews observed that human errors or instrument malfunctions occurred at an average of one every four minutes during an overseas flight (Perrow 1984). Each event was promptly recognized and corrected with no untoward effects. Pilots also willingly submit to an external authority, the air traffic controller, when within the constrained air and ground space at a busy airport.

Finally, safety in aviation has been institutionalized. In the USA, two independent agencies have government-mandated responsibilities: the Federal Aviation Administration (FAA) regulates all aspects of flying and prescribes safety procedures, and the National Transportation Safety Board investigates every accident. The adherence of airlines and pilots to required safety standards is closely monitored. The FAA recognized long ago that pilots seldom reported an error if it led to disciplinary action. Accordingly, in 1975 the FAA established a confidential reporting system for safety infractions, the Air Safety Reporting System (ASRS). If pilots, controllers or others promptly report a dangerous situation, such as a near-miss mid-air collision, they will not be penalized. This programme dramatically increased reporting, so that unsafe conditions at airports, communication problems and traffic control inadequacies are now promptly communicated. Analysis of these reports and of subsequent investigations appears as a regular feature in several pilots' magazines. The ASRS receives more than 5000 notifications each year (Perrow 1984).

The medical model

By contrast, accident prevention has not been a primary focus of the practice of hospital medicine. It is not that errors are ignored. Mortality and morbidity conferences, incident reports, risk management activities, and quality assurance committees abound. But, as noted previously, these activities focus on incidents and individuals. When errors are examined, a problem-solving approach is usually used: the cause of the error is identified and corrected. Root causes, the underlying systems failures, are rarely sought. System designers do not assume that errors and failures are inevitable and design systems to prevent or absorb them. There are, of course, exceptions. Implementation of unit dosing, for example, markedly reduced medication dosing errors by eliminating the need for the nurse to measure out each dose. Monitoring in intensive care units is sophisticated and extensive (although perhaps not sufficiently redundant). Nevertheless, the basic healthcare system approach is to rely on individuals not to make errors rather than to assume they will.

Second, standardization and task design vary widely. In the operating room, it has been refined to a high art. In patient care units, much more could be done, particularly to minimize reliance on short-term memory, one of the weakest aspects of cognition. On-time and correct delivery of medications, for example, is often contingent on a busy nurse remembering to do it, a nurse who is responsible for four or five patients at once and is repeatedly interrupted, a classic set up for a 'loss of activation' error.

On the other hand, education and training in medicine and nursing far exceed that in aviation, both in breadth of content and in duration, and few professions compare with medicine in terms of the extent of continuing education. Although certification is essentially universal, including the recent introduction of periodic recertification, the idea of periodically testing *performance* has never been accepted. Thus, we place great emphasis on education and training, but shy away from demonstrating that it makes a difference.

Finally, unlike aviation, safety in medicine has never been institutionalized, in the sense of being a major focus of hospital medical activities. Investigation of accidents is often superficial, unless a malpractice action is likely; non-injurious error (a 'near-miss') is rarely examined at all. Incident reports are frequently perceived as punitive instruments. As a result, they are often not filed, and when they are, they almost invariably focus on the individual's misconduct.

One medical model is an exception and has proved quite successful in reducing accidents due to errors: anaesthesia. Perhaps in part because the effects of serious anaesthetic errors are potentially so dramatic – death or brain damage – and perhaps in part because the errors are frequently transparently clear and knowable to all, anaesthesiologists have put great emphasis on safety. The success of these efforts has been dramatic. Whereas mortality from anaesthesia was one in 10,000 to 20,000 just a decade or so ago, it is now estimated at less than one in 200,000 (Orkin 1993). Anaesthesiologists have led the medical profession in recognizing system factors as causes of errors, in designing fail-safe systems, and in training to avoid errors (Gaba 1989; Cooper *et al.* 1984; Cullen *et al.* 1992).

Systems changes to reduce hospital injuries

Can the lessons from cognitive psychology and human factors research that have been successful in accident prevention in aviation and other industries be applied to the practice of hospital medicine? There is every reason to think they could be. Hospitals, physicians, nurses and pharmacists who wish to reduce errors could start by considering how cognition and error mechanisms apply to the practice of hospital medicine. Specifically, they can examine their care delivery systems in terms of the systems' ability to discover, prevent and absorb errors and for the presence of psychological precursors.

Discovery of errors

The first step in error prevention is to define the problem. Efficient, routine identification of errors needs to be part of hospital practice, as does routine investigation of all errors that cause injuries. The emphasis is on 'routine'. Only when errors are accepted as an inevitable, although manageable, part of everyday practice will it be possible for hospital personnel to shift from a punitive to a creative frame of mind that seeks out and identifies the underlying system failures.

Data collecting and investigatory activities are expensive, but so are the consequences of errors. Evidence from industry indicates that the savings from reduction of errors and accidents more than make up for the costs of data collection and investigation (Allnutt 1987). (While these calculations apply to 'rework' and other operational inefficiencies resulting from errors, additional savings from reduced patient care costs and liability costs for hospitals and physicians could also be substantial.)

Prevention of errors

Many healthcare delivery systems could be redesigned to reduce significantly the likelihood of error. Some obvious mechanisms that can be used are as follows:

- *Reduced reliance on memory.* Work should be designed to minimize the requirements for human functions that are known to be particularly fallible, such as short-term memory and vigilance (prolonged attention). Clearly, the components of work must be well delineated and understood before system redesign. Checklists, protocols and computerized decision aids could be used more widely. For example, physicians should not have to rely on their memories to retrieve a laboratory test result, and nurses should not have to remember the time a medication dose is due. These are tasks that computers do much more reliably than humans.
- *Improved information access.* Creative ways need to be developed for making information more readily available: displaying it where it is needed, when it is needed, and in a form that permits easy access. Computerization of the medical record, for example, would greatly facilitate bedside display of patient information, including tests and medications.
- *Error proofing.* Where possible, critical tasks should be structured so that errors cannot be made. The use of 'forcing functions' is helpful. For example, if a computerized system is used for medication orders, it can be designed so that a physician cannot enter an order for a lethal overdose of a drug or prescribe a medication to which a patient is known to be allergic.
- *Standardization.* One of the most effective means of reducing error is standardizing processes wherever possible. The advantages, in efficiency as well as in error reduction, of standardizing drug doses and times of administration are obvious. Is it really acceptable to ask nurses to follow six different 'K-scales' (directions for how much potassium to give according to patient serum potassium levels) solely to satisfy different physician prescribing patterns? Other candidates for standardization include information displays, methods for common practices (such as surgical dressings), and the geographic location of equipment and supplies in a patient care unit. There is something bizarre, and really quite inexcusable, about 'code' situations in hospitals where house staff and other personnel responding to a cardiac arrest waste precious seconds searching for resuscitation equipment simply because it is kept in a different location on each patient care unit.
- *Training.* Instruction of physicians, nurses and pharmacists in procedures or problem-solving should include greater emphasis on possible errors and how to prevent them. (Well-written surgical atlases do this.) For example, many interns need more rigorous instruction and supervision than is currently provided when they are learning new procedures. Young physicians need to be taught that safe practice is as important as effective practice. Both physicians and nurses need to learn to think of errors primarily as symptoms of systems failures.

Absorption of errors

Because it is impossible to prevent all error, buffers should be built into each system so that errors are absorbed before they can cause harm to patients. At minimum, systems should be designed so that errors can be identified in time to be intercepted. The drug delivery systems in most hospitals do this to some degree already. Nurses and pharmacists often identify errors in physician drug orders and prevent improper administration to the patient. As hospitals move to computerized records and ordering systems, more of these types of interceptions can be incorporated into the computer programs. Critical systems (such as life-support equipment and monitors) should be provided in duplicate in those situations in which a mechanical failure could lead to patient injury.

Psychological precursors

Finally, explicit attention should be given to work schedules, division of responsibilities, task descriptions and other details of working arrangements where improper managerial decisions can produce psychological precursors, such as time pressures and fatigue, that create an unsafe environment. While the influence of the stresses of everyday life on human behaviour cannot be eliminated, stresses caused by a faulty work environment can be. Elimination of fear and the creation of a supportive working environment are other potent means of preventing errors.

Institutionalization of safety

Although the idea of a national hospital safety board that would investigate every accident is neither practical nor necessary, at the hospital level such activities should occur. Existing hospital risk management activities could be broadened to include all potentially injurious errors and deepened to seek out underlying system failures. Providing immunity, as in the FAA ASRS system, might be a good first step. At the national level, the Joint Commission on Accreditation of Healthcare Organizations should be involved in discussions regarding the institutionalization of safety. Other specialty societies might well follow the lead of the anaesthesiologists in developing safety standards and require their instruction to be part of residency training.

Concluding remarks

Many of the principles described in this chapter fit well within the teachings of total quality management (Berwick 1989a). One of the basic tenets of total quality management, statistical quality control, requires data regarding variation in processes. In a generic sense, errors are but variations in processes. Total quality management also requires a culture in which errors and deviations are regarded not as human failures, but as opportunities to improve the system, 'gems' as they are sometimes called. Finally, total quality management calls for grassroots participation to identify and develop system modifications to eliminate the underlying failures.

Like total quality management, systems changes to reduce errors require commitment of the organization's leadership. None of the aforementioned changes will be effective, or, for that matter, even possible without support at the highest levels (hospital executives and department chiefs) for making safety a major goal of medical practice.

But it is apparent that the most fundamental change that will be needed if hospitals are to make meaningful progress in error reduction is a cultural one. Physicians and nurses need to accept the notion that error is an inevitable accompaniment of the human condition, even among conscientious professionals with high standards. Errors must be accepted as evidence of systems flaws, not character flaws. Until and unless that happens, it is unlikely that any substantial progress will be made in reducing medical errors.

Note

1 This article orginally appeared in the *Journal of the American Medical Association*, 21 December 1994, Vol. 272, no. 23, pp. 851–7. Copyright 1994 American Medical Association. Reprinted with permission.

References

Allnutt, M.F. (1987) Human factors in accidents, *British Journal of Anaesthesia*, 59: 856–64.

Anderson, R.E., Hill, R.B. and Key, C.R. (1989) The sensitivity and specificity of clinical diagnostics during five decades: Toward an understanding of necessary fallibility, *Journal of the American Medical Association*, 261(11): 1610–17.

Bates, D.W., Boyle, D., Vander Vliet, M. *et al.* (forthcoming) Relationship between medication errors and adverse drug events, *Journal of General Internal Medicine*.

Bedell, S.E., Deitz, D.C., Leeman, D. and Delbanco, T.L. (1991) Incidence and characteristics of preventable iatrogenic cardiac arrests, *Journal of the American Medical Association*, 265: 2815–20.

Berwick, D.M. (1989a) Continuous improvement as an ideal in health care, *New England Journal of Medicine*, 320: 53–6.

Berwick, D.M. (1989b) E.M. Codman and the rhetoric of battle: A commentary, *Milbank Quarterly*, 67: 262–7.

Brennan, T.A., Leape, L.L., Laird, N. *et al.* (1991) Incidence of adverse events and negligence in hospitalized patients: Results of the Harvard Medical Practice Study I, *New England Journal of Medicine*, 324: 370–6.

Cameron, H.M. and McGoogan, E. (1981) A prospective study of 1,152 hospital autopsies, I: Inaccuracies in death certification, *Journal of Pathology*, 133: 273–83.

Christensen, J.F., Levinson, W. and Dunn, P.M. (1992) The heart of darkness: The impact of perceived mistakes on physicians, *Journal of General Internal Medicine*, 7: 424–31.

Classen, D.C., Pestonik, S.L., Evans, R.S. and Burke, J.P. (1991) Computerised surveillance of adverse drug events in hospital patients, *Journal of the American Medical Association*, 266: 2847–51.

Cooper, J.B., Newbower, R.S. and Kitz, R.J. (1984) An analysis of major errors and equipment failures in anaesthesia management: Considerations for prevention and detection, *Anesthesiology*, 60: 34–42.

Cullen, D.J., Nemeskal, R.A., Cooper, J.B., Zaslavsky, A. and Dwyer, M.J. (1992) Effect of pulse oximetry, age, and ASA physical status on the frequency of patients admitted unexpectedly to a postoperative care unit, *Anesthesia and Analgesia*, 74: 181.

Deming, W.E. (1982) *Quality, Productivity and Competitive Position*. Cambridge, MA: MIT Press.

Deming, W.E. (1987) Written communication with author, November.

Dubois, R.W. and Brook, R.H. (1988) Preventable deaths: Who, how often, and why?, *Annals of Internal Medicine*, 109: 582–9.

Folli, H.L., Poole, R.L., Benitz, W.E. and Russo, J.C. (1987) Medication error prevention by clinical pharmacists in two children's hospitals, *Pediatrics*, 79: 718–22.

Gaba, D.M. (1989) Human errors in anesthetic mishaps, *International Anesthesiology Clinics*, 27: 137–47.

Goldman, L., Sayson, R., Robbins, S., Conn, L.H., Bettman, M. and Weissberg, M. (1983) The value of the autopsy in the three medical eras, *New England Journal of Medicine*, 308: 1000–5.

Gopher, D., Olin, M., Donchin, Y. *et al.* (1989) The nature and causes of human errors in a medical intensive care unit. Paper presented at the 33rd annual meeting of the Human Factors Society, Denver, CO, October.

Hilfiker, D. (1984) Facing our mistakes, *New England Journal of Medicine*, 310: 118–22.

Leape, L.L., Brennan, T.A., Laird, N. *et al.* (1991) Incidence of adverse events in hospitalised patients: Results of the Harvard Medical Practice Study II, *New England Journal of Medicine*, 324: 377–84.

Leape, L.L., Lawthers, A.G., Brennan, T.A. and Johnson, W.G. (1993) Preventing medical injury, *Quality Review Bulletin*, 8: 144–9.

Lesar, T.S., Briceland, L.L., Delcoure, K. *et al.* (1990) Medication prescribing errors in a teaching hospital, *Journal of the American Medical Association*, 263: 2329–34.

McIntyre, N. and Popper, K.B. (1989) The critical attitude in medicine: The need for a new ethics, *British Medical Journal*, 287: 1919–23.

Nightingale, F. (1863) *Notes on Hospitals*. London: Longman.

Norman, D.A. (1984) *To Err is Human*. New York: Basic Books.

Orkin, F.K. (1993) Patient monitoring during anaesthesia as an exercise in technology, in L.J. Saidman and N.T. Smith (eds) *Monitoring in Anaesthesia*, 3rd edn. London: Butterworth.

Palmer, R.H., Strain, R., Rothrock, J.K. *et al.* (1983) Evaluation of operational failures in clinical decision making, *Medical Decision Making*, 3: 299–310.

Perrow, C. (1984) *Normal Accidents: Living with High Risk Technologies*. New York: Basic Books.

Raju, T.N., Thornton, J.P., Kecskes, S. *et al.* (1989) Medication errors in neonatal and paediatric intensive-care units, *Lancet*, ii: 374–9.

Rasmussen, J. and Jensen, A. (1974) Mental procedures in real-life tasks: A case study of electronic troubleshooting, *Ergonomics*, 17: 293–307.

Reason, J. (1992) *Human Error*. Cambridge, MA: Cambridge University Press.

Schimmel, E.M. (1964) The hazards of hospitalisation, *Annals of Internal Medicine*, 60: 100–10.

Steel, K., Gertman, P.M., Crescenzi, C. *et al.* (1981) Iatrogenic illness on a general medical service at a university hospital, *New England Journal of Medicine*, 304: 638–42.

Tversky, A. and Kahneman, D. (1981) The framing of decisions and the psychology of choice, *Science*, 211: 453–8.

Wu, A.W., Folkman, S., McPhee, S.J. and Lo, B. (1991) Do house officers learn from their mistakes?, *Journal of the American Medical Association*, 265: 2089–94.

Yerkes, R.M. and Dodson, J.D. (1908) The relation of strength of stimuli to rapidity of habit formation, *Journal of Comparative Neurology and Psychology*, 18: 459–82.

Human factors approaches in medicine

Charles Vincent and James Reason

Introduction

Formal studies of the quality of care can be traced back to the early part of the twentieth century and beyond (Groves 1908) but the last twenty years have seen a massive increase in formal quality initiatives and the volume of studies published. In spite of this increased attention to quality, errors and adverse patient outcomes are still frequent and the risk of iatrogenic injury to patients in acute hospitals remains remarkably stable (Vincent 1997). Comparatively few studies in medicine have focused directly on adverse outcomes, with some important exceptions such as critical incident studies and the British confidential enquiries (Vincent 1993; Drife 1995). Serious incidents may be discussed with colleagues or in departmental meetings, but few studies or reports of such meetings are published, making it difficult to develop a systematic method of investigation (see Rosenthal, Chapter 10). Incidents that may lead to litigation are investigated intensively, albeit long after the event, with the focus on whether there was substandard care and on whether it caused identifiable injury. However, the full range of factors is unlikely to be revealed from an analysis of the medical records in isolation. Furthermore, lawyers are seldom interested in understanding why care was substandard, so clinically relevant factors such as a doctor or midwife being undertrained, exhausted or inadequately supervised are rarely considered (and are not seen as relevant in court).

In contrast, as Leape makes clear in Chapter 2, the formal investigation of adverse events in industry is a well-established practice. Studies of accidents in industry, transport and military spheres have led to a much broader understanding of accident causation, with less focus on the individual who makes the error and more on pre-existing organizational factors. This 'human factors' approach, as it is called, is a hybrid discipline which focuses on the human component within complex organizational systems. The assessment of accidents in large-scale systems has acquired a high profile in industry, after such disasters as Three Mile Island, the King's Cross London Underground fire, Chernobyl, Bhopal and the Piper Alpha oil disaster. The human factors community has developed a variety of methods of analysis, which have begun to be adapted for use in medical contexts (Reason 1992, 1995; Bogner 1994).

Initially, these collaborations were focused around the work of anaesthetists and intensivists (Gaba *et al.* 1987; Cook and Woods 1994), partly because their activities had much in common with those of more widely studied groups such as pilots and nuclear power plant operators. More recently, this interest in the human factors of healthcare has spread to a wide range of medical specialties (such as general practice, accident and emergency care, obstetrics and gynaecology, radiology and surgery). This burgeoning concern is reflected in a number of recent texts and journal issues devoted to medical accidents (Vincent *et al.* 1993; Bogner 1994; Vincent 1995) and in the creation of incident monitoring schemes that embody leading-edge thinking with regard to human and organizational contributions (Runciman *et al.* 1993). Critical incident and human factors analyses of individual cases have illustrated the complexity of the chain of events that may lead to an adverse outcome (Cooper *et al.* 1984; Cook and Woods 1994; Vincent and Bark 1995). The root causes of adverse medical events may lie in factors such as the use of locums, communication and supervision problems, excessive workload, educational and training deficiencies and so on. Some fundamental features of a unit, such as poor communication within a team, may be implicated in a wide variety of adverse clinical events.

One of the most significant consequences of this collaboration between medical and human factors specialists is the increasing acceptance that human factors models of accident causation, developed for domains such as aviation and nuclear power generation, can be adapted to many healthcare settings. The same is also true for many of the diagnostic and remedial measures that have been created within these non-medical areas.

In the remainder of this chapter, we will develop many of the themes introduced by Leape in Chapter 2. We will first consider the different ways in which human beings can contribute to the breakdown of complex, well-defended technologies. Then we will show how these various contributions may be combined within a generic model of accident causation and illustrate its practical application with two accident case studies. Finally, we will outline the practical implications of such models for improving risk management within the healthcare domain.

Human factors approaches in medicine

Human decisions and actions play a major part in nearly all accidents, contributing in two main ways: through *active* failures and *latent* failures

(Reason 1995). Active failures are unsafe acts or omissions committed by those at the 'sharp end' of the system (pilots, air-traffic controllers, anaesthetists, surgeons, nurses, etc.) whose actions can have immediate adverse consequences. The term 'active failures' includes both action slips or failures, such as picking up the wrong syringe, and cognitive failures such as memory lapses and mistakes due to ignorance or misreading a situation, which could also be seen as the preludes to unsafe acts. *Violations* – deviations from safe operating practices, procedures or standards – are another important form of unsafe act. In contrast to errors, which arise primarily from informational problems (forgetting, inattention, etc.), violations are more often associated with motivational problems such as low morale, poor examples from senior staff and inadequate management generally. These important distinctions are discussed only briefly here as they are described in more detail by Leape in the previous chapter. A full account can be found in Reason (1992).

The distinction between active and latent failures owes a great deal to Mr Justice Sheen's observations (Sheen 1987) regarding the capsizing of a British ship, the *Herald of Free Enterprise*. In his inquiry report, he wrote:

> At first sight the faults which led to this disaster were the . . . errors of omission on the part of the Master, the Chief Officer and the assistant bosun . . . But a full investigation into the circumstances of the disaster leads inexorably to the conclusion that the underlying or cardinal faults lay higher up in the Company. . . From top to bottom the body corporate was infected with the disease of sloppiness.
>
> (Sheen 1987: 6)

Here, the distinction between active and latent failures is made very clear. The active failures – the immediate causes of the disaster – were various errors on the part of the ships' officers and crew. But, as the inquiry revealed, the *Herald* was a 'sick' ship even before it sailed from Zeebrugge on 6 March 1987.

To sum up the differences between active and latent failures:

- Active failures are unsafe acts (errors and violations) committed by those at the 'sharp end' of the system (surgeons, anaesthetists, nurses, physicians, etc.). They are the people at the human–system interface whose actions can, and sometimes do, have immediate adverse consequences.
- Latent failures are created as the result of decisions, taken at the higher echelons of the organization. Their damaging consequences may lie dormant for a long time, only becoming evident when they combine with local triggering factors (the spring tide, the loading difficulties at Zeebrugge harbour, etc.) to breach the system's defences.

Thus, the distinction between active and latent failures rests upon two considerations: first, the length of time before the failures have a bad outcome; second, where in the organization the failures occur. Generally, medical active failures are committed by those in direct contact with the patient,

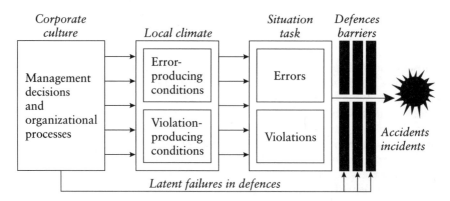

Figure 3.1   Stages in the development of an organizational accident

and latent failures occur within the higher echelons of the institution, in the organizational and management spheres. A brief account of a model showing how top-level decisions create accident-producing conditions in the workplace is given in Figure 3.1.

The aetiology of an organizational accident

The anatomy of an 'organizational accident' is shown in Figure 3.1. The direction of causality is from left to right. The accident sequence begins with the negative consequences of organizational processes (decisions concerned with planning, scheduling, forecasting, designing, policy-making, communicating, regulating, maintaining, etc.). The latent failures so created are transmitted along various organizational and departmental pathways to the workplace (the operating theatre, the ward, etc.), where they create the local conditions that promote the commission of errors and violations (understaffing, high workload, poor human–equipment interfaces, etc.).

Defences are measures designed to protect the system against hazards and to mitigate the consequences of human or equipment failure. The functions of such defences are to protect, detect, warn and aid recovery from potential problems. In industry this might be a fail-safe device to shut down a reactor, in medicine the warning sound of a monitor alerting an anaesthetist to falling blood pressure. In medicine, a 'hands-on' activity, defences are much less in evidence than in other settings. Many of these unsafe acts are likely to be committed, but only very few of them will penetrate the defences to produce damaging outcomes. The fact that engineered safety features, standards, controls, procedures and the like can be deficient due to latent as well as active failures is shown by the arrow connecting organizational processes directly to defences.

These organizational root causes are further complicated by the fact that the healthcare system as a whole involves many inter-dependent organizations, such as manufacturers, government agencies, and professional and patient organizations. The model shown in Figure 3.1 relates primarily to a given institution, but the reality is considerably more complex, with the behaviour of other organizations impinging on the accident sequence at many different points. Furthermore, high-level management and organizational decisions are shaped by economic, political and operational constraints. All strategic decisions will carry some negative safety consequences for some part of the system, even those that were judged to be essentially good decisions at the time. Resources, for example, are rarely allocated evenly. A decision to move resources from psychiatry to accident and emergency (or vice versa) is bound to have some adverse consequences, even though the overall outcome is for the better. The crux of the matter is this: we cannot prevent the creation of latent failures; we can only make their adverse consequences visible before they combine with local triggers to breach the system's defences.

In the next two sections we show how this model can be used in practice. The method is essentially to examine the chain of events that leads to an accident or adverse outcome, consider the actions of those involved and then, crucially, look further back at the conditions in which staff were working and the organizational context in which the incident occurred.

Case study 1: The Omnitron 2000 accident at the Indiana Regional Cancer Center, 1992

Although this event (see Box 3.1) has all the causal hallmarks of an organizational accident, it differed from the usual run of medical mishaps in having adverse outcomes for nearly 100 people. The accident, which is described in detail in Nuclear Regulatory Commission (1993), occurred as the result of a combination of procedural violations (resulting in breached or ignored defences) and latent failures.

Active failures
- The area radiation monitor alarmed several times during the treatment, but was ignored – partly because the physician and technicians knew that it had a history of false alarms.
- The console indicator showed 'safe' and the attending staff mistakenly believed the source to be fully retracted into the lead shield.
- The truck driver deviated from company procedures when he failed to check the nursing home waste with his personal radiation survey meter.

Latent failures
- The rapid expansion of HDR brachytherapy from one to ten facilities in less than a year had created serious weaknesses in the radiation safety programme.

Box 3.1   The Omnitron 2000 accident

An elderly patient with anal carcinoma was treated with high dose rate (HDR) brachytherapy. Five catheters were placed in the tumour. An iridium-192 source (4.3 curies or 160 gigabecquerels) was intended to be located in various positions within each catheter, using a remotely controlled Omnitron 2000 afterloader. The treatment was the first of three treatments planned by the physician, and the catheters were to remain in the patient for the subsequent treatments.

The iridium source wire was placed in four of the catheters without apparent difficulty, but after several unsuccessful attempts to insert the source wire into the fifth catheter, the treatment was terminated. In fact, a wire had broken, leaving an iridium source inside one of the first four catheters. Four days later, the catheter containing the source came loose and eventually fell out of the patient. It was picked up and placed in a storage room by a member of the nursing home staff, who did not realize it was radioactive. Five days later, a truck picked up the waste bag containing the source as part of the driver's normal routine. It was then driven to the depot and remained there for a day (Thanksgiving) before being delivered to a medical waste incinerator, where the source was detected by fixed radiation monitors at the site. It was left over the weekend, but was then traced to the nursing home. It was retrieved nearly three weeks after the original treatment. The patient died five days after the treatment session, and in the ensuing weeks over 90 people were irradiated in varying degrees by the iridium source.

- Too much reliance was placed upon unwritten or informal procedures and working practices.
- There were serious inadequacies in the design and testing of the equipment.
- There was a poor organizational safety culture. The technicians routinely ignored alarms and did not survey patients, the afterloader or the treatment room following HDR procedures.
- There was weak regulatory oversight. The Nuclear Regulatory Commission did not adequately address the problems and dangers associated with HDR procedures.

This case study illustrates how a combination of active failures and latent systemic weaknesses can conspire to penetrate the many-layered defences designed to protect both patients and staff. No one person was to blame for the disaster. Each individual acted according to his or her appraisal of the situation. Yet one person died and over 90 people were irradiated.

Case study 2: The analysis of an obstetric incident

The following case (see Box 3.2) has been reported in more detail elsewhere (Vincent and Bark 1995) and is presented here to illustrate the method and its applicability to clinical practice. We first examine the actions of the staff involved (as would be discussed in an audit meeting) and then the conditions in which these actions and decisions were taken and the latent failures that these imply. In practice, the extent to which latent failures are perceived depends on how far the active failures were influenced by more general conditions in the unit or were representative of wider problems. Thus a failure to pass on crucial information when the protocol clearly specifies that this should be done might be an isolated mistake, but possibly influenced by fatigue, in turn influenced by poorly designed shift patterns, a latent failure. Alternatively, the protocol or systems for conveying this information might be at fault, a latent failure of a different kind.

Active failures: unsafe acts

All the staff took decisions that were, to them, reasonable at the time given the constraints they were under. However, it is clear, at least in retrospect, that many of them constituted 'unsafe acts'. Some of the main ones, in chronological order, were:

- The significance of the decelerations on the CTG trace were not given sufficient weight, partly because CTGs produce a high rate of false positives.
- The midwife did not follow the midwifery protocol in that she did not turn down the syntocinon as soon as she saw the deteriorating trace.
- The consultant overrode the decision of the team without giving due weight to their reasons for considering that a Caesarean was urgently needed. The decision not to proceed with a Caesarean was probably influenced by the lack of confidence and ability of junior staff to present their case for intervention.
- The syntocinon was not administered correctly. The senior registrar and the midwives were reluctant to use the syntocinon when they judged there was an obstruction. In response, they alternately increased and decreased the syntocinon, neither stopping it nor allowing the dose to increase to an effective level.
- The sister felt forced to induce more evident signs of fetal distress in order to impress the doctors of the gravity of the condition of the baby.

Box 3.2   A problematic obstetric incident

This example concerns a healthy teenage mother in the late stages of labour. The staff involved were three experienced midwives and a student midwife on eight-hour shifts, a registrar in his first week in the department, an on-call senior registrar, a locum senior registrar and a consultant, also new to the department. The team were not used to working together.

The mother arrived on the labour ward at midnight, contractions were strong, and the baby's head was visible. Cardiotocograph (CTG) decelerations were observed – a possible indication of fetal distress. At 4 a.m. the mother had progressed to 7 cm dilation, but the head had not descended. Contractions were irregular and decelerations had increased. By 6 a.m. midwife A and the registrar were concerned that the labour was not progressing, and decided to use syntocinon to augment the labour. Uterine activity increased but the CTG trace became abnormal, so the syntocinon was reduced. The registrar phoned the senior registrar (on call at home) who said a Caesarean section should be carried out if there was no progress by 9 a.m. By 7 a.m. the midwife suspected an obstruction due to cephalopelvic disproportion (i.e., that the head was too big for the pelvis) and relayed her fears to midwife B at the handover. Midwife B changed the CTG monitor because she feared it was faulty as the trace was unclear. The registrar carried out a vaginal examination and found evidence of likely obstructed labour with a swollen cervix and blood staining of the urine, and agreed with the midwife that a Caesarean section was indicated. The midwife stopped the syntocinon and prepared the mother for theatre.

At 9 a.m. the consultant arrived, and disagreed with the registrar's interpretation, saying that the decelerations were not significant, there was no obstruction and that the syntocinon should resume. With syntocinon the contractions became stronger and the mother very distressed. The locum senior registrar and the midwife alternately increased and decreased the syntocinon. The baby was showing evidence of fetal distress, with tachycardia and decelerations. By noon the cervix was more swollen and still not dilating. The contractions were weaker and the fetal heart trace deteriorating further. Both the midwife and the locum senior registrar were convinced of an obstruction, but could not challenge the consultant.

At 1 p.m., with a student midwife now with the mother, the senior sister recognized the crisis and saw that she had to arrange a Caesarean without obviously overruling the consultant's decision. She sent the student midwife for a break and then deliberately increased the syntocinon to induce more marked abnormalities in the CTG, before reducing the syntocinon and calling the locum senior registrar. The increase in decelerations was then serious enough to justify delivery by Caesarean section. After further delays, a Caesarean section was performed without the consultant being informed. The baby was born at 4 p.m. in poor condition, not breathing and covered in meconium, an indication of severe distress. He was transferred to Special Care and recovered quickly, with no immediate signs of neurological damage. The baby has since proved to be healthy. Cephalopelvic disproportion was recorded in the medical notes as the indication for the section.

The case disturbed everyone involved. With hindsight, it was clear that the Caesarean should have been performed earlier. Some meetings were arranged to discuss the case, but then cancelled. In the end nothing was done to address the emerging concerns: the differences in CTG trace interpretation were not discussed, nor were conflicting ideas of care management, unreliable equipment, or deviations from protocols.

Conditions of work in the unit and implied latent failures

There were a number of background conditions that contributed to the problems in handling this case. Some of the most important were:

- There was inadequate training for CTG interpretation. Where there were disagreements there was no follow-up discussion.
- When decelerations were observed the tendency was to assume something was wrong with the machine rather than with the mother. Underlying this attitude were the recurrent problems associated with poorly maintained and unreliable equipment.
- There was a general acceptance of faulty equipment being the norm, with a lax system for reporting faults. Staff provided each other with inadequate information about prior problems with equipment, each one using equipment that had been found faulty by another.
- No one person was responsible for induction programmes, which were inadequate. Both the registrar and consultant were attempting to get to grips with a new job and a high workload after a very brief induction period. They were expected to assume full responsibilities before being integrated into the team.
- Shift rotas did not take new staff into account, or the need to have at least one experienced member of staff in the duty team. A registrar in his first week was working with a new consultant and a locum senior registrar.
- There was no system within the unit to learn from cases like this one by discussion among the staff. Mistakes were repeatedly compounded and lost confidence was not restored. There was also no mechanism for

addressing the potential dangerous conflict that had arisen in this case between the consultant and the rest of the team.
• The outstanding deficiency in the management of this case was the lack of definition of who was responsible for what and the lack of an agreed line of communication. When the consultant insisted on further augmenting labour, thereby increasing the risk to the fetus, the normal lines of communication broke down. No system existed to deal with such an eventuality, leading to a highly questionable desperate decision by the sister to induce fetal distress.

The above list of factors that precipitated the active failures, or at least made them more likely, implies latent failures at an organizational level. Action would seem to be needed on CTG training, equipment maintenance, reporting equipment faults, induction programmes, shift patterns, adverse incident reporting and forward planning for cases in which there were major disagreements between staff.

There are considerable advantages to investigating a 'near-miss', such as this obstetric case where an adverse outcome was narrowly avoided. Incidents with a serious outcome, where litigation may ensue, may lead to recrimination and feelings of guilt and shame. Near-misses, on the other hand, are less emotive and people are less likely to apportion blame. However, as the psychological and organizational precursors to near-misses are assumed to be similar to incidents with a serious outcome, the root unsafe features of organizations can be highlighted before a serious incident occurs. System deficiencies can be understood and changes implemented to enhance safety and reduce the chances of a real disaster after a 'free lesson'.

Responding to adverse outcomes

In medicine a common response to serious adverse outcomes is to issue new procedures that proscribe particular behaviour; to sanction, exhort and retrain the key personnel in an effort to make them more careful; and to introduce increased automation so as to take people 'out of the loop'. There are several problems with this 'anti-personnel' approach. First, people do not intend to commit errors. It is therefore difficult for others to control what people cannot control themselves. Second, the psychological precursors of an error (inattention, distraction, preoccupation, forgetting, fatigue and stress) are probably the last and least manageable links in the chain of events leading to an accident. Finally, accidents rarely occur as the result of single unsafe acts. They are the product of many factors, personal, task-related, situational and organizational. This means two things. First, the mere recurrence of some act involved in a previous accident will probably not have an adverse outcome in the absence of the other causal factors. Second, so long as these underlying latent problems persist, other acts – not hitherto regarded as unsafe – can also serve to complete an incipient accident sequence.

Serious incidents are rare events, but may cause considerable shock and a wave of procedural changes. However, hasty *ad hoc* corrective measures after single incidents are not likely to produce constructive changes. In other settings a broad range of accident and near-miss data is collected and subjected to analysis, so that common organizational problems can be discerned. If a series of similar incidents are investigated (post-partum haemorrhage, emergency Caesarean section due to fetal distress) and common factors revealed, then scientifically justified system changes and error reduction strategies can be implemented. This may be possible even with an apparently dissimilar set of clinical incidents as common organizational problems may underlie a quite disparate (diagnostically speaking) set of incidents. In the longer term a database of adverse and potentially dangerous incidents which have been subjected to detailed analysis can be established, in which clinical management failures, conditions of work and organizational factors are separately indexed.

Safety programmes in healthcare

Once problems have been identified, the solutions must be implemented. As we have seen, safety demands a wider approach than the traditional medical exhortations and retraining. The goal of effective risk management is not so much to minimize particular errors and violations as to enhance human performance at all levels of the system (Cook and Woods 1994). Perhaps paradoxically, most performance enhancement measures are not directly focused on what goes on inside the heads of single individuals. Rather, they are directed at team, task, situation and organizational factors. This section gives brief examples of approaches that have been taken in medicine and industry. For further details, see Reason (1992).

Task factors

Tasks vary widely in their liability to promote errors. Identifying and modifying tasks and task elements that are conspicuously failure-prone is an essential step in risk management. At the level of the task, some of the principal safety strategies include increased standardization, less reliance on memory, greater use of computers and various strategies to correct errors that are made. Increased standardization, while it might seem to limit clinicians' freedom, actually frees time and mental resources for those novel, urgent or dangerous situations where clinical experience and expertise is really needed.

Effective incident monitoring is an invaluable tool in the identification of error-prone tasks. On the basis of their corpus of nearly 4000 anaesthetic and intensive care incidents, Runciman and his colleagues at the Royal Adelaide Hospital have introduced many inexpensive equipment modifications guaranteed to enhance performance and to minimize recurrent errors. These include colour-coded syringes and endotracheal tubes graduated to assist the non-intrusive identification of endobronchial intubation (Runciman *et al.* 1993).

Team factors

The way a medical team functions and communicates can have a great impact on the staff concerned. However, the extent to which team performance and team characteristics are predictive of clinical outcomes has seldom been examined in formal studies, though they have been found to be strongly implicated in studies of aviation safety and in some preliminary studies in medicine (Driscoll and Vincent 1992; Helmreich and Schaefer 1994). Team factors are likely to be crucial in mental health, but possibly also in acute specialties such as obstetrics, where the relationships between midwives and doctors can be a powerful determinant of the way a unit functions.

Helmreich (one of the pioneers of crew resource management) and his colleagues at the University of Texas analysed 51 aircraft accidents and incidents, paying special attention to team-related factors (Helmreich and Schaefer 1994). Some examples of their findings are shown in Box 3.3, where the team-related factors are categorized as negative (having an

---

Box 3.3   Team factors in aviation accidents

- Crew members ask questions regarding crew actions and decisions (negative, 11; positive, 4).
- Crew members speak up and state their information with appropriate persistence until there is some clear resolution or decision (negative, 14; positive, 4).
- Captain coordinates flight-deck activities to establish proper balance between command authority and crew member participation, and acts decisively when the situation requires (negative, 18; positive, 4).
- Workload and task distribution are clearly communicated and acknowledged by crew members. Adequate time is provided for the completion of tasks (negative, 12; positive, 4).
- Secondary tasks are prioritized so as to allow sufficient resources for dealing effectively with primary duties (negative, 5; positive, 2).
- Crew members check with each other during times of high and low workload in order to maintain situational awareness and alertness (negative, 3; positive, 3).
- When conflicts arise, the crew remains focused on the problem or situation at hand. Crew members listen actively to ideas and opinions and admit mistakes when wrong (negative, 2).

adverse impact upon safety and survivability) or positive (acting to improve survivability). The numbers given in each case relate to the number of accidents or incidents in which particular team-related factors played a negative or a positive role. If one substitutes the phrase 'surgical team' or 'mental health team' for 'crew' in any of the examples, the relevance to medicine becomes apparent.

Recently, Helmreich and the anaesthetist, Hans-Gerhard Schaefer, have studied team performance in the operating theatre of a Swiss teaching hospital (Helmreich and Schaefer 1994). They noted that 'interpersonal and communications issues are responsible for many inefficiencies, errors and frustrations in this psychologically and organizationally complex environment'. They also observed that attempts to improve institutional performance have largely entailed throwing money at the problem through the acquisition of new and ever more sophisticated equipment, whereas improvements to training and team performance could be achieved more effectively at a fraction of this cost. As has been clearly demonstrated in aviation, formal training in team management and communication skills can produce substantial improvements in human performance as well as reducing safety-critical errors.

Situational factors

Certain conditions, both of the individual and of his/her immediate environment, that are guaranteed to increase the likelihood of error are summarized in Box 3.4 (Williams 1988). Here, the error-producing conditions are

---

Box 3.4 Error-producing conditions

- Unfamiliarity with the task ($\times$ 17)
- Time shortage ($\times$ 11)
- Poor signal–noise ratio ($\times$ 10)
- Poor human–system interface ($\times$ 8)
- Designer–user mismatch ($\times$ 8)
- Irreversibility of errors ($\times$ 8)
- Information overload ($\times$ 6)
- Negative transfer between tasks ($\times$ 5)
- Misperception of risk ($\times$ 4)
- Poor feedback from system ($\times$ 4)
- Inexperience, not lack of training ($\times$ 3)
- Poor instructions or procedures ($\times$ 3)
- Inadequate checking ($\times$ 3)
- Educational mismatch of person with task ($\times$ 2)
- Disturbed sleep patterns ($\times$ 1.6)
- Hostile environment ($\times$ 1.2)
- Monotony and boredom ($\times$ 1.1)

---

ranked in the order of their known effects and the numbers in parentheses indicate the risk factor (the amount by which the nominal error rates should be multiplied under the worst conditions). For convenience, we can reduce these error-producing conditions to seven broad categories: high workload; inadequate knowledge, ability or experience; poor interface design; inadequate supervision or instruction; stressful environment; mental state (fatigue, boredom, etc.); and change.

It is worth noting that three of the best-researched factors – sleep disturbance, hostile environment and boredom – carry the lowest penalties. The other point of significance is that those error-producing factors at the top of the list are also those that lie squarely within the organizational sphere of influence. This is a central element in the present view of organizational accidents. Managers and administrators rarely, if ever, have the opportunity to jeopardize a system's safety directly. Their influence is more indirect: top-level decisions create the conditions that promote unsafe acts.

Organizational factors

Accident and incident reporting procedures are a crucial part of any safety or quality information system. But, by themselves, they are insufficient to support effective quality and safety management. The information they provide is both too little and too late for this longer-term purpose. In order to promote proactive accident prevention rather than reactive 'local repairs', it is necessary to monitor an organization's 'vital signs' on a regular basis.

When a physician carries out a routine medical check, he/she samples the state of a number of critical bodily systems: cardiovascular, pulmonary, excretory, neurological and so on. From individual measures of blood pressure, electrocardiograph, cholesterol level, urinary contents, reflexes and the like, the doctor makes a professional judgement about the individual's general state of health. Assessing an organization's current state of 'safety health', as in medicine, involves the regular and judicious sampling of a small subset of a potentially large number of indices. But what are the dimensions along which to assess organizational 'safety health'?

Diagnostic techniques vary from industry to industry, but all of them have been guided by two principles. First, they try to include those organizational 'pathogens' that have featured most conspicuously in well-documented accidents (hardware defects, incompatible goals, poor operating procedures, understaffing, high workload, inadequate training, etc.). Second, they seek to encompass a representative sampling of those core processes common to all technological organizations (design, build, operate, maintain, manage, communicate, etc.). For instance, Tripod-Delta, commissioned by Shell International and currently implemented in a number of its exploration and production operating companies, on Shell tankers, and on its contracted helicopters in the North Sea, assesses the quarterly or half-yearly state of eleven general failure types (GFTs) in specific workplaces: hardware; design;

Table 3.1 The measures of organizational health used in different industries

Oil exploration and production	Railways	Aircraft maintenance
Hardware	Tools and equipment	Organizational structure
Design	Materials	People management
Maintenance management	Supervision	Provision and quality of tools and equipment
Procedures	Working environment	Training and selection
Error-enforcing conditions	Staff attitudes	Commercial and operational pressures
Housekeeping	Housekeeping	Planning and scheduling
Incompatible goals	Contractors	Maintenance of buildings and equipment
Organization	Design	Communication
Communication	Staff communication	
Training	Departmental communication	
Defences	Staffing and rostering	
	Training	
	Planning	
	Rules	
	Management	
	Maintenance	

maintenance management; procedures; error-enforcing conditions; housekeeping; incompatible goals; organizational structure; communication; training; and defences (Table 3.1). A discussion of the rationale behind the selection and measurement of these GFTs can be found elsewhere (Hudson *et al.* 1994).

Concluding remarks

Full human factors analyses of medical incidents can only be undertaken on occasion. Any method which is routinely used must be quick and effective to be useful in a medical setting. However, a basic active/latent failure analysis can be conducted quite quickly by, say, a maternity risk

Box 3.5   Managing risk, promoting safety

- Human rather than technical failures now represent the greatest threat to complex and potentially hazardous systems. This includes healthcare systems.
- Managing the human risks will never be 100 per cent effective. Human fallibility can be moderated, but it cannot be eliminated.
- Different error types have different underlying mechanisms, occur in different parts of the organization and require different methods of risk management. The basic distinctions are as follows:
  - Slips, lapses, trips and fumbles (execution failures) and mistakes (planning or problem-solving failures).
  - Errors (information-handling problems) and violations (motivational problems).
  - Active versus latent failures. The former are committed by those in direct contact with the patient. The latter arise in the organizational and managerial spheres, and their adverse effects may take a long time to become evident.
- Safety-significant errors occur at all levels of the system, not just at the sharp end. Decisions made in the upper echelons of the organization create the conditions in the workplace that subsequently promote individual errors and violations. Latent failures are present long before an accident and hence are prime candidates for principled risk management.
- Measures that involve sanctions and exhortations (moralistic measures directed to those at the sharp end) have only very limited effectiveness, and especially so in the case of highly trained professionals.
- Human factors problems are a product of a chain of causes in which the individual psychological factors (momentary inattention, forgetting, etc.) are the last and least manageable links. States of mind contributing to error are extremely difficult to manage; they can happen to the best of people at any time.
- People do not act in isolation. Their behaviour is shaped by circumstances. The same is true for errors and violations. The likelihood of an unsafe act being committed is heavily influenced by the nature of the task and by the local workplace conditions, which are the product of 'upstream' organizational factors. Great gains in safety can be achieved through relatively small modifications of equipment and workplaces.
- Automation and increasingly sophisticated equipment do not cure human factors problems, they merely relocate them. In contrast, training people to work effectively in teams costs little,

> but has achieved significant enhancements of human performance in aviation.
> - Effective risk management depends critically upon a confidential and preferably anonymous incident monitoring system that records the individual, task, situational and organizational factors associated with incidents and near-misses.
> - Effective risk management means the simultaneous and targeted deployment of limited remedial resources at different levels of the system: the individual or team, the task, the situation and the organization as a whole.

manager talking to one or two members of staff, particularly when guided by check-lists of task, team, situational and organizational factors (Stanhope *et al.* 1997). Cases such as the obstetric one described above are, of course, often discussed in morbidity and mortality meetings or in audit sessions, but several cases are usually discussed in the course of an hour, so there is usually only time to decide whether care was substandard in any way and, if so, to identify the main deficiencies – the 'active failures' as we have described them. There will not be time to address the deeper causes of the errors, the latent failures and the triggering factors, or to begin to generate ideas for implementing change. We suggest that a more systematized approach dealing with a smaller number of cases in more depth is likely to yield greater dividends than the 'many' cases currently analysed quite briefly and hence less effectively.

Systemic change, at both the clinical and organizational level, involves a commitment to safety and quality at all levels of an organization, a fact long recognized by proponents of total quality management. The examination of individual incidents in a risk management programme is a powerful way of examining the range of factors that may be implicated in adverse outcomes, but thoroughgoing change will require a range of quality and safety techniques embedded in a comprehensive strategy. The principles underlying such an approach are summarized in Box 3.5. Total quality management approaches in turn, with their roots in industry, will benefit from approaches such as risk management which are grounded in clinical practice. If the true costs of adverse events are recognized, rather than the comparatively trivial costs of litigation, then resources may be made available to implement the comprehensive strategies that are needed.

References

Bogner, M.S. (ed.) (1994) *Human Error in Medicine*. Hillsdale, NJ: Lawrence Erlbaum.

Cook, R.I. and Woods, D.D. (1994) Operating at the sharp end: The complexity of human error, in M.S. Bogner (ed.) *Human Error in Medicine*. Hillsdale, NJ: Lawrence Erlbaum.

Cooper, J.B., Newbower, R.S. and Kitz, R.J. (1984) An analysis of major errors and equipment failures in anesthesia management: Considerations for prevention and detection, *Anesthesiology*, 60: 34–42.

Drife, J. (1995) Reducing risk in obstetrics, in C.A. Vincent (ed.) *Clinical Risk Management*. London: BMJ Publishing Group.

Driscoll, P.A. and Vincent, C.A. (1992) Organizing an efficient trauma team, *Injury*, 23(2): 107–10.

Gaba, D.M., Maxwell, M. and DeAnda, A. (1987) Anesthetic mishaps: Breaking the chain of accident evolution, *Anesthesiology*, 66: 670–6.

Groves, E.W. (1908) A plea for the uniform registration of operation results, *British Medical Journal*, 2: 1008–9.

Helmreich, R.L. and Schaefer, H. (1994) Team performance in the operating room, in M.S. Bogner (ed.) *Human Error in Medicine*. Hillsdale, NJ: Lawrence Erlbaum.

Hudson, P., Reason, J., Wagenaar, W., Bentley, P., Primrose, M. and Visser, J. (1994) Tripod-Delta: Proactive approach to enhanced safety, *Journal of Petroleum Technology*, 46: 58–62.

NUREG (1993) *Loss of an Iridium-192 Source and Therapy Misadministration at Indiana Regional Cancer Center, Indiana, Pennsylvania, on November 16th, 1992. Report-1480*. Washington, DC: US Nuclear Regulatory Commission.

Reason, J.T. (1992) *Human Error*. Cambridge, MA: Cambridge University Press.

Reason, J.T. (1995) Understanding adverse events: Human factors, in C.A. Vincent (ed.) *Clinical Risk Management*. London: BMJ Publishing Group.

Runciman, W.B., Sellen, A., Webb, R.K., Williams, J.A., Currie, M. and Morgan, C. (1993) Errors, incidents and accidents in anaesthetic practice, *Anaesthesia and Intensive Care*, 21: 506–19.

Sheen, Mr Justice (1987) *MV Herald of Free Enterprise. Report of Court No. 8074 Formal Investigation*. London: Department of Transport.

Stanhope, N., Vincent, C.A., Adams, S., O'Connor, A.M. and Beard, R.W. (1997) Applying human factors methods to clinical risk management in obstetrics, *British Journal of Obstetrics and Gynaecology*, 104: 1225–32.

Vincent, C.A. (1993) The study of errors and accidents in medicine, in C.A. Vincent, M. Ennis and R.J. Audley (eds) *Medical Accidents*. Oxford: Oxford University Press.

Vincent, C.A. (ed.) (1995) *Clinical Risk Management*. London: BMJ Publishing Group.

Vincent, C.A. (1997) Risk, safety and the dark side of quality, *British Medical Journal*, 314: 1775–6.

Vincent, C.A. and Bark, P. (1995) Accident investigation: Discovering why things go wrong, in C.A. Vincent (ed.) *Clinical Risk Management*. London: BMJ Publishing Group.

Vincent, C.A., Ennis, M. and Audley, R.J. (eds) (1993) *Medical Accidents*. Oxford: Oxford University Press.

Williams, J.A. (1988) A data-based method for assessing and reducing human error to improve operational performance, in W. Hagen (ed.) *IEEE Fourth Conference on Human Factors and Power Plants*. New York: Institute of Electrical and Electronic Engineers.

Part two | International perspectives

4 Medical accidents in the UK: a wasted opportunity for improvement?

Kieran Walshe

Introduction

Medical accidents, medical mishaps or adverse events happen in the UK's healthcare system, just as they do in every other healthcare system in the world. And, like other countries, the UK has a number of overlapping systems designed (though that is perhaps too kind a word for the way they have come about) to identify and deal with medical accidents. But, crucially, the UK lacks effective mechanisms for learning from medical accidents when they occur, translating that learning into changes in clinical or organizational practices, and so ensuring that worthwhile and lasting improvements in the quality of care result. If, as the gurus of quality improvement would argue, 'every defect is a treasure' because each one presents us with an opportunity to improve, we are wasting most of those opportunities.

This chapter presents an overview of the current understanding of medical accidents or adverse events in healthcare in the UK. It begins by setting the context, with a brief description of the way in which health services are funded and provided in the UK. Then the rather limited literature on the epidemiology of medical accidents in the UK is reviewed. Next, some of the systems in place for identifying and dealing with adverse events are described, and some current developments in this area are discussed. Finally, some conclusions are drawn about the place of medical accidents in UK healthcare, the way they are dealt with at present and how they could be managed and learned from rather better in the future.

An overview of healthcare in the UK

In the UK, healthcare is largely both funded and provided by the state. The UK spends about £42 billion on healthcare each year, or around 7 per cent of its gross national product (Levitt *et al.* 1995; Key Note 1993). Almost all of that money comes from central government taxation revenues. Some additional healthcare funds come from private citizens and employers purchasing private healthcare insurance to supplement or replace the services they would be entitled to in the state healthcare system (about 15 per cent of the population has some additional health insurance cover). Some healthcare funding is also raised through the levying of user charges for drug prescriptions in primary care, dentistry and opticians' services, though many categories of patient are exempted from payment for various reasons. But private funds and user fees make up a small proportion of overall healthcare financing and the bulk comes from general taxation. There is no specific tax levied to pay for health services – the funds come from the pool of government revenue generated by a range of direct and indirect taxes on individuals and corporations.

Just as most healthcare is funded by the state, so most healthcare provision takes place in the public hospitals and healthcare providers which make up the NHS. While the UK has a small but thriving independent hospitals system, with both charitable and for-profit hospitals, the great majority of in-patient care takes place in the NHS. The independent sector only really plays a significant role in a few areas, such as elective surgery and long-term nursing home care. The structure and management of the NHS vary slightly in the four countries which make up the UK (England, Wales, Scotland and Northern Ireland) but the general arrangements are the same. There is a network of geographically based health authorities, each responsible for commissioning or purchasing health services for a population of about half a million people. They contract for health services with NHS hospitals, community healthcare organizations and primary care providers. Both health authorities and NHS hospitals are run by boards made up of executives and non-executives appointed by the government's Department of Health. The performance of health authorities and hospitals is managed and monitored by the Department of Health through the NHS Executive. In short, the NHS is made up of healthcare purchasers (health authorities) and providers (hospitals and community healthcare providers) which, though they have a high degree of local autonomy, are all public sector bodies, managed by central government appointees with no local democratic involvement and accountable to the Department of Health.

State funding and provision in healthcare has advantages and disadvantages. In comparison with other developed countries, the UK spends less on healthcare but on most indicators of mortality and morbidity its population is just as healthy. It has a strong primary care sector which has acted to manage and control access to expensive secondary care services. It has also been able to use the centralized control of healthcare funding to resist the pressures for health spending growth that afflict all counties. Spending on administering the healthcare system, with no need to cost and bill for care on a patient-by-patient basis, has traditionally been very low. In addition, public support for our healthcare system has generally been very strong, with such commitment to the principle that healthcare should be provided free at the point of use and in accordance with clinical need that no major change to these arrangements seems likely.

However, constraints on government spending have meant some patients having to wait for healthcare, particularly for elective surgery, and have left some healthcare facilities under-resourced, dilapidated and overcrowded. There have been few incentives for NHS organizations to provide a customer-focused and user-friendly service, or to be dynamic and innovative in seeking to improve performance. In many ways the NHS has seemed inflexible, slow to change, unresponsive to patients' demands and too often led by the views and wishes of the professionals who work within it rather than the needs of the community it serves.

In this context, it is probably not surprising that the NHS has not paid much attention in the past to medical accidents and their consequences. It has been somewhat slow to act to ensure it can identify accidents when they occur, manage them in ways that benefit both patients and NHS organizations and learn from them so that future medical accidents are prevented. In the past there have been few incentives for either individual clinicians or NHS healthcare providers to take medical accidents seriously.

The epidemiology of medical accidents in the UK

We know surprisingly little about the incidence of medical accidents or adverse events in healthcare in the UK – how often they happen, what kinds of accidents occur, what effects they have on patients, what causes them, or how they are best prevented in the future. No investigations of the scope and sophistication of the Harvard Medical Practice Study (Brennan *et al.* 1991) or the Quality in Australian Health Care Study (Wilson *et al.* 1995) have been carried out. There are three main sources of data on which we can draw: some studies of quality of care which report on rates of medical accidents or adverse events; information collected on the numbers of complaints made by patients; and records of the numbers of claims for clinical negligence made against NHS healthcare providers.

Only one major study of the incidence of medical accidents or adverse events in healthcare in the UK has been undertaken at an acute hospital in Brighton on the south coast. Between 1990 and 1992, a total of over 15,000 patient admissions to that hospital in 12 specialties were reviewed to identify adverse events – instances of poor-quality care, resulting from the actions of healthcare providers, which have or may have some adverse consequences for the patient concerned (Walshe *et al.* 1995). The results varied from specialty to specialty. For example, in ophthalmology, where 1088 patient admissions were reviewed, the study found that about 35 per cent of patients had at least one adverse event during their stay in hospital, but that the majority of these events were relatively trivial and had no real impact on the patients' care or on their health. However, significant numbers of patients suffered more serious adverse events. Four per cent had some form of non-clinical problem while in hospital (such as missing records, delays in discharge or other administrative failures). About 3 per cent had some form of unintended injury or repair during surgery, 1 per cent had incomplete or missing consents to surgery, 1 per cent had unplanned returns to theatre for second procedures and 4 per cent suffered some specific ophthalmic surgical complications. Of course, not all of these adverse events were preventable, but of those that were subjected to peer review, 21 per cent were judged to have been avoidable and 11 per cent were assessed as having had a major impact on the patient's health. The study also found that patients with adverse events stayed significantly longer in hospital, suggesting that adverse events result in increased healthcare cost for NHS providers as well as unnecessary morbidity for patients.

There have been other studies of the characteristics and causes of medical accidents in the UK, but they generally lack the denominator data which would tell us how frequently such accidents occur. For example, reviews of malpractice claims in obstetrics have shown that many result from avoidable human or system errors (Ennis and Vincent 1989). Studies of critical incidents in general practice have highlighted failures in communication and follow-up as common causes of adverse events (Berlin et al. 1992) and the use of adverse events in clinical audit in general practice has been described (Pringle et al. 1995).

Nationally collected statistics on the incidence of complaints give us some idea of the frequency of some sorts of medical accidents. In a 12-month period in 1997–98 there were 93,000 complaints about hospital care in the NHS in England (Department of Health 1998). About a quarter of these complaints concern communication and staff attitudes; a quarter hotel services (such as portering or catering); about 30 per cent the quality of medical care; and most of the rest concern access to healthcare services – delays and waiting lists, etc. (Allsop and Mulcahy 1996). But since there were about 10 million hospital admissions in that year, this would suggest that only about 1 in 115 patients had a complaint. It seems likely that complaint statistics underestimate the number of dissatisfied patients (since many do not bother to raise or pursue their complaints) and will also not include many significant incidents because patients themselves do not realize they have suffered a medical accident (Mulcahy and Tritter 1994).

Available information on levels of medical negligence claims suggests that there are about 6000 new claims each year in the NHS – or about 11 claims for each NHS hospital or healthcare provider (Dingwall and Fenn 1995). Of course, large acute hospitals see many more claims than this, and small providers of community health services have rather fewer.

However, given the incidence of negligent adverse events observed in other countries, we have to conclude that the vast majority of medical accidents in the UK do not result in legal action.

How medical accidents are managed in the UK

Like many other countries, the UK healthcare system has multiple, over-lapping mechanisms aimed at identifying medical accidents; investigating and resolving medical accidents; and preventing future medical accidents. To an outsider, these arrangements may seem confusing, and it might seem hard to see how they interrelate. In fact, there is considerable scope for greater integration and collaboration, not only to eliminate unnecessary duplication of effort but also to promote the more effective management of medical accidents.

Clinical audit

Until relatively recently, little of the care provided in the British NHS was subject to any systematic form of quality measurement, and there were few formal systems for quality assurance and improvement. Of course, there were always some pioneers, sufficiently interested in healthcare quality to examine their own and others' performance and to publish the results, but they were very much the exception rather than the rule (Groves 1908). There were also some long-standing informal professional mechanisms for addressing quality problems, such as 'mortality and morbidity' meetings in hospitals at which cases of complications and potential quality problems would sometimes be discussed, but these rather casual and limited ex-plorations of healthcare quality were usually fairly ineffectual in changing practice and effecting improvements in the quality of care. When a Royal Commission examined the working of the NHS in 1979 it observed, with a degree of understatement, that 'we are not convinced that the professions generally regard the introduction of audit or peer review with a proper sense of urgency' (Merrison 1979). Rather more directly, Robert Maxwell, a respected health policy specialist and former chief executive of the King's Fund in London, commented that the medical profession 'seemed collec-tively allergic to rational examination of the case for medical audit in any form' (Maxwell 1984).

During the 1980s, things began to change. A number of the organizations representing clinical professionals established initiatives aimed at encourag-ing or developing quality measurement and improvement. For example, the Royal College of General Practitioners (RCGP) developed detailed standards for the quality of primary care (Royal College of General Practitioners 1985) and the Royal College of Nursing (RCN) created its Dynamic Qual-ity Improvement Programme, which involved a network of practitioners in developing and using standards for nursing care, supported and coordinated by a team at the RCN (Royal College of Nursing 1990). Research studies aimed at developing quality improvement activities at a local level were supported (Walshe *et al.* 1991) and some influential national organizations charged with evaluating public sector services began to focus much more explicitly on the quality of care in the NHS (National Audit Office 1987; Audit Commission 1992). Just as importantly, there were a number of changes in the NHS, and in society more widely, which made the quality of healthcare an increasing priority. The management of NHS organizations was strengthened, and clinicians (particularly doctors) became much more directly involved both in managing and in being managed. Society became more consumerist, and there was a dramatic growth in the attention paid to accountability and performance management across the public sector – in education, social services and local government as well as in healthcare.

When the government launched a controversial set of reforms to the NHS in 1989, the package included proposals for the development of formal structures and mechanisms for clinical audit – the systematic, critical analysis of the quality of care – in all NHS healthcare providers (Department of Health 1991). For the first time ever, the government made participation in clinical audit mandatory for doctors and strongly encouraged other clinical professionals to play their part. It also invested some dedicated funding in establishing clinical audit structures and systems at a local level – about £220 million in England between 1989 and 1994. In general, the government's proposals on clinical audit were cautiously welcomed by the professions. A *British Medical Journal* editorial declared that 'the whole profession needs to claim ownership of audit and see a constant search for improvement as a central part of being a doctor' (Moss and Smith 1991) – an admirable sentiment, but one which the medical profession had not endorsed before.

Since the beginning of the 1990s, there has been a dramatic growth in clinical audit activity in NHS hospitals and healthcare providers. Almost every healthcare organization now has some form of clinical audit programme, usually with an audit committee directing activities and reporting to the board; a department of perhaps three or four staff responsible for facilitating, coordinating and monitoring audit activities; and a network of audit groups in departments or specialties, each undertaking a series of audit projects on quality problems in their own areas. There are few clinicians who have not had any contact with clinical audit in recent years and almost all hospital doctors now take part in some kind of audit activity (Walshe and Buttery 1995).

It is difficult to provide a concise description of what all this clinical audit actually involves in practice, because it is so heterogeneous. While some have focused on developing and using guidelines, others have undertaken case reviews or standards-based audits. Some have used clinical databases to compare outcomes and performance, while others have set about obtaining patients' views of services. Most have held some form of regular audit meeting in departments or specialties, and set about doing a number of projects each addressing a particular condition, patient group, procedure or area of care. However, it has been clear that relatively few audits have been undertaken that focus on adverse events or medical accidents. A survey of clinical audit practice showed that adverse event audits were the second least common form of audit to be undertaken, and revealed that in 70 per cent of NHS providers no audit projects relating to patients' complaints had been initiated (Buttery *et al.* 1994).

Moreover, there are serious questions about the effectiveness of clinical audit in the NHS. Research suggests that while some audit programmes have produced very worthwhile improvements in patient care, many others have not (Walsh and Buttery 1995). Clinicians and audit staff have, of course, been learning as they go along how to undertake clinical audit and what measurement and improvement techniques they can use, and some allowance should be made for this. Nevertheless, it is clear that there are widespread problems in clinical audit, particularly concerning the translation of audit findings into real and lasting changes in clinical practice.

Confidential enquiries

For over forty years, obstetricians in the UK have operated a 'confidential enquiry' into all maternal deaths. The principles of the scheme, which has some claim to be the first and longest-running continuous adverse event study in the world, are simple. Local reporters in hospitals pass details of any maternal death (a woman dying during or around childbirth) to regionally based coordinators, who then send questionnaires to the staff who were involved in the care of the patient. These questionnaires are confidential and effectively anonymous, and they collect data about the circumstances surrounding the death and particularly about any avoidable or preventable factors which have affected the woman's care. A report is published every three years, which draws on the data from the confidential enquiry to make recommendations to obstetricians, midwives and others involved in the care of women in pregnancy and childbirth (Department of Health and Social Security 1989). Since the Confidential Enquiry into Maternal Deaths (CEMD) was established, maternal death rates have fallen dramatically, for several reasons, but it seems that this study can take at least some of the credit for the reduction in mortality.

With this example in mind, the Royal College of Surgeons established a similar, but much larger and more ambitious, study in 1987. The National Confidential Enquiry into Perioperative Deaths (NCEPOD) examines the care of patients who have died within 30 days of undergoing surgery. Local reporters pass information to a coordinating unit at the Royal College of Surgeons. Given that there are very large numbers of such deaths, a sample of cases is selected and questionnaires are sent to the surgeons and anaesthetists involved in those patients' care. NCEPOD has published a number of influential reports, based on the data drawn from the review of these cases, which are widely credited with leading to some important changes in practice. For example, NCEPOD reports have recommended a reduction in the numbers of operations undertaken by junior doctors without supervision, more appropriate use of out-of-hours operating and better control over both surgeons and anaesthetists undertaking work outside their main areas of expertise (for example, adult general surgeons operating on children). Two further confidential enquiries have also been established more recently, one dealing with perinatal and neonatal deaths and another, organized by the Royal College of Psychiatrists, examining cases of suicide and serious self-harm.

The confidential enquiries are a form of clinical audit – powerful, professionally-led adverse event studies which have considerable capacity to influence practice and prevent future adverse events. They are perhaps the best and most encouraging example of the use of data on medical accidents or adverse events in quality improvement in the UK to date. Of course, the design of these enquiries imposes some important limitations on their effectiveness. The confidentiality, which helps to ensure frank and honest reporting, also prevents action being taken over individual cases, however poor the care is revealed to have been. Participation is voluntary, and some clinicians simply refuse to provide data on their cases. Furthermore, although the Royal Colleges have considerable influence over their members, the important recommendations from confidential enquiry reports are often not taken up by hospitals and health authorities, especially when they have financial consequences. Nevertheless, the confidential enquiries demonstrate that it is perfectly feasible to collect data about medical accidents with the cooperation and support of clinical professionals, and to use such data to bring about important quality improvements.

Risk management

As recently as the early 1990s, almost no hospitals or healthcare providers in the UK had any form of risk management programme or system, designed to identify, manage and minimize risk to patients and the organization. Risk management had not been seen as a priority, because the costs of claims for medical negligence were traditionally low. However, as litigation became more frequent and more costly, risk management began to be seen as more important. In 1993, the Department of Health issued very detailed guidance to all healthcare providers, encouraging them to establish arrangements for risk management (Department of Health 1993). It also set up a risk pooling scheme called the Clinical Negligence Scheme for Trusts (CNST) in which NHS providers share responsibility for funding the costs of litigation for medical negligence. The development of medical negligence litigation in the UK is discussed in more detail below. However, because the size of the financial contributions required from NHS providers to the CNST is linked to their use of risk management, there are now important incentives for NHS providers to put risk management systems in place.

As a result, many NHS providers have now established formal arrangements for risk management. In line with the CNST's published standards for risk management in healthcare organizations, most now have a written risk management strategy, a named executive director (on the organization's board) with responsibility for risk management, a designated risk and claims manager and systems for incident reporting, following up serious incidents and managing complaints.

Risk management is managed in different ways by different healthcare providers. Some have given responsibility for the issue to the executive director who also has responsibility for quality – commonly the director of nursing in many NHS providers. Others have made it part of the role of the medical director, arguing that because of the sensitivity of many clinical risk management issues and the importance of medical staff commitment and involvement, it needs to be managed through the medical representative on the board. In a few cases, it falls within the remit of the director of finance or some other executive director. While none of these approaches is necessarily better than the others, it does seem important that risk management gains acceptance and support among all clinical staff groups (not just medical staff), that there is a genuine top-level commitment to making risk management work and that risk management is integrated into other activities and structures within the organization.

Although most NHS providers have introduced some form of incident reporting, with clinicians completing paper forms to report medical accidents or adverse events which may have a consequence for the patient concerned or for the organization, anecdotal evidence suggests that there is some way to go before these incident reporting systems provide a meaningful and accurate picture of the incidence of medical accidents. At present, the quality of reported data is often poor, and there are important differences in reporting behaviour in different clinical groups, making the interpretation of incident rates problematic. However, incident reporting seems likely to be the main source of data on medical accidents in the future for the NHS, so there are good reasons to try to ensure it is done rigorously.

More importantly, risk management activities in many NHS providers are not linked to the clinical audit or quality improvement programmes which also take place. Although incident reporting and other risk management data should be an ideal starting point for clinical audit, in practice communication is often poor. Risk managers, who frequently also carry responsibility for non-clinical risk issues (such as health and safety at work) and/or claims management and litigation, often do not have time to deal properly with risk prevention.

Complaints

Complaints from patients about the quality of care they have received should be an invaluable source of information about medical accidents, but in practice complaints have often been treated more as an irritation and a distraction than as an important channel for identifying areas where improvements or changes in practice are indicated (see Allsop and Mulcahy, Chapter 9).

In the past, complaining in the NHS was a complex business (Allsop and Mulcahy 1996). There were different systems in place for managing complaints in primary and secondary care, and different procedures for dealing with complaints about non-clinical and clinical matters. In primary care, the systems were quasi-legal and adversarial in the extreme, with hearings held before a service committee made up in large part of other doctors. The remit of complaint hearings was limited to the fairly narrow terms of the doctor's contract with the health authority, and so it was difficult, for example, to complain about a general practitioner being rude, insensitive or abrasive. Things were scarcely better in secondary care, where clinical complaints were largely passed on to the clinician concerned, and non-clinical matters were dealt with by local managers. Patients who were dissatisfied with the response to their complaint could appeal to the Health Service Commissioner (HSC), an ombudsman who is directly responsible to Parliament, but his remit was limited in a number of ways. Overall, complaining was difficult for all but the most motivated and vocal complainants, and complaints were rarely treated as important opportunities to improve practice.

Following a detailed review (NHS Executive 1994), the arrangements for managing complaints in the NHS have now been substantially revised, though it is still too early to tell how well they are now working. In both secondary and primary care, there is now a two-stage process in place. Initially, complaints are to be dealt with informally and immediately, in a conciliatory and non-defensive way. It is expected that when they are not resolved by local staff, including both clinicians and managers, they may, at the discretion of a 'convenor', be passed on to a more formal process, with an independent panel comprised of lay representatives and, where necessary, independent clinical assessors. There is also a requirement to collect more management information about the way in which complaints are handled, including data to demonstrate that NHS organizations have effective complaints procedures in place and some information about patients' views of the way those procedures have worked. The remit of the HSC has also been broadened to cover bad handling of clinical complaints at service level.

However, complaints remain a largely underused resource in quality improvement. There are still no formal mechanisms for trying to ensure that NHS healthcare providers use complaints to trigger wider reviews of services and processes, so that they learn from instances of poor-quality care and act to prevent future similar problems. In many NHS providers, the arrangements for dealing with patients' complaints, though they may now work much better than they used to, are still curiously disconnected from systems for clinical audit and quality improvement.

Litigation

For many years, litigation against NHS healthcare providers arising from clinical negligence was relatively rare. While other countries experienced dramatic growth in both the frequency and size of claims, the UK saw only modest rises in costs (Dingwall and Fenn 1995). From the inception of the NHS, liability for medical negligence was shared between doctors and the hospitals or healthcare providers which employed them. Doctors subscribed to medical defence organizations which provided them with insurance cover against their share of the cost of any claims. As recently as 1978, the annual subscription for a doctor in the UK was about £40, and the annual cost of claims against the NHS was of the order of £1–2 million. However, during the 1980s there was a huge growth in both the number of claims (up by about 500 per cent) and in the costs of settling clams (up by around 250 per cent). The resulting cost pressures made the price of medical defence organization subscriptions increasingly hard for doctors to pay from their own salaries, and led eventually in 1990 to NHS providers assuming full responsibility for liabilities resulting from the actions of the doctors they employed – something which they had always accepted for all other staff.

However, NHS providers were increasingly concerned that the costs of medical negligence claims could adversely affect the services they were there to provide, especially for those providers who faced a number of very large claims. Effectively, compensating claimants for clinical negligence takes priority over all other claims on healthcare providers' resources, and a few large claims could seriously threaten the viability of some providers' health services. With this in mind, the Department of Health created a risk pooling scheme aimed at sharing the costs of liability between providers. Named the Clinical Negligence Scheme for Trusts, it effectively acts as a self-insurance scheme for the NHS providers who join it. The CNST is administered by a specially created health authority called the NHS Litigation Authority, which also has responsibility for managing the backlog of claims which existed before the CNST came into being. Current estimates suggest that clinical negligence claims now cost the NHS between £150 million and £200 million a year, and costs continue to grow (Vincent 1997).

Litigation for medical negligence remains at best a blunt instrument for dealing with medical accidents and for influencing the quality of care in the UK (Allsop and Mulcahy 1996). First, the number of actual claims is clearly far short of the number of accidents which occur, and the number of potentially valid claims which could be made. Second, many claims for clinical negligence arise from cases in which there has been no medical accident or negligent adverse event.

Many patients do not sue, because they are not aware that they have suffered a preventable medical accident, because they are not strongly motivated to seek financial recompense (they may be more interested in an explanation, apology or assurance that such an incident will not happen again) or because they cannot afford to go to law. But it is probably the latter reason which, more than anything else, has served to keep the lid on levels of clinical negligence litigation in the UK. Litigation is only open to the very poor (who can obtain financial aid which covers their legal costs, so long as their claim is deemed to have some merit), the very rich (who can afford the legal fees involved) and the exceptionally determined (who may need to be willing to mortgage their houses and risk financial ruin if they lose). Claims from children, particularly those who have suffered some form of accident during childbirth, make up an unrepresentatively large proportion of all claims simply because children can apply for and receive legal aid in their own right. Recently, lawyers have been permitted to accept clinical negligence cases on a contingency fee basis, only charging their client for their services if the case is won, but we have yet to see how this will affect the incidence of claims. Nevertheless, for the great majority of adults, litigation for clinical negligence is simply not a realistic option.

There has been some sporadic discussion in the UK of the advantages of some form of no-fault compensation scheme, akin to those in Sweden and New Zealand, which would take the whole issue of medical accidents out of the legal realm, with all the adversarial attitudes and defensive behaviours it engenders. However, the likely costs of no-fault compensation and the problems of defining the nature of compensable accidents have both discouraged serious attempts to introduce such a scheme. Less radical proposals to alter the way in which clinical negligence claims are handled by the courts, as part of a wider review of civil justice, are now in train (Woolf 1997). In short, they envisage the much wider use of mediation (see Mulcahy, Chapter 11), a more open approach to the use of evidence, reforms to speed up the handling of cases and the introduction of greater specialization among the judiciary.

Professional competence and regulation

As in most countries, the healthcare professions in the UK operate with a degree of autonomy and self-regulation, under statutory governing bodies, made up largely of the professionals themselves. These bodies are responsible for admitting applicants to the profession, monitoring their behaviour or performance to ensure it meets with the standards of the profession and disciplining or otherwise dealing with those who do not come up to the agreed standards of the profession. For doctors, this task is the remit of the General Medical Council, while for nurses the United Kingdom Central Council for Nursing, Midwifery and Health Visiting (UKCC) fulfils this role.

In theory, both bodies could act to gather information about instances of poor-quality care, in order to monitor proactively the performance of the professionals for whom they are responsible, and one might expect data on medical accidents to form an important part of such data collection. In practice, both the GMC and the UKCC generally wait for incidents to be reported to them, by colleagues of the professional concerned, health authorities or hospitals, other agencies or patients themselves. They then conduct an investigation, may call the professional concerned to a hearing and can deploy a range of sanctions of which the most serious is removing the professional from the register so that he/she can no longer practise.

The GMC has been much criticized for interpreting its mandate in a rather limited fashion. It has traditionally concerned itself largely with issues such as dishonesty, fraud, sexual misconduct and drug or alcohol abuse, and has paid rather less attention to the clinical competence and performance of doctors. It has also set a high threshold for action, sometimes allowing quite remarkable lapses in the quality of care to go unremarked because they have not constituted 'serious misconduct'. Latterly, the GMC's remit has been widened, and it is now specifically tasked with examining instances of poor performance by doctors (see Irvine, Chapter 14). However, the most important weakness of both the UKCC and the GMC is still their reliance on healthcare professionals, NHS organizations, other agencies and patients to report matters to them. All the evidence suggests that most clinicians are reluctant to report matters to the GMC or UKCC, and as a result these regulatory bodies see only a fraction of the true volume of clinical performance or behaviour problems. Only the most serious and obvious medical accidents will ever reach them.

There are other formal and informal mechanisms which serve to regulate professional practice and deal with instances of incompetence or misconduct – managerial action to redeploy staff, adjust workloads or arrange early retirement; informal agreements to steer referrals elsewhere; and, of course, the usual arrangements for disciplining and ultimately dismissing employees on performance grounds. But research suggests that these arrangements are often weak and slow-acting, and that it is frequently difficult to assemble the evidence needed to take action, so that many problems of performance in clinical staff go unchallenged and unresolved.

Conclusions

The UK has a number of overlapping mechanisms which serve to identify and deal with medical accidents, but some are clearly of more use than others. It seems clear, for example, that clinical negligence litigation, though it undoubtedly affects the behaviour of both NHS providers and the clinicians who work within them, is of rather limited use in identifying, dealing with or preventing medical accidents. Similarly, the professional regulatory bodies, while they can and do deal with the grossest manifestations of poor performance, hear nothing and do nothing about the much larger number of less serious quality problems, and are unable to tackle the many medical accidents which arise from lapses in organizational rather than individual performance.

It is also clear that much has changed since the late 1980s. If this chapter had been written then, it would have been both shorter and markedly less positive about the way in which medical accidents were dealt with in the UK. Some important developments have taken place in NHS hospitals and healthcare providers – in particular, the establishment of clinical audit, the creation of risk management structures and the wholesale revision of arrangements for handling patient complaints. In these three initiatives, we have the building blocks for an effective and highly productive system for identifying medical accidents, dealing properly with their consequences for patients and clinicians and learning from them in ways that lead to improvements in the quality of care which make such accidents less likely in the future. Of course, our systems of clinical audit are still evolving, our understanding of risk management is still developing and our new arrangements for managing complaints have yet to be properly tested. But, despite their present imperfections, we have most of the tools we need to make medical accidents less frequent and to manage those that do occur much better.

Yet, there are still two fundamental weaknesses in our approach to medical accidents. First, we seem unable or unwilling to make the connections between activities such as clinical audit, risk management and patient complaints in ways that promote the learning and quality improvement described above. All too frequently, there seem to be organizational or cultural barriers between departments or professions which militate against achieving these highly desirable and feasible aims. Second, we continue to lack effective strategies for promoting changes in clinical practice. There is no point in having wonderful systems for identifying and understanding medical accidents if we cannot persuade clinicians and managers in the health service to change the way things are done as a result.

References

Allsop, J. and Mulcahy, L. (1996) *Regulating Medical Work: Formal and Informal Controls*. Buckingham: Open University Press.

Audit Commission (1992) *Minding the Quality: A Consultation Document on the Role of the Audit Commission in Quality Assurance Health Care*. London: Audit Commission.

Berlin, A., Spencer, J.A., Bhopal, R.S. *et al.* (1992) Audit of deaths in general practice: Pilot study of the critical incident technique, *Quality in Health Care*, 1: 231–5.

Brennan, T.A., Leape, L., Laird, N. *et al.* (1991) Incidence of adverse events and negligence in hospitalized patients: Results of the Harvard Medical Practice Study I, *New England Journal of Medicine*, 324: 370–6.

Buttery, Y., Walshe, K., Coles, J. and Bennett, J. (1994) *Evaluating Medical Audit: The Development of Audit – Findings of a National Survey of Healthcare Provider Units in England*. London: Caspe Research.

Department of Health (1991) *Medical Audit in the Hospital and Community Health Service*, HC(91)2. London: Department of Health.

Department of Health (1993) *Risk Management in the NHS*, EL(93)111. London: Department of Health.

Department of Health (1998) Handling Complaints: Monitoring the NHS Complaints Procedure, England 1996–97, Yorkshire: Department of Health.

Department of Health and Social Security (1989) *Report on Confidential Enquiries into Maternal Deaths in England and Wales*. London: HMSO.

Dingwall, R. and Fenn, P. (1995) Risk management: Financial implications, in C.A. Vincent (ed.) *Clinical Risk Management*. London: BMJ Publications.

Ennis, M. and Vincent, C. (1989) Obstetric accidents: a review of 64 cases, *British Medical Journal*, 300: 1365–7.

Groves, E.W. (1908) A plea for the uniform registration of operation results, *British Medical Journal*, iii: 1008–9.

Key Note (1993) *Private Health Care: A Market Sector Overview*. London: Key Note Publications.

Levitt, R., Wall, A. and Appleby, J. (1995) *The Reorganised National Health Service*, 5th edn. London: Chapman & Hall.

Maxwell, R.J. (1984) Quality assessment of health, *British Medical Journal*, 288: 1470–2.

Merrison, A. (1979) *Royal Commission on the National Health Service*. London: HMSO.

Moss, F. and Smith, R. (1991) From audit to quality and beyond, *British Medical Journal*, 288: 1470–2.

Mulcahy, L. and Tritter, J. (1994) Hidden depths, *Health Services Journal*, July, 24–6.

National Audit Office (1987) *Quality of Clinical Care in National Health Service Hospitals*. London: HMSO.

NHS Executive (1994) *Being Heard: The Report of the Review Committee on NHS Complaints Procedures* (chair: Professor Alan Wilson). London: HMSO.

Pringle, M., Bradley, C.P., Carmichael, C.M. *et al.* (1995) *Significant Event Auditing: A Study of the Feasibility and Potential of Care-based Auditing in General Practice*. London: RCGP.

Royal College of General Practitioners (1985) *What Sort of Doctor? Assessing Quality of Care in General Practice*. London: RCGP.

Royal College of Nursing (1990) *RCN Standards of Care Project: The Dynamic Standard Setting System*. London: RCN.

Vincent, C.A. (1997) Risk, safety and the dark side of quality, *British Medical Journal*, 314: 1775–6.

Walshe, K., Lyons, C., Coles, J. and Bennet, J. (1991) Quality assurance in practice: Research in Brighton Health Authority, *International Journal of Health Care Quality Assurance*, 8(1): 7–14.

Walshe, K. and Buttery, Y. (1995) Measuring the impact of audit and quality improvement activities, *Journal of the Association for Quality in Healthcare*, 2(4): 138–47.

Wilson, R.M., Runciman, W.B., Gibberd, R.W. *et al.* (1995) The Quality in Australian Health Care Study, *Medical Journal of Australia*, 163: 458–71.

Woolf, Lord (1997) The medical profession and justice, *Journal of the Royal Society of Medicine*, 90: 364–7.

5 Research on errors and safety in Dutch general and hospital practice

M.H. Conradi and B.A.J.M. de Mol

Introduction

Errors made in Dutch medical practice are probably comparable in frequency and consequences to those made in other northern European countries and the USA. Awareness of errors among doctors and the public alike is largely determined by the way medical practice is organized and the societal status of the medical profession. The public's confidence in so-called medical high-technology solutions for disease appears unshakeable. Surveys indicate that the Dutch population of 15.5 million people attaches the greatest value to good health. They also show that doctors, especially heart surgeons, enjoy the highest social status in The Netherlands. General practitioners (GPs) are of slightly lower status, but are considered by policy-makers and the public to be indispensable as case managers and gatekeepers.

A complex system of interests and influences renders the healthcare system in The Netherlands stable and highly effective, but also insensitive to new developments in human resources and slow in meeting new challenges (de Mol 1994). The system is evolving into a form of managed care and a national health service. The gross value of the Dutch healthcare system is estimated at $35 billion and accounts for approximately 9 per cent of the gross national product. There are eight university hospitals and approximately 230 other hospitals and institutions. The number of medical specialists is approximately 11,500, and the number of GPs more than 8000. The facilities can safely be called luxurious. A Minnesota newspaper has described the Mayo Clinics as 'a corner gas station' in comparison to the Academic Medical Centre of the University of Amsterdam built in 1984.

In this chapter, we describe medical error research in Dutch general and hospital practice, but concentrate on the former. We also focus on risk management and the exposure of malpractice within the system.

Error control by means of disciplinary action and civil law

Error control and prevention are only implicit aspects of the efforts to improve the quality of healthcare in The Netherlands. Despite the $35 billion healthcare budget, the total costs of liability insurance to healthcare providers is estimated at less than $25 million. Medical malpractice liability, irrespective of the cause, is not a significant stimulus for risk prevention. Apart from some professional databases and complication registers, there are no sources which provide figures on adverse events in hospitals. Poor communication and an inadequate attitude towards the patient's needs have been recognized as major causes of complaints and claims. Moreover, research has demonstrated that nearly 5 per cent of specialist physicians should be considered unfit to practise (van der Wal 1996). Prompted by such concerns, in 1997, the Dutch Society for Surgery started a nationwide registry for reporting surgical complications.

The Netherlands has two systems of external auditing for punishing errors in medicine. The vast majority of instances become known through medical board decisions, which may result in disciplinary sanctions. There are five boards, made up of one appointed physician and two lawyers. Two or more specialist physicians and several experts may join the board when considered necessary by the chairman, who is a professional judge. From 1998, paramedics and nurses also became subject to board supervision. Complaints can be brought to the attention of the secretary of the board in an informal manner by patients, relatives and the Health Inspectorate.

A recent review of disciplinary activity over a ten-year period examined 5333 decisions of such boards. The annual number of complaints registered with these boards doubled over the period from 379 to 720 (van der Wal 1996). The vast majority of complaints, 92 per cent, were levelled against doctors, but the claims were unevenly distributed among the various specialties: plastic surgery received 6.9 complaints per 100 specialists; surgery, 4.6; gynaecology, 3.1; anaesthesiology, 0.8; and general practice, 2.4. While the investigators did report consistency in the seriousness of the complaints, only 20 per cent of the complaints resulted in the imposition of sanctions. A specific review of complaints against surgeons revealed that only 10 per cent of the claims had this result.

The other system of external auditing is provided by the civil law system. The number of civil personal injury claims due to a medical error is not known. Competition among the three major medical malpractice insurers prevents joint publication of the numbers and types of damages claims awarded. As mentioned above, the estimated costs of malpractice insurance in The Netherlands are low, based on the number of claims and the foreseen damages. However, given the level of resources and practice there is no reason to believe that the true numbers of adverse events, errors and complications, and justified tort claims should differ from those in the USA, UK or Scandinavia. We must conclude that the societal burden of medical malpractice in The Netherlands remains concealed. It is also clear that serious under-reporting exists and that the burden of insurance costs reflects only the tip of the iceberg.

The picture is different for injuries inflicted by drugs and medical devices. Aided by advocates hired by consumer organizations, and on occasion supported by the Ministry of Health, patients are active and well informed about such mishaps. Post-marketing surveillance is immediate, and thorough follow-up studies on fractured heart valves and moving hip prostheses have been carried out. Not only manufacturing deficiencies but also errors in specialists' practice related to diagnosis, information about the patient, and device mishandling have been publicized. By exposing the aetiology and risk control of fractured Björk–Shiley mechanical heart valves, Dutch patients and doctors played a leading role in their evaluation (van der Graaf et al. 1992; de Mol et al. 1995).

Quality systems

A general Quality Law for Hospitals and Institutions enables the government to enforce standards of quality of care and cost containment. The major instruments aimed at ensuring professional quality, including that of general practitioners, are the system of (re)certification, permanent education and single disciplinary auditing.

The auditing system is not accessible to non-specialists and reflects a rather conservative approach to setting professional standards. A review of disciplinary board cases against surgeons also revealed that peers judge errors of colleagues mildly. Their expert opinions are rarely tested against a normative professional standard and reflect only a limited awareness of skills-based and organizational errors (Koornneef et al. 1996; Leape 1994; Reason 1995). With respect to safety standards, and warrants of specific procedures in particular, medical professionals and the public, represented by judges, hold different opinions on standards setting.

A recent landmark verdict by the Supreme Court involved a case of a patient who had fallen out of his bed in the recovery room after minor ear, nose and throat surgery. It was decided that doctors and nurses had deliberately violated safety standards. The verdict stated that the nurse who had been assigned to the man in question had also been assigned to three other patients, all more seriously ill, and that she was very busy at the time of the accident. Hospital and medical experts described this as a standard practice, and, furthermore, did not view the absence of a fall protection rail as abnormal. The judges at three courts upheld the opinion that all reasonable measures must be taken to protect patients from falling after operations where disturbance during recovery is likely and that the use of simple and cheap safety devices is to be considered part of such measures. In another case, involving an infant, the courts determined on the basis of expert opinion that medical negligence was involved. However, experts disagreed about the consequences and the final disability. According to tort law no compensation should have been awarded, but in order to sanction the evident negligence, the courts decided to compensate the child partially.

Internal auditing is based on complaints filed by patients, claims for financial compensation and the reporting of accidents and near-accidents. The latter category primarily involves medication errors and falls, and nurses write the vast majority of the reports. As in industry and air transportation, the confidential reporting of near-accidents is encouraged by management, but rarely undertaken by workers. However, in some surgical practices, evaluation of nursing and medical practice takes place on a regular basis. Sophisticated software will assist in confidential reporting and allow analysis of errors and failures and their root causes. Moreover, clinical risk management is gaining in popularity and is particularly encouraged by malpractice insurers, who will offer advice and action in the hospital. This situation has raised some questions, similar to those relating to the health and malpractice insurance debate in the USA. The almighty insurer appears to be determining the appropriateness of medical care. At the same time, the professional standards to test this care are controlled by insurance-guided risk managers and medical experts. In future, rising interest in reports on adverse events in hospital care is expected as is curiosity about the effectiveness of risk management strategies and observations related to error and safety awareness in hospitals.

General practice and medical errors

The general practitioner occupies a central position within the healthcare system of The Netherlands. GPs live among their patients, to whom they, or their locums, are available 24 hours a day. All Dutch residents are registered with a GP, with whom they tend to have a long-term relationship. This means that patients can only consult their own GP. On average, each patient has four GP consultations per year. Specialized healthcare can be accessed only by obtaining GP referral. As 'gatekeepers' of intramural care, GPs guard and determine access to hospitals and out-patient clinics. As the pivot of the healthcare system, GPs care for their patients from cradle to grave, and guide them through the healthcare system.

Healthcare policies have set the GP an important task – to protect patients against medical overconsumption, and in turn to prevent exhaustion of the country's finances. Low rates of referral and prescription are generally viewed with pride by GPs, not so much because they are consistent with official policy aims, but because of professional pride and in light of the goal of providing care efficiently. It will be obvious that this attitude can have its drawbacks – failure to make a necessary referral can harm the patient. It is in this context that research in the area of errors and iatrogenic damage in Dutch general practice must be viewed.

Research

The first reports of errors in general practice appeared from within the profession itself in the form of case studies. GPs described their own errors, usually followed by advice about the prevention of similar errors. The early academic interest in errors in general practice culminated in the appearance in 1978 of the book *Valkuilen in de Huisartspraktijk* ('Traps in General Practice'), written to mark the tenth anniversary of the creation of the first academic chair of general practice in The Netherlands (Vanes *et al.* 1978). In this collection, 13 GPs describe the 'traps' in which they have found themselves, often with fatal consequences for the patient. Following on from this GPs began to research errors and iatrogenic damage within their own practices, or within their own locum group. This usually took the form of necrologic analysis (Crebolder 1980; Schadé 1981; Post 1984; van den Bosch 1985; Tempelaar 1986). The research demonstrated that a portion of deaths (estimates ranged from just a few to 15 per cent) were caused or contributed to by physicians. This initial reporting of errors from within the professional community can in retrospect be viewed as a break with tradition. It ran counter to the reflexive tendency to hush up errors.

Once it had become commonly known that GPs were responsible for harmful errors, it became possible to undertake more intensive exploratory research. In 1988, Conradi conducted such a research project among 17 GPs to examine, by means of open-ended interviews, the types of errors GPs make and their subsequent means of dealing with them (Conradi *et al.* 1988). Sixteen GPs admitted having made errors, and provided over 100 examples. Fourteen cited errors with fatal or disabling consequences. It was concluded that it is likely that all GPs make errors, and that the making of errors does not signify that the GP in question functions in a consistently poor manner – errors are of an incidental nature. The research also focused extensively on the way GPs conceptualize 'errors' and generated useful definitions. It appears that GPs apply the term 'error' in the event that a patient is affected detrimentally and the GP has contravened professional regulations.

Within this framework, GPs distinguish between three types of errors. First, in the case of medical-technical errors, the conduct of the GP runs counter to the norms set by the professional community as the measure of proper medical-technical practice. Second, in relational errors the relationship between the GP and the patient is interfered with. This interference does not result from the medical-technical conduct of physicians, but rather from their social conduct. For example, they fail to exhibit normal interpersonal skills that would express politeness, interest or attentiveness. Finally, errors based on carelessness reflect a lack of prudence and/or inadequate intent on the part of the GP, such as working under the influence of alcohol or refusing to make a house call.

A fourth type of error identified by GPs is incorrect decisions, apparent only in hindsight. These only become clear once the results of the treatment of the diagnosis are known. The GP will have acted in accordance with professional regulations and guidelines, and other GPs would have acted similarly in the given situation, so it is not an error, but unfortunately, the consequences of the actions are not as expected, because the diagnosis and/or the treatment proved incorrect.

Since the availability of diagnostic tools to GPs in The Netherlands is limited (electrocardiograph equipment is rarely available in general practice, for example), GPs often base their diagnosis on its probable accuracy. The GP considers the probabilities in relation to potential consequences and, mindful of the individual needs and situation of the patient, subsequently formulates the diagnosis and selects a medical approach. Frequently, the GP must choose between diagnosing the patient as having a common and relatively innocent condition, and a rare and serious one. In light of his/her epidemiological knowledge – acquired through exposure to the random population sample characteristic of the general practice – the GP is likely to opt in favour of the more common diagnosis. The GP thus takes a risk. He/she balances this risk against the potential benefit of a referral, the potential of iatrogenic damage and the costs. Professional pride may also exert some influence. GPs do not like to make 'unnecessary' referrals. In some cases, however, the less probable, and often the most serious, diagnosis turns out to be the correct one and the chosen course of action is proved inappropriate. As long as the medical regulations have been adhered to, errors, as defined in general practice, are not considered to have been made in such instances. Nevertheless, GPs do feel responsible.

The analysis of 67 cases cited in this research, with mostly serious consequences for the patient, demonstrated that more than three-quarters (78 per cent) of the cases concerned a faulty diagnosis (Conradi 1995). Myocardial infarction, 'acute abdomen' and children with fever (collectively representing 40 per cent of the cases) are examples of frequently missed diagnoses where the condition deteriorated quickly and where a rapid intervention might have prevented damage. In 43 per cent of these cases the patient died, not as a direct result of the GP's actions, but as a consequence of the illness which could have been better treated if the GP had diagnosed the condition accurately.

Having determined that GPs do make harmful mistakes, and having gained insight into the types of errors made, it would be appropriate to determine the number of errors made in general practice, their causes and consequences. Extensive research regarding the number of errors and their consequences has not been carried out. A secondary analysis was performed of a 1991 study of Dutch registration data pertaining to morbidity within general practice (Foets *et al.* 1992; van der Velden *et al.* 1992). Diagnoses, including the International Classification of Primary Care (ICPC) codes A-85 (adverse effect medical agent proper dose) and A-87 (complication surgery/medical treatment, X-ray), were analysed in detail because these two ICPC codes represent a significant portion of iatrogenic damage (Lamberts and Wood 1987; Conradi *et al.* 1996). The most significant findings were that, in 2 per cent of the diagnoses, 'side-effects' or 'complications' were involved. Among these patients, the occurrence of life-threatening situations, as well as disability, was twice the average of the entire research sample. These diagnoses were made or considered for women twice as often as for men. They were also more likely among the elderly.

This type of large-scale quantitative study has thus far not been undertaken in relation to medical-technical and relational errors, errors based on carelessness or incorrect decisions apparent only in hindsight. Plans for such a project do not currently exist, because of methodological and related financial problems.

It is generally known and recognized that all GPs make errors, with at times very serious consequences for the patient. Is it, however, possible to prevent errors and their consequences? Three studies have been undertaken over the past three years concerning the possibility of preventing errors. The first study involved an analysis of a variety of errors, and an attempt was made to identify sources of error for each phase of a regular interaction between GP and patient (Conradi 1995). Such interaction occurs in four chronological phases. First, *contact* must be established with the GP or his assistant. The GP then produces a *diagnosis* during a consultation. Subsequently, a *therapy* is selected or a referral is made. Finally, a *follow-up* is agreed on. Specific sources of errors were found within each phase.

In the contact phase, sources of error develop in part from inadequate accessibility and availability of the GP. Lack of clarity regarding appointments and technical problems with communication devices all contribute. Problems arise in particular during the first telephone call from the patient, when a choice has to be made between an (emergency) call, an appointment, or advice over the phone. This choice is often made by a practice assistant. Another typical problem for GPs is the 'informal consultation'. Patients will approach GPs with questions in the grocery store, during a sporting event or at a party. Problems can easily arise, specifically since patients may be reassured even though, at the time, the GP does not have all of the necessary information available. A proper consultation has not taken place.

Many things can and do go wrong in the diagnostic phase. Sources of error relate to the emotions of the GP. Both a particularly poor relationship with a patient (marked by conflict) and a very good relationship (in the case of friends or family members as patients) can apparently be too taxing for the GP. Communication skills and thought processes can be affected to the extent that they prevent a correct diagnosis or prognosis from being made. Lack of knowledge and skill also play a role in this phase, as does the inadequate use of available information. Finally, physical and/or psychological problems on the part of the GP (such as addiction and burnout) can also represent a source of error.

The patient can also facilitate errors by, for instance, holding back information or by making frequent but unnecessary medical demands upon the GP. The GP then must continually weigh the net results of an intensive diagnosis with the risk of a somatic fixation, and opting against a diagnosis with the risk of failing to identify a dangerous condition. Finally, the involvement of third parties, such as specialists or laboratories, can produce problems in communication, especially when erroneous information is reported.

In the therapeutic phase, errors made by GPs are usually not very harmful. Therapies that carry high risks are offered only by specialists. In this phase, the most serious harm results from errors in writing out prescriptions. The consequences can be particularly grave for the elderly.

The last phase, the follow-up, involves administrative errors and results in patients being 'lost' by the system. In particular, the responsibilities of GPs and patients for keeping track of appointments are not always clear.

A second study sought to identify sources of error. Each GP reported one error per month sampled. The resulting 39 errors were classified by cause. Most of the errors had multiple causes. The most frequent sources of error were 'communication with the patient' (25 cases), 'attitude of the GP' (irritability, fatigue: 25 cases) and failure to use or incorrect 'use of medical information' (12 cases) (van Pelt-Temeer and van den Berg 1995).

Following this causal analysis of errors, the third study investigated the level of interest in the development and use of a system of error prevention (Conradi *et al.* 1994b). A model was developed, in consultation with the professional community, for a 'committee of investigation of incidents in general practice'. The committee would receive reports from GPs regarding errors, analyse the cases and consider ways of preventing their recurrence. The findings and preventative recommendations would be reported back to the GPs involved and, if necessary, to the professional community at large. A survey conducted among 600 GPs indicated that 83 per cent of the respondents agreed that such a commission should be established. A large majority (89 per cent) also expressed a willingness to report errors. A small-scale experiment demonstrated that GPs will indeed make such reports – of the 49 participating GPs, 22 collectively reported 50 errors (Conradi *et al.* 1994a). Plans are currently in place to introduce such a standing committee of investigation.

These studies demonstrate that, within general practice, it is possible to learn from errors and that GPs are willing to participate in such a process. In general, it can be observed that GPs make diagnostic errors. As a result

of the limited availability of diagnostic tools in general practice as compared to hospitals, there is a significant degree of uncertainty regarding the
accuracy of diagnoses. In terms of risk taking, there is a clear difference
between GPs in The Netherlands and those in surrounding countries. In an
international comparative study regarding the willingness of GPs to take
risks in medical decisions, 60 per cent of respondents in Belgium, 54 per
cent of respondents in England and a mere 24 per cent of respondents in
The Netherlands were unwilling to take risks (Grol *et al.* 1990). It should
be noted that malpractice suits against GPs are unusual in The Netherlands, although the number is increasing. Complaints are almost never
lodged, certainly not against GPs, with the aim of winning compensation.

Conclusion

The above gives an impression of the state of research pertaining to errors
made within general practice in The Netherlands. It appears that the time
has come for larger-scale research in the area of errors, and specifically the
prevention of errors in general practice. It is now possible to speak with
GPs about their errors (Conradi and Jansen 1997). The next step would be
the actual prevention of errors, by learning mishaps which occur.

We conclude that the managerial and professional quality control by
professionals and authorities is not transparent in terms of standards to be
tested. Awareness of human and organizational error in general and of
hospital practice is increasing. However, a multidisciplinary approach to
analysing care programmes is still lacking. Therefore, measures to improve
safety and reduce errors are absent or ineffective in comparison to initiatives taken in other industrialized countries. The excellent infrastructure in
which to conduct patient research in general practice and hospitals may be
used more intensely to increase knowledge about errors and treatment
failures.

References

Conradi, M.H. (1995) *Fouten van huisartsen*. Amsterdam/Meppel: Boom.
Conradi, M.H. and Jansen, F. (1997) Fouten, feiten en valkuilen in de huisarts-
    praktijk. Evaluatie van een nascholingscursus over fouten, *De Huisarts in Neder-
    land*, 1: 19–21.
Conradi, M.H., Schuling, J. and Mulder, H. (1988) Fouten in de huisartspraktijk.
    1. De fouten, *Huisarts en Wetenschap*, 31: 222–7.
Conradi, M.H., de Bruijn, M., Schuling, J., Broer, J. and Meyboom-de Jong, B.
    (1994a) Naar preventie van fouten in de huisartspraktijk. Een vergelijking van
    verschillende meldingssystemen, *Huisarts en Wetenschap*, 37(9): 381–6.
Conradi, M.H., Groenier, K., Hutten, J. *et al.* (1996) Complications and side effects:
    A problem in general practice?, *International Journal of Risk Safety in Medicine*,
    8: 225–30.

Conradi, M.H., Schuling, J., de Bruijn, M. and Meyboom-de Jong, B. (1994b) Towards a model on prevention of errors in general practice, *International Journal of Risk Safety in Medicine*, 6: 47–56.

Crebolder, H.F.J.M. (1980) Over sterven en stervensbegeleiding: Een kwantitatieve analyse van honderd sterfgevallen, *Huisarts en Wetenschap*, 23: 439–46.

de Mol, B.A.J.M. (1994) Homage to the quack: From 'Earn as you learn' to 'Profit by safety'. Inaugural professorial oration. Delft University of Technology.

de Mol, B.A.J.M., Koornneef, F. and van Gaalen, G.L. (1995) What can be done to improve the safety of heart valves?, *International Journal of Risk Safety in Medicine*, 6: 157–68.

Foets, M., van der Velden, J. and de Bakker, D.H. (1992) *Dutch National Survey of General Practice. Summary of the Survey Design*. Utrecht: Nederlands Instituut voor Onderzoek van de Gezondheidszorg (NIVEL).

Grol, R., Whitfield, M., de Maeseneer, J. and Mokkink, H. (1990) Attitudes to risk taking in medical decision making among British, Dutch and Belgian general practitioners, *British Journal of General Practice*, 40: 134–6.

Koornneef, F., van Gaalen, G.L. and de Mol, B.A.J.M. (1996) A risk assessment and control model for the failing Björk–Shiley convexo-concave heart valve, *International Journal of Technical Assessment in Health Care*, 12: 141–5.

Lamberts, H. and Wood, M. (1987) *International Classification of Primary Care*. Oxford: Oxford University Press.

Leape, L.L. (1994) Error in medicine, *Journal of the American Medical Association*, 272: 1851–7.

Post, D. (1984) *Iatrogene Ziekten. Een Onderzoek naar de Oorsprong en Omvang*. Alphen aan den Rijn and Brussels: Stafleu.

Reason, J. (1995) A systems approach to organizational error, *Ergonomics*, 38: 1708–21.

Schadé, E. (1981) Het bestuderen van de doodsoorzaken bij patiënten in de huisartspraktijk: de opzet van een toetsing, *Nederlands Tijdschrift voor Geneeskunde*, 125: 1414–17.

Tempelaar, A.F. (1986) Sterfte en iatrogene schade, *Huisarts en Wetenschap*, 29: 34–7.

van den Bosch, W. (1985) Het lentse dodenboekje, *Huisarts en Wetenschap*, 28: 99–104.

van der Graaf, Y., de Waard, F., van Herwerden, L.A. and Defauw, J.J. (1992) Risk of strut fracture of Björk–Shiley valves, *Lancet*, 339: 257–61.

van der Velden, J., de Bakker, D.H., Claessens, A.A.M.C. and Schellevis, F.G. (1992) *Dutch National Survey of Morbidity in General Practice*. Utrecht: Nederlands Instituut voor Onderzoek van de Gezondheidszorg (NIVEL).

van der Wal, G.A. (1996) Medical disciplinary jurisprudence in The Netherlands: A 10-year survey, *Netherlands Journal of Medicine*, 140(52): 2640–4.

Vanes, J., Gill, K. and Tielens, V. (1978) *Valkuilen in de Huisartspraktijk*. Utrecht: Bohn, Scheltema & Holkema.

van Pelt-Temeer, A.M.M. and van den Berg, F.A. (1995) Hoe heeft het kunnen gebeuren? Beoordeling van fouten en bijna-ongelukken in een toetsgroep, *Huisarts en Wetenschap*, 38: 7–9, 29.

6 | Medical accidents and mishaps: the Swedish situation

Lars H. Fallberg and Johan Calltorp

Introduction

Medical mishaps and identification of problem doctors are not the subject of extensive public debate in Sweden. Existing systems, such as the Patient-skadeförsäkringen, (PSF) (Patient Compensation Insurance), largely exclude individual responsibility for medical mishaps. Instead, a preventive approach is taken, whereby efforts are made to provide information to healthcare professionals on adverse incidents in order that they can be encouraged to change their care accordingly. A number of information sources exists. In particular, data are available from formal and informal complaints procedures. However, the procedures could be used in a more effective and coordinated way that facilitates comparative analysis across Sweden.

The Swedish system

The Swedish healthcare system is a predominantly public service in terms of financing, ownership of healthcare facilities and control of the system. It is organized into national, regional and district levels. Swedish health providers are decentralized, with locally elected boards (county councils) in 26 geographically defined areas having an obligation to provide health services for citizens.

Health financing is closely linked to the county councils' right to levy taxes. Currently, around 80 per cent of health financing is allocated through this mechanism. A relatively insignificant fraction comes from patient fees (around 1–2 per cent) and the rest from central government contributions allocated to the county councils according to an essentially *per capita* formula.

This taxation power gives Swedish county councils a strong and relatively independent position in relation to central government (Calltorp 1996).

Specialized hospital care has dominated the Swedish healthcare system in the post-war era. No more than 20 per cent of the physicians have training in a primary care specialty. Recent attempts by the liberal coalition government of 1991–94 to change this long-term pattern included the introduction of a British GP-style 'house doctor system' where the population had to register with individual GPs. Introduction of a capitation payment to the GPs was planned, but when a new social democratic government came into power in the autumn of 1994, this new mandatory scheme was turned into a voluntary system dependent on the agreement of individual county councils.

Another major configuration has been the emergence of a purchaser–provider split, a development initiated by a few county councils in 1990. This scheme has evolved gradually and currently involves about half of the county councils. It is typical of the decentralized structure and power in Swedish healthcare that different county councils operate the internal market in different ways. Generally, the purchaser–provider split has increased productivity and customer awareness. It has also helped the system to cope with the rapidly growing demand for services which is the result of the combined pressures of an ageing population, rapid biomedical technological advances and the rising public expectations of the system. Sweden's population still has the world's highest proportion aged over 80 years.

Healthcare resources

Up until the beginning of the 1980s Sweden allocated a steadily increasing fraction of its Gross Domestic Product to health services. Since 1982 there has been a steady decrease, and at present around 7 per cent of gross domestic product is devoted to health. Around 1 per cent of the decrease can be accounted for by a shift of non-medical long-term care from the county councils to the municipalities. Even taking this into account, among the Organization for Economic Co-operation and Development (OECD) countries, Sweden has one of the most pronounced and active system-level cost containment programmes. At present a number of diverging initiatives are evident in Sweden. Under the umbrella of the purchaser–provider split, efforts are being made to develop organizational systems in health services. There is a marked interest in quality, chains of care and a process perspective. Typically different approaches are taken in different county councils, and this in turn has encouraged a new diversity.

Key players and decision-making

The traditional Swedish health services model attempted to strike a balance between centralized power held by national institutions and local power held by the different county councils. However, during the 1990s the structural changes mentioned above prompted a significant move towards decentralization. Consultancy and cooperation are very marked aspects of the Swedish way of decision-making. Despite this, at national level there remain a number of key actors involved in the regulation of healthcare. The National Board of Health and Welfare (Socialstyrelsen, SoS) has the task of supervising the performance and safety of health services. The Federation of County Councils (Landstingsförbundet) has a coordinating function for the 26 county councils. In addition there is the Swedish Institute for Health Services Development (Hälso- och sjukvårdens utvecklingsinstitut, SPRI) and the Swedish Council on Technology Assessment in Health Care (Statens beredning för medicinsk utvärdering, SBU), which is linked to an office of government. Parliament has a role in determining the overall rules for the healthcare system, and the Minister of Social Affairs executes the decisions of the Parliament. In addition, at regional level, Swedish healthcare is divided into six medical regions, each responsible for planning and coordination of medical services.

Research on medical mistakes

An important new focus for health policy is the need to control regulation of different types of mistakes in the system. But what is a medical mistake, and who is a problem doctor? Rosenthal (1995 : 8) has included the following in her definition of a problem doctor:

> impaired doctors by virtue of substance abuse, physical illness, mental illness, or manifestations of ageing; doctors whose knowledge or skills are poor by the standards of their peers: doctors who are 'burnt out', over-worked or are having personal problems; doctors whose personalities or personal behaviour are seen as problematic in the work environment; doctors who may be having a 'run' of bad results.

What is known of the real occurrence of medical mistakes in Swedish healthcare? Research on adverse events, problem doctors and medical mistakes is scarce and there has been no attempt in Sweden systematically to study and analyse errors and mistakes. In part this is due to a lack of coordination between different procedures and a tradition of medical paternalism.

Adverse events in surgery

In order to explore the nature of errors, complications and adverse outcomes in Swedish clinical surgery, a retrospective review of hospital records for 273 patients with 285 admissions was undertaken by researchers at Lund University (Troëng 1992). The selected records were studied for surgical and general complications and for errors according to classifications developed by Coach *et al.* (1981). The study suggests that error and adverse events occur at a rate similar to those in other developed countries. Errors were identified in 39 admissions, which represented 1 per cent of all admissions. A therapeutic error of commission was the most common. The study suggests that longer-term adverse outcomes, (that is, a lack of improvement over one year) are not uncommon, and in peripheral vascular surgery for chronic leg ischaemia a considerable number of patients did not improve clinically after one year (Troëng 1992).

The work environment of Swedish physicians

In the late 1980s the Swedish Medical Association started an investigation into the working environment of physicians which provide data on why mistakes might occur. The aim was to analyse the effects of the major changes in working environment which had occurred in previous decades. Progress in technical 'know-how' – as well as social, economical and political developments – had influenced working conditions considerably. One in ten physicians was surveyed using a postal questionnaire and 79 per cent responded. The survey focused on physicians' views about working on call, working hours, and feeling 'burnt out', as well as their use of tobacco and alcohol.

When on call, 21 per cent judged their performance to be worse than in 'ordinary' work and over half felt that their performance was lowered the first working day after being on call. Ten per cent felt themselves to be less empathetic in consultations with patients after a number of years of practice. About one-third said that they had no time to keep 'up to date' and develop their professional medical skills during their office hours. Twenty-three per cent indicated that they spent less than an hour a week on keeping their medical knowledge up to date.

As far as continuing education was concerned, about one-third did not participate regularly in any formalized education programme, and only 15 per cent were satisfied that they had the opportunity for further education in their medical speciality. Another problem identified by the study was the physician's exposure to alcohol and drugs. Physicians have easy access to addictive drugs and alcohol, since they are permitted to prescribe in *manum medici*. A quarter of physicians said they 'needed a drink' after work to calm down. Only 6 per cent said they needed a drink in order to sleep, but as many as 19 per cent said they personally knew one or more colleagues who were addicted to alcohol. When it comes to sedatives, 24 per cent of female and 16 per cent of male physicians admitted to using them from time to time.

The perioperative study

The Perioperative Risk Project (Ouchterlony *et al.* 1995) was a clinical and epidemiological prospective study of perioperative risk and its determinants in anaesthesia and surgery. The records of 1361 patients subjected to elective general and orthopaedic surgery were examined. General anaesthesia was given to 59 per cent and regional or local anaesthesia to 41 per cent. Adverse preoperative events occurred in 19 per cent. The most common problems were circulatory (11 per cent), respiratory (4 per cent) and allergic reactions (1 per cent). However, only one-eighth of the adverse events were detected through the official registration system. The authors concluded that simplified registration systems, like the official Swedish cipher-like coding used at the time of the study, were hampered by human error both in the coding process and at data entry (Ouchterlony *et al.* 1995).

Nurses and medical mistakes

Attention has also been paid to mistakes by other clinicians. The Swedish Nurses' Association (Svensk Sjuksköterskeförening) undertook a study to compare medical mistakes made by nurses educated in traditional nursing schools with those who had had alternative postgraduate education. The research was based on complaints to the Medical Disciplinary Board (Hälso- och sjukvårdens ansvarsnämnd, HSAN) between 1984 and 1989. The most frequent causes of complaint concerned lack of knowledge in relation to delegation, handling of drugs and documentation. Medication mistakes related to the handling of drugs were caused by lack of control rather than mistakes in measuring the right dosage. All complaints were within areas of expertise covered by the education programmes. There was no correlation between education and the number of complaints. However, the study revealed that 33 per cent of the nurses in the survey had not been working within their field of competence.

Gender disparities in patient care

Attempts have also been made to explore the part that gender has to play in understanding medical mishaps. The National Committee on Gender Disparities in Patient Care analysed information from five sources of patient dissatisfaction: the HSAN, the PSF, the National Register of Medical Incidents, the SoS and one of the 33 county council complaints boards (CCB). When these sources are combined, female patients account for 60 per cent of all reports and represent a slightly higher percentage of the number of 'successful' complaints resulting in financial compensation or disciplinary sanctions. The report shows that 70 per cent of all complaints to the HSAN and the CCBs are related to physician–patient interactions and 90 per cent of complaints to the CCBs are about lack of sufficient information during the care and treatment process. The study discovered that a major part of patients' complaints to the HSAN and the CCBs concerned general practice and psychiatric care. However, a majority of financially compensated cases are generated by surgical specialities, especially orthopaedics.

Tracking mistakes and mishaps

A number of other sources of data are available within the Swedish healthcare system which can contribute to the identification of medical mishaps. In this section eight major resources are described: the SoS; the National Register on Medical Incidents; the Medical Access and Results System (MARS); quality registers in different specialities; the HSAN; the CCBs; the PSF; and quality management systems.

National Board of Health and Welfare

The SoS is the supervisory body of all healthcare services, including dentistry and the private sector. It has six regional offices, and its primary goals are to promote patient safety and a high quality of care. It attempts to achieve this goal through preventive measures, regulation and the imposition of sanctions such as fines on healthcare institutions or a partial or total closing down of activities. The SoS regularly publishes guidelines, recommendations and other information for healthcare providers to apply. Actions taken by the SoS are often initiated by healthcare providers or patient reports. The SoS undertakes an analysis of complaint reports and, where appropriate, sends them to the HSAN for a decision. However, patients may also address the HSAN directly.

National Register on Medical Incidents

Each healthcare provider in Sweden has an obligation to report all adverse incidents, or risk of them, to the SoS (Lagen om tillsyn över hälso- och sjukvården, 1996: 785) in the interest of improving the quality of health services. A reportable *incident* is one where a patient has been injured, or exposed to such a risk, by healthcare providers. All such incidents are registered and classified in a national register according to a number of indicators, such as whether they involved diagnosis, level of care, or medical or pharmaceutical injury. The SoS regularly publishes anonymized information bulletins from this database which are distributed to hospitals, primary care centres and education centres. Researchers, healthcare institutions and others are free to use this material without restriction. However, by reporting an incident to the SoS, healthcare personnel are at risk of being reported to the HSAN, and this significantly limits their willingness to make reports. Consequently, the number of unreported incidents is high, and this makes it difficult to draw any general conclusions from the material.

The MARS database

The MARS database was created by the SoS as a response to the rapid changes in medical technology and treatment procedures. The objectives of the database are threefold:

- to level out regional differences in the availability and capacity of sources;
- to facilitate effective use of all available resources in the care-providing units; and
- to develop measurement and outcome standards, as well as evaluation tools, locally and regionally.

Quality registers in different medical specialities

In addition to the sources of information reviewed so far, there are 33 national registers in different medical specialities. The registers often evolved at the initiative of local researchers and physicians and are now run with financial aid from the state. The collection of information is voluntary and depends on the cooperation of different clinics around the country. In a study of all clinics (134) in one participating speciality, undertaken in 1994, around 80 per cent of clinics asserted that the information collected was important and 39 per cent believed that it had affected the care and outcome of medical treatments they had undertaken (Garpenby and Carlsson 1994). The information in the register is not public (Johansson 1995), although participating clinics can, if they wish, evaluate the outcome data for the public.

The Medical Responsibility Board

In spite of the fact that it is extremely unusual for patients in Sweden to sue their doctor for medical mistakes, recent research (Arnetz 1997) has revealed that physicians fear the possibility. The Swedish healthcare system offers a number of complaint procedures and other systems for managing medical mistakes. Where a service user has a grievance there are informal complaints procedures which operate in parallel with formal ones. The purpose of the informal systems is to handle patient dissatisfaction with medical services without the need for the courts and other formal procedures. As is the case in the UK, it is estimated that a large number of complaints (around 85–95 per cent) are related to lack of communication between patients and carers. As a result the informal processes aim to promote good communication.

The most important task of the HSAN is to contribute to patient safety in health services, including dentistry. Unlike its Nordic counterparts, the HSAN is separate from the supervisory board, the SoS. The HSAN consists of eight members representing patients and professionals, and an independent chairman, who is a judge. It has the power to decide whether the standard of care provided by healthcare professionals who are the subject of complaint was acceptable. The HSAN has the power to sanction anyone licensed to work within the health service. However, the number of sanctions received or their severity does not affect the professionals' right to practice. Available sanctions also include the ability to withdraw the licences of healthcare personnel and to limit their right to prescribe drugs.

The HSAN has been criticized for non-systematic feedback of its decisions to the profession and lack of usable statistics on medical mistakes. However, since its decisions became computerized at the beginning of the 1990s, the distribution of information has improved. The HSAN is now required by statute to make its decisions public.

County complaints boards

Patients may also complain to one of 30 CCBs. Every county is obliged to provide a complaints board for its citizens. The purpose of the board is to provide patients with the information they need about making a complaint and to facilitate communication with healthcare personnel. The CCB has no right to take disciplinary action or to decide on compensation for patient injury. A recent government report criticized the unsystematic approach of the CCBs and came to the conclusion that comprehensive statistics of patient complaints to CCBs should be made available. The lack of data makes it difficult to analyse trends, and renders it impossible to make comparisons with other information sources and evaluate CCBs' present and future role in quality management (Statens Offentliga Utredningar 1996).

Patient Compensation System

The Swedish PSF was introduced in 1975 as a voluntary insurance scheme for healthcare providers, and has since been used as a model for other Nordic countries. The PSF is used when patients claim financial compensation for injuries caused to them. Up to 1994, the PSF had received 82,500 applications for financial compensation, which it granted in 35,400 cases. Table 6.1 shows details of the patient complaint reports made in 1996. The PSF database includes information about the year of the injury, the employer involved (county council), the reason for treatment, the reason for the injury and the effect of the injury. In 1997 the PSF changed from being a voluntary insurance scheme, based upon agreement between care providers and the state, to a statutory compulsory insurance scheme for all healthcare providers. Compensation can be awarded for injuries caused to patients in all Swedish hospitals, as well as in primary care. All Swedish patients are covered by this legislation. The statute has resulted in a substantial increase in awards to patients. Before the introduction of PSF in

Table 6.1 Patient complaint reports in 1996

Organization	Number of complaint reports
Medical Responsibility Board	2,660
No Fault Liability Insurance Scheme	7,011
Medical incident register	1,388
County council complaints boards	15,400

1975, an average of only ten cases per year received compensation for maltreatment (Oldertz 1988). The figure is now 200 times higher.

As part of this scheme, a special analysis group, including medical experts, continuously monitors the development of patient injuries and makes suggestions about how they might be prevented. Guidelines are developed based on evidence and lessons of cases handled by the insurer. In the beginning of 1991, a project (Rosén and Jonsson 1992) was launched by the PSF in collaboration with SPRI. The aim was to find out how useful the PSF database was as a source of information concerning the kinds of damage and why they occurred. In addition, the project was to develop the existing classification system in order to better aid continuous quality improvement by care providers.

Quality management systems

Other initiatives promise to generate data which will be of use for the identification of future mishaps. In 1997 statutory provisions for the use of quality systems in healthcare services and dentistry were issued by the SoS. The provisions require every healthcare provider to implement a quality system and define the ambit of professional responsibility at managerial level. However, they do not include instructions as to what kind of quality method should be used. The purpose of the legislation is to make it mandatory for every care provider to have a quality management system. Although it has been within organizations' discretion to decide the type of system to be introduced, recently considerable effort has been put into development of peer review models and many of these are currently being implemented (Calltorp 1990). The legislation has granted supervisory powers to the SoS over these quality management systems, but these powers are severely limited. The SoS's jurisdiction in this field does not extend beyond ensuring that a system is in place.

Questions for further investigation

In summary, a review of available data raises a number of important questions about the identification of medical mishaps in practice and the inter-organizational handling of data. Are some medical specialities more likely to make mistakes than others? Are some more exposed to sanctions? A number of factors need to be taken into account when addressing these questions. One important factor is the visibility of the care. Procedures undertaken by surgeons might, for instance, have more serious and more immediately observable consequences than the actions of a general practitioner. In the USA, medical specialities, such as gynaecologists and neurosurgeons have been more exposed to lawsuits than other specialities. In Sweden, preliminary studies indicate a similar pattern.

Does it make any difference to quality and risk management initiatives if health service managers have a medical background? On the one hand, lay managers might see themselves as not responsible for medical issues, while a medical director might be more prone to regard these issues as top managerial ones. On the other hand, there might be examples of collegiality inhibiting action.

To what extent will repeated changes in the organizational structure of an institution, and high turnover among leaders, be mirrored in insufficient attention to issues of malpractice? It is easy for managers to be diverted from important operational issues when they are subjected to frequent organizational changes and leadership turnover. There is evidence of a lack of 'organizational memory' and of low priority given to quality issues, in situations of organizational turmoil. This can cause a distraction from such important managerial issues as malpractice.

Concluding remarks

The 'social innovation' of no fault compensation, for which Sweden is well known, was expected to have a number of positive effects on medical practice, leading to increased openness, honesty and generosity. However, the scheme can also have negative effects. In particular, it might shield incapable physicians in cases of serious damage to patients. Since the PSF focuses on legal protection of patients and their financial 'recovery', no disciplinary action is taken in relation to medical professionals. Physicians, nurses and others are encouraged to report, or to help injured patients report, any injuries that might be subject to compensation. For disciplinary matters, other organizations and other complaints procedures have to be sought for and applied. In pursuing a case through the PSF, the incentive is money. In the disciplinary complaints system, it is justice – not wanting anyone else to be injured by that physician.

A study by the Swedish National Audit Office (Riksrevisionsverket 1996) found that too much of the SoS's time is devoted to dealing with complaints from patients. Systematic analysis with a view to facilitating the prevention of accidents receives little time or effort. The study also found that incentives for physicians to report serious accidents are lacking. The fear of being punished reduces the willingness to report. The consequence of this is that the majority of mistakes will remain undiscovered.

In the analysis of the situation presented here, we have found that there has not been sufficient emphasis on tracking problem doctors and taking preventive action. There are high expectations of physicians, and from the user perspective all physicians are perceived as more or less 'equally competent'. The Swedish system does not allow the patient to choose his or her physician. This shifts the focus away from patient choice based on assessment of competence. The PSF tends to review the medical system in a lukewarm way. It forgives physicians and provides patients with inadequate compensation (Fallberg and Borgenhammar 1997).

The Swedish system for dealing with medical mistakes has sufficient information sources, which researchers, administrators and others can use to obtain valuable information. However, these sources are not properly coordinated. Information systems overlap each other and it is difficult to identify systematic efforts to track down and deal with individuals who make medical mistakes. We believe that efforts are needed to systematize and distribute information on medical mistakes in such a way that preventive measures can be taken. Some kind of social safety net also needs to be set up. Anyone identified as a 'problem doctor' or 'problem nurse' in healthcare is facing a personal disaster which demands the establishment of rehabilitation and training programmes before professionals will be encouraged to invest in such a system.

References

Arnetz, B. (1997) Unpublished data from a study at the Karolinska Hospital, Stockholm, Sweden.

Calltorp, J. (1990) Physician manpower politics in Sweden, *Health Policy*, 15: 105–18.

Calltorp, J. (1996) Swedish experiences with fixed regional budgets, in F.W. Schwartz, H. Glennerster and R.B. Saltman (eds) *Fixing Health Budgets: Experiences from Europe and North America*. Chichester: Wiley.

Coach, N.P., Tilney, N.L., Rayner, A.A. and Moore, F.D. (1981) The high cost of low-frequency events, *New England Journal of Medicine*, 301: 604.

Fallberg, L. and Borgenhammar, E. (1997) Problem doctors in P. Lens and G. Wal (eds) *Problem Doctors: A Conspiracy of Silence*. Amsterdam: IOS Press.

Garpenby, P. and Carlsson, P. (1994) Utvärdering och förslag till organisation av nationella register. Centre for Medical Technology Assessment Report. Linköping: Universitetet i Linköping.

Johansson, A. (1995) Utvidgad sjukvårdsinformation. Vårdresultat och kvalitetsmått. (förstudie). Unpublished report. Stockholm: SPRI.

Oldertz, C. (1988) The patient, pharmaceutical and security insurance, in C. Oldertz and F. Tidefelt (eds) *Compensation for Personal Injury in Sweden and Other Countries*. Stockholm: Juristförlaget.

Ouchterlony, J., Arvidsson, S., Sjöstedt, L. and Svärdsudd, K. (1995) Perioperative and immediate postoperative adverse events in patients undergoing elective general and orthopaedic surgery. The Gothenburg study of perioperative risk (PROPER), part II, *Arta Anaesthesiologica Scandinavica*, 39: 643–52.

Riksrevisionsverket (1996) *Statens tillsyn över hälso-och sjukvården – en effektivitetsrevision*. Stockholm: Riksrevisionsverket. (State inspection over health and medical services.)

Rosén, B. and Jonsson, P.M. (1992) *Patientförsäkringens skademateral som underlag för skadeförebyggande verksamhet*. Stockholm: SPRI.

Rosenthal, M. (1995) *The Incompetent Doctor: Behind Closed Doors*. Buckingham: Open University Press.

Statens Offentliga Utredningar (1996) Rapporterade brister och problem ur ett könsperspektiv, in *Jämställd vård på lika villkor*. Stockholm: Norstedts.

Troëng, T. (1992) On errors and adverse outcomes in surgery: learning from experience. Doctoral dissertation. Malmö: University of Lund.

7 Safety of healthcare in Australia: adverse events to hospitalized patients

Ross McL. Wilson, Robert Gibberd, John Hamilton and Bernie Harrison

Iatrogenic injuries or adverse events to patients have always been a possible outcome for hospitalized patients. From the perspective of patients, as well as healthcare providers and funders, this is an issue of increasing importance. Determination of the size and nature of the problem is essential in fashioning and prioritizing an appropriate response. Furthermore, monitoring the frequency of adverse events is required in order to measure the effectiveness of future interventions, as well as to detect new causes of adverse events as they might arise. Hence there is increasing interest in the regular reporting of these events as an essential part of any quality of care programme. The main constraint, however, is that the processes involved in obtaining data on the nature and the extent of adverse events are considerably more complex and difficult than those required for many other hospital statistics. For example, clinical indicators such as readmission rates and infection rates, although not necessarily a valid or reliable measure of quality, can be more easily documented and recorded than adverse events, which involve measuring the 'unintended patient injury caused by medical management rather than the disease process'. The need to use clinical judgement in order to determine 'unintended patient injury' has so far prevented the use of standard clinical indicators. To establish a simple coping schedule is still a major research challenge.

Despite these limitations, Australia is one of the few countries to have made a serious attempt to make national estimates of the magnitude of patient injury caused by healthcare. Such estimates have involved different sources of data, and we summarize the divergent results below. There are at least seven sources of data that can be used (Commonwealth of Australia 1994), and we list them from least to most valid as a measure of the adverse event rate.

1 Medical defence organizations, which provide professional indemnity for medical practitioners in Australia, receive claims from patients demanding financial compensation for perceived poor outcome from the healthcare that they have received. These organizations provide minimal data on these claims, but the number is estimated to be about 1600 per annum, for the years 1987–91 (Commonwealth of Australia 1994). The number of successful claims and the relationship of the complaint to the presence of an adverse event are not known. A US study (Localio *et al.* 1991) suggests that most adverse events do not result in claims, and that not all claims relate to adverse events, nor successful claims to adverse events resulting from negligence.

2 Anaesthetic-related mortality collections in Australia report that there were over 1300 deaths in the three years 1985–87, and that approximately 20 per cent of these reported deaths were partly or wholly due to the anaesthetic or an aspect of its management (Commonwealth of Australia 1994). This estimate is likely to be an underestimate according to a Working Party that reviewed the results, and represents a mortality rate from anaesthesia of about 25 per million population.

3 In 90 hospitals throughout Australia, anaesthetists were invited to report (voluntarily and anonymously) any unintended incident that reduced or could have reduced the safety margin for a patient. This study, the Australian Incident Monitoring Study, has received more than 2000 reports of incidents relating to anaesthesia. These reports of incidents have been analysed and the results published in a special volume of the journal on anaesthesia and intensive care (Runciman 1993). Voluntary reporting of incidents can be useful for providing information on the nature and immediate context for errors as they occur, but there are considerable limitations in the types of adverse events that are documented (errors that are not recognized at the time of patient contact are missed). Incident reports are also unable to provide population estimates of the number of adverse events, since the quality of reporting incidents varies dramatically within and between hospitals, and with time.

4 The Adverse Drug Reactions Advisory Committee received 4920 voluntary adverse drug reaction reports in 1990 (Commonwealth of Australia 1994), while other estimates based on in-patient data suggest that there were 30,000–40,000 admissions to hospitals related to adverse drug reactions (National Health Strategy 1992). Not all adverse drug reactions will qualify as an adverse event, using the definition given below, since they may not result in disability or prolonged length of stay.

5 The hospital in-patient data provide some information on the incidence of adverse events through the use of the E-code (a code, from the International Classification of Diseases to indicate that an external cause was associated with the hospitalization), which allows for the coding of misadventures during surgical and medical care. Using data from public and private hospitals in Australia, it was estimated that 4 per cent of all admissions (or 146,000 admissions), were possible adverse events

(Commonwealth of Australia 1994). O'Hara and Carson (1997) have recently reported that for 1994–95, 5 per cent of all admissions in Victoria had an E-code that indicated an adverse event. The increase is likely to be due to better reporting of E-codes as a result of the increased use of these data for funding purposes. Most of the E-codes were for surgery or other procedures (81 per cent), indicating that those adverse events that occur as a result of medical or diagnostic care are less well reported. E-codes have also been used to determine the adverse event rate in laparoscopic cholecystectomy, which was found in Victoria to be 6.7 per cent from 1987 to 1994 (Ackland *et al.* 1997).

6 The above studies were used to provide estimates of the number of adverse events and the extra bed-days resulting from these adverse events in Australia. The estimate was that there were 58,000 to 146,000 adverse events, with the costs being A$213 million to A$536 million, based on a per diem rate of A$367 (Commonwealth of Australia 1994).

7 Finally, there are the results of the Quality in Australian Health Care Study (QAHCS 1996; Wilson *et al.* 1995). This study was designed to produce national estimates of the level of adverse events, where an adverse event is defined as involving three components: (1) an unintended injury or complication which (2) results in disability, death or prolongation of hospital stay, and (3) is caused by healthcare management rather than the patient's disease. This study was based on a retrospective medical record review of over 14,000 admissions in 1992 and found that 16.6 per cent of hospital admissions were associated with an adverse event. These adverse events occurred either during the 'index' hospitalization, or before it, or were substantially responsible for it. This adverse event level translated into an annual estimate of 470,000 adverse events, or 3.3 million bed-days, and hence a cost of nearly A$1 billion for 1992. Thus, this study revealed that the methods listed above in items 1–6 provided estimates that were 20 per cent or less of the QAHCS estimate. The estimates in source no. 6 above were also influenced by the results of the Harvard Medical Practice Study (Brennan *et al.* 1991), which estimated the ratio of adverse events to admissions as 3.6 per cent (the ratio for the QAHCS study was 13 per cent). If the methodologies are comparable, this implies that the level of injury and the cost to the healthcare system in Australia is four times as high as expected, and that therefore there is now a greater potential benefit from developing a systematic approach for describing the nature of the adverse events, their preventability and level of disability. Methods to reduce the number of adverse events are an important area for future research.

The QAHCS data also provide information on why the other methods listed above underestimated the level of adverse events. In the 14,000 records sampled, only 16 medical records had documentation indicating litigation, and of these only seven were judged to be adverse events. Thus, the data from the medical defence organizations are an invalid measure of adverse events. Similarly, only 4 per cent of admissions had E-codes, of which 36 per cent were judged not to be adverse events. The sensitivity of E-codes is low for predicting adverse events, being 24 per cent. The recording of anaesthesia incidents and adverse drug reactions, considered important events, was found to make up only 2.2 per cent and 10.8 per cent of adverse events respectively in the QAHCS. That is, only 13 per cent of all adverse events are possibly recorded in the data collections of sources 3 and 4 above. The areas of greatest concern, the technical and cognitive performance of practitioners, are discussed in a later section.

The Australian healthcare system

The concern about measurement of adverse events in Australian hospitals may suggest that there are some aspects of Australian healthcare that require special attention, thus distinguishing it from that of other countries. Comparison of the results in the Harvard Medical Practice Study and the QAHCS may also lead to a conclusion that quality of care is inferior in Australia. However, Australia rates very highly relative to other OECD countries when performance is compared in terms of health expenditure, life expectancy and supply of services. Taylor and Salkeld (1996) have summarized the 1993 OECD database on health-related indices. Out of 24 OECD countries, Australia has improved its ranking in life expectancy to eighth in 1990, ahead of the USA and the UK, while being similar to Canada. The acute hospital bed supply of 5.3 per 1000 ranks sixth highest, with 170 admissions per 1000 population being the eighth highest, and bed-days per capita 2.8 (rank of 11th). Australia is also similarly placed in expenditure on health per capita (US$1310) and total expenditure on health as a proportion of GDP (8.2 per cent). Healthcare prices have been relatively stable from 1975 to 1990. The one area where Australia is different from many European countries is in public expenditure on health as a proportion of total health expenditure (68 per cent, rank 20th) which makes Australia more like the USA.

Thus, using these crude indices, it would seem reasonable to expect that the adverse event rates in Australia might be similar to those in other OECD countries. It is difficult, however, at this time to make any direct comparisons due to the lack of data in other countries, and even if these were available, there remains the underlying problem associated with all international comparisons: namely that the data are often not comparable. Given the importance of the findings in the QAHCS, the next section summarizes some of the results.

The quality in Australian health care study

The QAHCS was commissioned by the Australian government. The main findings have been published (Wilson *et al.* 1995) and two additional reports expand on the material already published (QAHCS Consortium 1996). The methodology was based on that used in the Harvard Medical Practice Study. The major modification was to replace the Harvard Medical Practice Study measure of negligence with a measure of the degree of preventability of the adverse event. The aim was not to determine the amount of negligence in Australian healthcare, as this would not provide a complete picture of the level of poor patient outcome. An additional component added to the study was not only to collect quantitative data, but also to use narrative text fields to describe the clinical situation, to provide a description of the unintended injury and to identify the errors and the causes leading to the adverse events.

The details of the sampling methodology, the measure of agreement between the reviewers for classifying adverse events, detailed tabulations and their implications are contained in the references, but the important results are summarized below:

- 16.6 per cent of admissions were associated with an adverse event, and for 8.3 per cent of admissions the adverse events were judged to have high preventability.
- 46.6 per cent of adverse events caused minimal disability (resolved in less than one month); in 77.1 per cent of adverse events the disability had resolved within 12 months; 13.7 per cent of adverse events resulted in permanent disability (excluding death); and 4.9 per cent of adverse events resulted in death. For 4.3 per cent of adverse events, it was not possible to determine the disability.
- The proportion of admissions associated with an adverse event increased with age: 10.8 per cent for ages 0–14, increasing to 23.3 per cent for ages over 65. The relationship with age was much stronger for adverse events that resulted in permanent disability: 0.9 per cent and 6.1 per cent for ages 0–14 and over 65, respectively.
- A significantly lower proportion of the adverse events were reported for obstetrics (7.2 per cent) and ear, nose and throat surgery (7.9 per cent) than for other specialties, while a higher proportion were associated with digestive (23.2 per cent), musculoskeletal (21.9 per cent) and circulatory (20.2 per cent) disorders.
- Adverse events resulting from problems with 'decision-making' were generally associated with increased preventability, permanent disability and death.
- Errors of omission (52 per cent of adverse events) were almost twice as common as errors of commission (27 per cent of adverse events).
- Half of the adverse events (50 per cent) were associated with an operation, and 14 per cent with a diagnostic clinical category. Adverse events for which the 'system' within the hospital could be regarded as partly responsible accounted for 16 per cent.

The findings above refer to the quantitative fields in the study, and we present in tabular form the results obtained from reviewing the text data.

Table 7.1   Human cause codes and the percentage of adverse events with these codes

Description	%
Complication of, or failure in, the technical performance of an indicated procedure	43.3
Failure to synthesize, decide and/or act on available information	19.8
Failure to request or arrange an investigation, procedure or consultation	14.7
Lack of care/attention, failure to attend	13.6
Misapplication of, or failure to apply, a rule; or use of a bad or inadequate rule	11.0
Violation of a protocol or rule (failure to practise basic medicine)	6.0
Do not know/cannot tell	3.9
Other	3.5
Acting on insufficient information	2.3
Slips and lapses; errors due to 'absent-mindedness' in activities in which the operator is skilled	2.0
Failure to continue established management	1.8
Lack of knowledge	1.4
Electively practising outside area of expertise	1.3
Questionable practice ethics	0.6

The adverse events were classified by human cause codes, system cause codes and clinical situation summary codes. The results are presented as frequencies.

Eighty-two per cent of adverse events had at least one human cause code associated with them, and five of the possible 13 human cause codes accounted for over 80 per cent of all codes (Table 7.1). These findings are consistent with the clinical category findings summarized above, which highlight the major source of adverse events as technical and cognitive performance errors.

One of the aims of QAHCS was to focus on possible system errors within the hospital environment, rather than focusing on the medical staff's errors. The contribution of the 'system' to the causation of an adverse event was judged by the reviewers who were required to indicate the system causes. Given that the medical record was the original data source for the QAHCS, it is reasonable to propose that the contributions of individuals will overshadow the contributions of the 'system' in which they function. Fifty-nine per cent of the adverse events had a system cause code, which is a low percentage given the studies of Deming (1986) who found that over 90 per cent of quality problems within industry can be assigned to 'system' problems. The most frequent system cause codes were problems with policies and protocols (33 per cent) and education and training (24 per cent); see Table 7.2.

In an attempt to determine the areas for the possible prevention of adverse events to patients, the clinical situation in which the adverse event

Table 7.2 Percentage of adverse events associated with a system cause code

Description	%
Policies and protocols	32.7
Education and training	24.4
Unable to determine appropriate category	13.8
Organization, flow, storage and/or display of information	4.6
Organization culture	2.7
Organization management	2.6
Other	2.0
Personnel: the number available or their quality	2.0
Patient placed or managed in an inappropriate facility	1.0
Equipment and other physical resources: their availability or quality	0.7

occurred was categorized as a shorthand way of 'setting the clinical scene'. This has value for developing the context for the discussion on preventative strategies. Five per cent of the adverse events were without a clinical situation code. Of the remaining adverse events, technical problems, failed care processes and infections were the top three clinical situation codes and were associated with 36 per cent, 31 per cent and 23 per cent of the adverse events, respectively (Table 7.3).

The future effect of these data on policy in healthcare in Australia is difficult to determine at this stage, due to the political sensitivities of the material. Initially the government of the day formed a Taskforce on Quality in Australian Health Care whose task was to recommend improvements in the safety of healthcare. Its report (Task Force Report 1996) was released by the Australian government in December 1996 without any endorsement of its recommendations, and to date there has been no national systematic action. However, various medical bodies have begun to express interest in the Taskforce recommendations and have begun using the QAHCS data for their own specific roles in the monitoring of quality of healthcare. Further, some hospitals have begun to use methods similar to the QAHCS protocol to monitor the adverse event rates in their own hospital, and to use the results with clinicians to reduce the adverse event rate. One hospital has reported a successful reduction in the adverse event rate as a result of this approach (Wolff 1996), although the study does suffer from the lack of a control hospital.

One of the main issues arising from these studies is to determine the advantages of the different approaches to measure adverse events. The cheapest method involves the use of voluntary reporting of adverse events, but there are clear limitations to interpreting the results, since there is no denominator and no control over the criteria used to report them. The review of medical records within a single hospital provides data for clinicians to use for monitoring their work and determining possible improvements.

Table 7.3   Percentage of adverse events with the given clinical situation summary code

Description	%
Technical problem	36.0
Failed care process	30.8
Infection	23.3
Delay	20.0
Treatment	19.6
Patient factors (psychiatric, frail or disabled, poor cooperation, language)	17.4
Acute care problem	16.9
Orthopaedic problem	13.1
Investigation	10.7
Drug problem	8.0
Cancer or oncology problem	8.0
Acute cardiology problem	6.2
Early or inappropriate discharge	5.4
Vascular surgery problem	3.3
Pain	2.9
Deep vein thrombosis or pulmonary embolism	2.7
Anaemia	2.6
Unnecessary procedure	2.6
Diabetes	2.5
Anti-coagulant therapy	2.3
Hepatobiliary problem	2.2
Peptic ulcer or GI haemorrhage	2.2
Fall	2.2
Urinary catheter problem	2.0
Asthma	1.0
Problem with intravenous access or cannula	0.6

However, these results are not easily used for national estimates due to the differences in coding practices. The major advantages of the studies such as Harvard Medical Practice Study and QAHCS are that they allow a measure of between-hospital variation, and that high variation between hospitals in patient outcome may indicate that the processes used in the different hospitals are causing the variation. The QAHCS showed that the adverse event rate across hospitals was highly variable (8–25 per cent), but that the adverse event proportion was not associated with whether the hospital was a teaching or non-teaching hospital, or whether the hospital was a public or private hospital. The level of variation between hospitals can be used to establish possible target levels for future adverse event rates that could be achieved under an ideal system.

The major disadvantage associated with the QAHCS methodology is that only summary data on admissions without adverse events are collected. There is information on diagnoses, procedures, diagnostic related groups, age and sex for these admissions, but no data are collected on the technical performance for the procedure carried out or the patient outcome. This information would add considerably to the costs of the study. This means that there is not a complete data set with which to assess the differences between admissions with and without adverse events.

Ideal systems to monitor and prevent adverse events

The ideal system for recording adverse events would be valid, reliable and cost-effective. In reality, the tools or methods are not currently available that would allow such a system to be implemented on a routine basis. It is not yet clear that a continuous measurement system is required to improve the quality of healthcare, compared with a series of 'snapshot' studies. No 'snapshot' study to date has been followed by a series of interventions and a post-intervention analysis. One must assume that the impetus that led to the initial studies has passed, and hence that much of their value related to the monitoring of change has therefore been lost.

In order to obtain a quantitative estimate of the incidence or prevalence of adverse events, medical record review is the only proven methodology. Its limitations are based on the very nature of the medical record, which provides little contextual information about what else was happening at a particular moment in time around but not directly involving the patient in question. But it does provide a valid and reliable measure of patient safety for that patient (Wilson *et al.* 1995). Obtaining this information from clinical indicators or E-codes has not been shown to be reliable or valid. Obtaining this information from incident reporting has the advantage of providing the contextual data, but, given the lack of a denominator, incident reporting is unable to provide quantitative rates and the reliability of the numerator is poor, given that it is obtained on a voluntary basis.

Hence, medical record review is the only proven means of measuring patient safety through adverse events. Initially, the resource implications may appear to be too large. However, major resources are currently expended on financial and activity data systems in healthcare and these data are valued by the funders and administrators of healthcare. As the significant cost of adverse events becomes established, and the potential to reduce this cost becomes a priority, the data obtained from the medical record review will become valued by patients and providers.

It is interesting to consider the recent research into public health, since it may provide an indication into what may occur in the field of patient injury in hospitals. Public health interventions that relate to smoking reduction, heart disease and cancer prevention were trialled in towns (COMMIT Research Group 1995; CART Project Team 1997). Each study used ten or more intervention towns, which were matched with a control town. There were before and after measurements to determine the impact of the interventions. These projects required large financial resources. A similar research design could be used for patient injury, with hospitals replacing towns. Half of the hospitals would receive a major intervention to reduce the adverse event rate, and the other half would be controls. Before and after measurements would be required to evaluate the intervention. To carry out such a study, a valid and reliable measure of adverse events is required, and at this stage this would need to be a medical record review.

Organizations dealing with complaints and discipline procedures

In Australia there is now a national policy on the need for an independent patient 'ombudsman' and complaints body for each state. The titles vary from Health Care Complaints Commission to Health Rights Commission, but the essential functions are consistent from state to state. These are to provide an independent recipient of, and investigator of, patients' complaints about their healthcare. It is funded and accountable to government at a senior level. In New South Wales this body works closely with the professional registration boards for medical and other healthcare practitioners, both referring and acting as an investigatory arm. It has no specific disciplinary powers, other than access to the civil jurisdiction, but none the less is a powerful body in providing support for patients and external accountability for health services and providers.

Professional disciplinary powers rest with the professional registration boards, which depend on specific referrals against providers from a wide range of sources, but mainly patients. These boards have the power to suspend or terminate the legal right of an individual practitioner to continue in clinical practice. In addition, some boards have the capacity to offer identification of, and assistance to, the impaired practitioner. These boards do not cover all healthcare providers, but do cover doctors, nurses, pharmacists and so on. The providing of board registration to healthcarers from so called 'alternative' areas such as herbal medicine is currently being explored, but the issue is not clear-cut. From the perspective of the patient, having a professional registration board provides reassurance about the training and qualification of the practitioner, but few boards have mandatory recertification, with most having certification for 'life'. On the other hand, registration with a professional board can facilitate a monopoly for the registered providers, and hence may not necessarily be in the patient's best interest in the longer term. This dilemma is still being explored.

As far as litigation is concerned, the level in Australia is apparently lower than in the USA, but accurate figures on rates of claim and the outcomes of claims are not publicly available. The cost to medical practitioners of annual premiums for medical indemnity continues to rise, and has moved from approximately A$500 annually in 1982 to approximately A$15,000 annually in 1997 for a general surgeon. This vastly exceeds the rate of inflation for the period, and can be used as a surrogate for the costs being incurred by insurers. Successful civil litigation for negligence seems to be increasing, as does the dollar value of the settlement. Successful criminal litigation for gross negligence has not yet occurred in New South Wales, but is occurring in the different jurisdiction of New Zealand. The prospect of criminal proceedings would seem anecdotally to be a powerful stimulus to risk management programmes, but there are few if any published data.

There is evidence that the use of litigation and accreditation, while necessary, does not provide the best outcome in terms of reducing the adverse event rate.

Conclusion

The conclusion of this review is that a retrospective review of hospital medical records is the most reliable method for estimating patient injury caused by healthcare. The costs of carrying out these studies are high, but could be justified if there were a corresponding reduction in patient injury. Extrapolating the data on the proportion of admissions and the additional bed-days associated with adverse events to all hospitals in Australia in 1992 indicated that about 470,000 admissions and 3.3 million bed-days were attributable to adverse events. These national estimates provide empirical data for further studies on quality of care in Australian hospitals.

Given the similarity between the Australian health system and those of other OECD countries, the implications of this study in terms of preventable adverse outcomes for patients and the use of health resources are substantial. There is now evidence that similar studies should be carried out in other countries. The study of the epidemiology of adverse events will have major implications for policy on litigation in healthcare, quality of care programmes, including the development of safe protocols or practices, and possibly patient education on aspects of healthcare.

References

Ackland, M.J., Jolley, D.J. and Ansari, M.Z. (1997) Postoperative complications of cholecystectomy in Victorian public hospitals, *Australian and New Zealand Journal of Public Health*, 20: 583–8.

Brennan, T.A., Leape, L.L., Laird, N., *et al.* (1991) Incidence of adverse events and negligence in hospitalized patients: Results of the Harvard Medical Practice Study I, *New England Journal of Medicine*, 324: 370–6.

CART Project Team (1997) Community Action for Health Promotion: A review of methods and outcomes 1990–1995, *American Journal of Preventive Medicine*, 13(4): 229–39.

COMMIT Research Group (1995) Community Intervention Trial for Smoking Cessation (COMMIT): I. Cohort results from a four-year community intervention, *American Journal of Public Health*, 85(2): 183–92.

Commonwealth of Australia (1994) Review of professional indemnity arrangements for health care professionals: compensation and professional indemnity in health care. An interim report. Australian Government Publishing Service: National Library of Australia.

Deming, W.E. (1986) *Out of the Crisis*. Cambridge, MA: MIT Press.

Localio, A.R., Lawthers, A.G., Brennan, T.A. *et al*. (1991) Relation between malpractice claims and adverse events due to negligence: Results of the Harvard Medical Practice Study III, *New England Journal of Medicine*, 325: 245–51.

National Health Strategy (1992) *Issues in Pharmaceutical Drug Use in Australia. Issue Paper no. 4*. Canberra: Treble Press.

O'Hara, D.A. and Carson, N.J. (1997) Reporting of adverse events in hospitals in Victoria, 1994–1995, *Medical Journal of Australia*, 166: 460–7.

Runciman, W. (1993) Anaesthesia and intensive care, *J. Australian Society of Anaesthetists*, 21: 501.

Taylor, R. and Salkeld, G. (1996) Health care expenditure and life expectancy in Australia: How well do we perform?, *Australian and New Zealand Journal of Public Health*, 20: 233–40.

Wilson, R.M., Runciman, W., Gibberd R.W. *et al*. (1995) The Quality in Australian Health Care Study, *Medical Journal of Australia*, 163: 458–71.

Wolff, A.M. (1996) Limited adverse occurrence screening using medical record review to reduce hospital adverse patient events, *Medical Journal of Australia*, 164: 458–61.

Wolff, A.M. (1996) *Report of the Taskforce on the Quality of Health Care*. Australian Government Publishing Service.

Wolff, A.M. (1996) QAHCS Consortium, *Quality in Australian Health Care Study: Final report volumes 1 and 2*. Health Services Research Group, University of Newcastle, Newcastle Australia.

Part three | The escalation and mitigation of mishaps

8 | Calling doctors and hospitals to account: complaining and claiming as social processes

Sally Lloyd-Bostock

A wide range of factors determine whether a patient or relative will complain or claim, and the interrelationships among complaints, claims, medical mishaps and *perceived* medical mishaps are by no means straightforward (see, for example, Brennan *et al.* 1991; Mulcahy and Lloyd-Bostock 1992). We cannot assume that complaints and claims provide a representative picture of medical mishaps. But it is clear that perceived or suspected medical mishaps can give rise to legal claims and complaints that are among the most bitter and distressing of legal disputes for all concerned. As NHS managers are well aware, dissatisfaction with healthcare can all too easily be exacerbated by dissatisfaction with the response to a complaint or claim.

Attitudes to litigation and complaints within the NHS have changed greatly since the early 1990s. Mulcahy *et al.* (1996) describe a new, non-adversarial ethos in the management of complaints and negligence claims, placing greater importance on satisfying the complainant or plaintiff, and learning from medical mishaps. Allsop and Mulcahy (1996) see complaints systems as lying on a continuum from the 'prosecutory-disciplinary model' to the 'consumer orientated/learning model', and see a shift occurring from the first to the second. At the same time as NHS complaints procedures are undergoing change, civil litigation procedures are the target of reform. Again the emphasis is increasingly on settling disputes as early as possible, avoiding escalation and minimizing the adversarial aspect of claims (Lord Chancellor's Department 1996). But designing and implementing a non-adversarial approach is no easy task. Complaints and claims are inherently adversarial processes, and a natural response to being criticized is to offer a defence. An already difficult situation can be exacerbated by the very different experience, purposes and social and professional situation of doctors, patients and other actors in the process. Those who deal with patients and their relatives following a medical mishap can feel they are walking on eggshells.

This chapter sets out a broad social psychological framework for understanding the processes of making and responding to complaints and legal claims about healthcare. As well as physical or financial needs, medical mishaps can create psychological needs to understand and come to terms with what has happened, and can set in motion complex social psychological processes. The chapter draws on data from two research projects, which will be referred to as the 'Complaints Project' and the 'Medical Negligence Project'. The principal data are from the Complaints Project, which was a study of complaints to NHS hospitals (Lloyd-Bostock and Mulcahy 1992; 1994).[1] Files on 399 complaints received in one calendar year (1 July 1989 to 30 June 1990) were studied in two NHS districts, and face-to-face interviews were conducted with a sub-sample of 74 complainants whose complaints had been received by the hospital during the second six months of the study period. The chapter draws in particular on a content analysis of letters exchanged between the complainant and the hospital in a sub-sample of 218 cases, and complainants' replies to interview questions about their satisfaction with the handling and outcome of their complaint. The study included non-clinical as well as clinical complaints. In addition, data are drawn from the Medical Negligence Project, which was a study of the operation of the tort system in medical negligence cases from the perspectives of the various parties involved (Genn and Lloyd-Bostock 1995).[2] It included a postal survey of plaintiffs in medical negligence claims, in which a questionnaire was sent to a sample of 400 people who had contacted Action for Victims of Medical Accidents (AVMA). The sample cannot be taken as representative, but is nevertheless illustrative of the views and experiences of plaintiffs in medical negligence cases. A total of 106 completed questionnaires were returned. Of those responding, 92 had actually embarked on a negligence claim. Details of the methodology of the two studies can be found in Lloyd-Bostock and Mulcahy (1992) and Genn and Lloyd-Bostock (1995).

What do complainants and plaintiffs want?

An obvious first step towards successful management of claims and complaints is to ask what complainants and plaintiffs want. Taken at face value, a negligence claim has the goal of compensation, and complaints are usually similarly thought of as attempts to obtain a remedy of some kind. But this is only a partial and sometimes misleading indication of the reasons why people make claims or complaints. Negligence claims by definition involve a quest for financial compensation, but it cannot be assumed that this is the plaintiff's main goal, or even a goal at all. The plaintiff in a medical negligence case may, ironically, not particularly wish for financial compensation, and indeed may be frustrated by settlement if it ends a case without having achieved other goals. Complaints, for their part, often have no obvious material goal at all. Sometimes it seems clear that the complainant wants some matter put right – to have a long-awaited operation; to have lost possessions restored to them. But many complaints about healthcare are not obviously instrumental in this sense. The goal or goals are not clear from the substance or from the expression of the complaint. The event complained of is often over and done with – for example, a complaint about nursing care made after the patient has returned home. In the Complaints Project only 26 per cent of the allegations made in complaints related to events or circumstances that were continuing or might be expected to recur at the time the complaint was made (see Lloyd-Bostock and Mulcahy 1994).

We need to ask, therefore, what outcome or response plaintiffs and hospital complainants actually wish for when they make a complaint or claim. Both the Complaints Project and the Medical Negligence Project provide relevant data.

What complainants ask for in letters of complaint

Complaints files analysed in the Complaints Project give one indication of the extent to which complainants aim to achieve a clear further goal beyond the expression of dissatisfaction. A content analysis of 342 letters of complaint was conducted. Any statement, however general, of what the complainant wanted the hospital to do was coded and categorized. The results are summarized in Table 8.1.

In 98 (29 per cent) of cases, there was no statement at all indicating what the complainant wished the hospital to do, or hoped to achieve by the complaint. For the remaining cases, statements of the response or action requested were grouped into the four main categories shown in Table 8.1. The first category consisted of specific requests that something should be done to put matters right *for this complainant* (or the person on whose behalf the complaint was made). Fifty-three letters (15 per cent) included at least one statement in this category. The second category was made up of requests that steps should be taken to put matters right *for others* in the future. As Table 8.1 shows, this was more frequent than the first category: 68 letters (20 per cent) contained a statement in this category. Some were quite general – for example, 'Please please don't let any more people suffer in this manner'. Sometimes a specific change to procedures and practices might be suggested for the benefit of others in the future – for example, improvements to appointments systems; providing separate-sex wards. The third category grouped together requests for information about what has gone wrong, or asking the hospital to conduct an investigation. Seventy-one letters (21 per cent) contained statements in this category. Finally, in the fourth category were unspecific, 'vague' requests that the hospital should 'resolve the matter', 'take some action' or 'let me have your comments'. Seventy-three (21 per cent) letters contained

Table 8.1   Statement of what the complainant wants

	No.	(%)
Specific remedy for this complainant/patient		
Arrange/help arrange treatment	10	2.9
Expenses/charges paid/compensation	9	2.6
Other specific request, e.g., to see notes, transport,		
letter written to GP	11	3.2
Punish/reprimand/sack/discipline	7	2.0
Apology	6	1.8
Ensure will not recur for this complainant/patient	5	1.5
Meeting arranged/interview	5	1.5
Remedy for others/future		
Suggested specific change in policy/procedure	17	5.0
Ensure will not recur/improve/stop it happening		
(for the future)	25	7.3
Ensure others will not suffer in future	13	3.8
Use the feedback/pass on information to someone		
who can do something	15	4.4
Investigation/explanation		
Answer questions/provide information	38	11.1
Investigate/look into/find out	32	9.4
Treat as formal complaint	8	2.3
'Vague' request		
Put right/resolve matter/sort out	32	9.4
Let me have your comments/reply	45	13.2
'Help' (unspecified)	13	3.8
Give attention to problem	9	2.6
No statement	98	28.7
Total no. of letters analysed	342	

statements in this category; and in 67 of these (20 per cent of all letters analysed) there was no other codeable statement of what the complainant wanted.

Purposes plaintiffs give for making a medical negligence claim

One might expect negligence claims to be much more clearly instrumental than complaints, and that the goal would be compensation. Plaintiffs in the Medical Negligence Project postal survey were asked 'Please give your most important purpose or purposes in making a claim', and were prompted for the 'most important', 'second most important', and 'third most important'. The results are shown in Table 8.2.

Compensation does rank comparatively highly in what these plaintiffs say they wanted, but a quest for compensation by no means constitutes the whole picture: 73 per cent of respondents named something other than

Table 8.2 Purpose(s) in making a medical negligence claim

Purpose	Most important		2nd most important		3rd most important	
	No.	(%)*	No.	(%)*	No.	(%)*
Compensation						
unspecified	12	14	13	15	9	10
to meet financial needs	9	10	11	13	7	8
as redress/make pay	2	2	–	–	1	1
Make doctor/hospital admit						
mistake	19	22	5	6	6	7
Justice/put matters right (no						
mention of compensation)	4	5	4	5	1	1
Explanation, find 'the truth'	19	22	5	6	6	7
Prevent reoccurrence	10	12	12	14	19	22
Apology	3	3	9	10	3	3
Obtain treatment	6	7	1	1	4	5
Damage caused/negligence	3	3	5	6	3	3
Publicize what happened	–	–	3	3	1	1
Other	1	1	5	6	4	5
Column total	88		73		64	

* Percentages of the sample of 88 who answered this question: not all respondents named three purposes.

compensation or meeting financial needs as their most important purpose in making the claim. Often those who named financial compensation specifically phrased their answer in terms of meeting a particular need or making good a significant financial loss caused by the medical accident – for example, 'To provide financial security for my handicapped daughter'; 'To pay for the best care'; 'I had lost my business'. Much less frequently, respondents phrased their answer in terms of seeking redress or 'making someone pay'.

A substantial proportion of stated purposes relate to making the doctor or hospital respond appropriately – to admit they had made a mistake, apologize, tell the truth about what happened. As with the sample of complainants, preventing the same thing happening again is also important, especially when one looks at plaintiff's second or third most important purpose. The desire for the truth or an explanation is also found in both samples. Vincent *et al.* (1993) show the importance of an adequate explanation in reducing the patient's distress after a medical accident, while the natural reaction of staff faced with an angry or grieving person who has been injured by treatment may be to withdraw. The need for an explanation appears to evolve into a more aggressive search for 'the truth' and admissions of fault when the patient meets difficulties finding out what happened. In the Medical Negligence Project, 83 per cent of respondents said they had had 'a lot of difficulty' obtaining information and a further 11 per cent said they had encountered 'some difficulty'.

Although there are differences between the stated purposes of complainants and plaintiffs, there are common threads. Both complainants and plaintiffs express a range of goals, only some of which concern redress or their own material benefit. For both, the desired response in many cases relates as much to the *process* of responding to the claim as to *outcome*, and indeed the distinction between process and outcome becomes difficult to draw. The next section summarizes an 'account' model of complaints processes developed on the basis of the Complaints Project and explores its application to claims as well as complaints.

Complaints and claims as processes of calling to account

Complaints and claims, and responses to them, both involve a series of interchanges in which a patient (or a patient's relative or friend) calls a doctor or hospital to account and in which the doctor or hospital makes its response, possibly followed by further exchanges. Taken together, these interchanges can be described as an 'account episode' (Schonbach 1990; Lloyd-Bostock 1992).

Claims are likely to be regarded as more hostile than complaints. However, like making a legal claim, making a complaint involves making an accusation, even if only implicitly, that there has been a failure to meet expected standards, and perhaps that someone is at fault. Both are thus to some degree hostile and threatening acts, and the interaction between the complainant or plaintiff and the hospital or doctor has potential to become emotionally charged. A complaint or claim is likely to provoke a defensive rather than conciliatory response.

It is frequently said that complainants and plaintiffs 'want an apology', but the idea that they will be so readily satisfied is sometimes met with scepticism. It is, of course, unlikely that a simple, possibly insincere expression of regret will be sufficient. Rather than reject the idea that an apology may satisfy complainants or plaintiffs, we need to ask what, more exactly, it means to wish for or to offer an apology. Goffman (1971) suggests that *full* apologies have several elements, including that the person making the apology must acknowledge that something blameworthy has occurred, must sympathize with the censure of others, and must evidence this repentant attitude by making amends or indicating that he or she will do better in future. An apology viewed this way is something much more than simply an expression of regret. Rather than examining whether the complainant or plaintiff succeeds in obtaining redress or a remedy, we can look at the extent to which the response amounts to a *full* apology. In this expanded sense, the response as a whole can be evaluated as an apology; and it can be predicted that the satisfaction of the complainant will relate to the extent to which the response amounts to a full apology by acknowledging that the complaint is justified, showing regret, and indicating intention to improve, as well as (perhaps instead of) offering compensation. Indeed, compensation itself, as a way of making amends, can be viewed as a component in a full apology.

In what follows, data from the Complaints Project will first be used to illustrate the model in more detail. Its application to claims as well as complaints will then be discussed.

Applying the account model to complaints

Letters of complaint

Where the interaction between a complainant and a hospital takes place in writing, it is possible to explore the process by analysing what is said in letters. As part of the Complaints Project, letters of complaint and replies from the hospital were analysed in 218 written complaints. Phrases or passages from letters were placed in categories developed during preliminary phases of the research, based on many hours spent reading complaints files, and drawing on concepts in attribution theory (see, for example, Kelley 1967; Hewstone 1989), the social psychology of explanation and accounting (Scott and Lyman 1968; Antaki 1988; Schonbach 1990) and Goffman's work on apologies (Goffman 1971).

Despite the great variety of complaints, the content of letters of complaint fell into clear patterns. As well as stating the matter complained of, letters comprised statements making the case (implicitly as well as explicitly) that something worthy of complaint had occurred; recognizing that making a complaint is a hostile act that may need justifying, and may evoke a defensive response; pre-empting the hospital from dismissing the complaint as, for example, unjustified, mistaken or trivial; and calling on the hospital to make an appropriate response. Table 8.3 summarizes the main results.

Substance of the complaint. By definition, every letter of complaint included a statement of the substance of the complaint. This varied from a short sentence to several pages setting out details of events with dates and times – see Lloyd-Bostock and Mulcahy (1994) for a full breakdown of allegations made.

Effects of the event/circumstances complained of. Statements showing that the event was significant and worthy of complaint included statements of negative emotions experienced (such as 'distressed', 'worried', 'embarrassed') or other effects such as expenses or interference with plans. Thirty-five per cent of complaints explicitly alleged that physical harm had been caused,

Table 8.3   Frequencies of main categories of statement in 218 letters of complaint

Category	Frequency	(%)
1 Statement of substance of complaint		
Specific allegation	218	100
General statement (e.g., 'the ward was in chaos')	73	33
2 Effects of event/circumstances		
Physical harm	76	35
Negative emotion/other effects on complainant or patient	156	72
3 Reasons event/circumstances significant	163	75
4 Appeals to standards	90	41
5 Asking for response	163	75
6 Consensus/distinctiveness		
Consensus (other(s) agreed there was a problem)	50	23
Praise for other visits/aspects of visit	76	35
Complainant not prone to making complaints	43	20
7 Anticipating hospital's justifications	61	28
(e.g., 'I know the clinic was busy, but . . .')		
8 Attempts to put matters right	63	29
9 Difficulties not part of the complaint	54	25
(e.g., continued ill health of patient; difficulties coping at home)		

ranging from temporary cold and discomfort to severe and lasting pain or permanent harm.

Significance of the event/circumstances complained of. Seventy-five per cent of letters contained a statement or passage indicating why the matter is important or significant, even if it might seem unimportant or trivial to the hospital. For example, complainants pointed out that the vulnerable or frail state of the patient magnified the importance of an incident (69 letters); that although no serious outcome had occurred on this occasion, the consequences could have been be far more serious (26 letters); and that the incident, though not serious in itself, indicated a more general problem (23 letters). Thus, one complainant wrote that, while it may seem unimportant, the offhand manner of a member of staff is significant:

> because my mother is 80 years old, frail and suffering from angina and osteoporosis . . . I wonder what effect such a man has on people visiting patients about whom they are desperately worried.

Sixteen of the statements in this category remarked that non-medical considerations such as dignity, politeness and comfort are important to patients. For example:

I had to use the toilet in the same room. Another person came in and out of the room part of the time and though I felt almost too ill to care I found it very humiliating. I realise that to hospital staff this is a familiar routine but to the patient it is not . . . I left the hospital angry at being degraded.

Appeals to standards. Statements referring to failure to meet standards are of particular interest here since they support the suggestion that complainants are, in essence, calling the hospital to account for violating a normative expectation. They included professional standards (for example, that doctors or nurses should be more caring; should protect confidentiality); moral standards or standards of humanity ('how can you let a child suffer in this way'); and standards of fairness (why should others be given priority?).

Calls for a response. Analysis of 'what the complainant wants' (see Table 8.1) showed that rather few complainants actually expressed a clear and specific goal. However, the majority made some form of statement calling for a response, including general statements asking for (or 'looking forward to') the hospital's explanation, comments, reply, etc. It is perhaps questionable whether such statements as 'I look forward to your reply' are sensibly counted as statements of the complainant's goals, but they are readily seen as indicating that an appropriate reply is expected, in the context of an account episode the complainant has initiated.

Other categories. The remaining categories in Table 8.3 contain statements that do not concern the complaint-worthiness of the event or circumstance that is the subject of the complaint, but instead explain and justify the complaint itself, and pre-empt excuses or justifications the hospital might offer or dismissal of the complaint as arising from the complainant's ignorance, unreasonableness or complaining nature. In particular, complainants sometimes seem to anticipate (quite rightly) that the complaint might be seen as arising from their complaining nature rather than more objectively from the event or circumstances (Mulcahy 1996). Statements pre-empting that conclusion (category 6) included, for example, 'I don't usually complain' (16 letters); 'I don't like to complain' (14 letters); 'I felt I had to write' (25 letters); mentioning that others also felt that something worthy of complaint had happened (50 letters) or praising other visits or other aspects of the hospital stay (76 letters).

Statements anticipating justifications (category 7) can again be understood as pre-empting dismissal of the complaint by displaying that the complainant has considered the hospital's point of view and possible excuses, and still regards the matter as complaint-worthy. Mention of attempts to put matters right (category 8) implies that the complainant has not complained lightly, but tried to remedy matters before resorting to complaining. Less frequent categories (not shown in Table 8.3) included statements about the complainant's status (32 letters) or medical knowledge or contacts

(26 letters), again perhaps pre-empting reasons why the hospital might not take the complaint seriously. In addition, many (25 per cent) mentioned difficulties and problems that were not part of the substance of the complaint, such as the continued poor health of the patient, or difficulties coping at home. While apparently irrelevant to the complaint, these statements tend to explain or justify the complaint, as well as throwing an obligation on the hospital to reply sympathetically.

Letters of response

The analytical framework developed for letters of response was largely the converse of that used for complainants' letters. A natural response to being called to account is to offer a defence, though defensiveness is likely to be counterproductive if the aim is to settle the dispute. Whereas complainants were putting forward a case for complaint-worthiness, letters of response commonly corrected (17 per cent of replies) or cast doubt on details of the complainant's account (15 per cent), included comments to the effect that if the event did occur, it was not complaint-worthy (18 per cent), or in some other way undermined the complainant's account or competence. Sometimes more specific allegations (for example, that the patient was left in a wet bed for several hours; that a nurse stubbed out a cigarette in a pot plant) were illustrations of a more general or global complaint. It can be a source of frustration to complainants when the response is to 'pick off' the examples and fail to respond to the more general complaint. For example (correcting the complainant's account):

I don't think the bath would actually have been uncleaned for the whole week your mother was in hospital – though it is possible the bath wasn't clean whenever she went . . .

Or, questioning complaint-worthiness:

I know no-one likes having a barium enema done, but we do try to be as nice as we can . . . One has to expect a little bit of non-privacy in an x-ray department. As for the room opening from the room where you were examined, this is the main dark room and film sorting area and we cannot expect people there to be entirely quiet.

Only 26 per cent of replies clearly accepted that all the alleged events occurred as described by the complainant.

Apologies. Sixty-three per cent of letters of response contained some form of expression of regret (excluding condolences on a bereavement). However, as indicated above, Goffman (1971) suggests that *full* apologies have several elements. The person making the apology must acknowledge that something blameworthy has occurred, must sympathize with the censure of others and must evidence this repentant attitude by making amends or indicating that he or she will do better in future. Thus, one full apology (at the end of a letter acknowledging that the complainant is quite right) read as follows:

> Can I offer you and your sister my apologies and assurances that we will do everything we can to avoid inflicting such discomfort on our patients in the future.

Another, concerning a rude remark by a nurse, said:

> We have identified the person concerned... May I once again offer you my apologies on behalf of the hospital and nursing staff, and thank you for drawing the problem to my attention, as without important feedback we may never have known.

The mere use of words or phrases such as 'I am sorry' or 'I apologize' is not by itself a full apology in this sense. Many of the apologies offered to complainants might on analysis be called incomplete or 'pseudoapologies' (Lloyd-Bostock 1992). They contained the word 'apology', 'apologize', 'sorry' or 'regret' but did not acknowledge that anything complaint-worthy had happened, or indicate a willingness to improve matters. If an apology states 'I apologize *if you felt that* [X occurred]' it does not actually concede that X did occur. For example:

> I am sorry that you felt as you did, but we try to be as kind as we can and I think that our staff go out of their way to do this.

> I apologise for any misunderstanding that may have arisen over the reason for her visit.

What at first glance may seem to be an apology may not relate to the substance of the complaint at all, but rather be an expression of regret about something else – for example, 'I was sorry to learn of your husband's continued ill-health'; 'I was sorry to get your letter'; 'I am sorry that you felt you had to complain'.

Complainant's views of the hospital's response: interview data

Interviews with complainants confirmed that hospitals' replies frequently appeared defensive; and that the elements of a full apology related strongly to their satisfaction with the response. Thirty-six per cent rated the hospital as 'not at all' accepting responsibility for the event complained of; 57 per cent rated the hospital as 'very much' or 'rather' trying to defend itself. Forty-one per cent said that they had been given an 'unsatisfactory explanation'. Complainants interviewed were asked to rate their satisfaction overall with the handling of their complaint on a ten-point scale. It was explained that a score of 5 or less indicated that they were more dissatisfied than satisfied; and 6 or over that they were more satisfied than dissatisfied. The average overall satisfaction rating was 4.8, with 58 per cent giving a rating of 5 or less. Twenty per cent rated their dissatisfaction at the extreme of the scale.

Table 8.4   Correlations between complaint satisfaction and ratings of hospital's responses

Statement rated	Correlation with satisfaction*
The hospital understood the complaint	0.41
The hospital accepted responsibility for what had happened	0.59
The hospital was trying to defend itself	−0.34
The hospital took the complaint seriously	0.53
The hospital saw that there was a problem	0.39
The hospital doubted that events had occurred as described	−0.39
The hospital felt the complaint was a nuisance	−0.43
The hospital regretted what happened	0.45
The hospital intended to improve matters for the future	0.67

* $p < 0.001$ (one-tailed).

Table 8.4 shows the correlations (Pearson's product moment correlation) between the satisfaction measure and other aspects of the complainants' views about the response to their complaint, rated on four-point scales. The results indicate again the importance of an appropriate social response to the complaint. It is evidently important to complainants that their complaint be acknowledged and taken seriously, and that the hospital accept responsibility. It is particularly interesting to note the strong positive correlation between satisfaction and the complainant's belief that the hospital intended to 'improve things for the future'. This finding suggests that when complainants state that they are complaining in order to prevent others suffering in future, they genuinely wish for this, and are not merely justifying their complaint with reference to altruistic goals. It also confirms that if an apology is to fulfil a mitigating and conciliatory function then doctors or hospitals need to give substance to explanations and statements of remorse by conceding that matters are unsatisfactory and indicating, credibly, that they intend to take remedial action.

Extending the account model to claims

The account model should in principle apply as much to claims as to complaints. Obviously a number of different considerations apply to claims, and it is a mistake to see claims as a next step after complaints, along the same pathway as complaints (Lloyd-Bostock and Mulcahy 1994). But, as we have seen, complainants and plaintiffs frequently express similar purposes or goals, and a view of claims as a quest for compensation is too narrow. A familiar pattern emerges across both complaints and claims.

Data from the Medical Negligence Project show that plaintiffs, like complainants, frequently express dissatisfaction with the response of the hospital or doctor, and report encountering defensiveness, not being taken seriously, and being treated in a dismissive or patronizing manner. As quoted earlier, 83 per cent of respondents in the Medical Negligence Project said they had had 'a lot of difficulty' obtaining information and another 11 per cent said they had encountered 'some difficulty'. Asked whether the doctor was defensive, 74 per cent chose the highest rating of 'very much so', and 80 per cent rated as 'definitely true' the statement that the medical profession was protecting itself. When asked whether the doctor took their concerns seriously, 51 per cent chose the extreme response 'not at all'.

Conclusion

Medical mishaps (or perceived mishaps) can create psychological and emotional needs to comprehend and come to terms with what has happened, and can set in motion lengthy and delicate processes of seeking and responding to explanations, admissions, apologies and redress. The management of claims and complaints is embedded in these processes, and calls for understanding of the psychology of claims and complaints processes from the perspectives of all concerned. The approach outlined in this chapter attempts to broaden our conception of what it is to make a claim or complaint. The focus on processes moves us away from the idea that an expression of grievance centrally involves seeking redress, and emphasizes the interactions and social goals of complainants and plaintiffs, areas where mediation may be a more appropriate means of exploring settlement of the dispute than adjudication or negotiation through solicitors (see Mulcahy, Chapter 11). The chapter has argued that part if not all of the desired outcome is often a satisfactory *social* response to the complaint or claim, so that the concepts of 'process' and 'outcome' become blurred. Complainants' satisfaction ratings were highly correlated with their sense of having been understood, taken seriously, and offered a satisfactory explanation; and with whether the hospital evidenced its repentant attitude by showing that it intended to improve matters for the future. Similarly, many who make claims say that they are not primarily interested in compensation, but in an explanation, apology or preventing the same thing happening to others in the future.

Concentration on dispute processes should not obscure the importance of redress or compensation in some cases, and indeed appropriate redress can be a necessary part of a full apology. Sometimes compensation is the central concern, and the potential role of mediation may become more questionable if its effects are to bring added pressure to bear on plaintiffs to settle for less than they might be awarded by a court. As the medical negligence data show, there is a substantial subset of cases where money is needed, perhaps to provide long-term care. In such cases, families may be satisfied with the explanations and apologies they have been given, and bear no ill feeling towards the doctor, but remain obliged to go through the costly and distressing process of a negligence claim for purely financial reasons.

The variety and complexity of complaints, claims and medical mishaps means that systems of response need to be flexible and adaptable. Obviously no simple formula will work in all cases. An attempt to satisfy patients and their relatives as quickly and cheaply as possible is likely to be seen for what it is and to be counterproductive. None the less, it seems clear that considerable expense and distress on all sides could be avoided by appropriate management of claims and complaints. Though many pieces of the puzzle are still missing, there is surely considerable potential for mediation to develop as a way of offering much of what complainants and claimants seek, exploring solutions that could not be offered within formal claims or complaints procedures, and forestalling unnecessary escalation of disputes.

Notes

1 The research was supported by ESRC award number YE13250007, held by Sally Lloyd-Bostock, Paul Fenn and Alistair McGuire at the Centre for Socio-Legal Studies, Oxford University. The chapter draws on an earlier publication (Lloyd-Bostock and Mulcahy 1994).
2 The project was supported by a grant from the Nuffield Foundation held jointly by Hazel Genn at Queen Mary and Westfield College, London University, and Sally Lloyd-Bostock at the Centre for Socio-Legal Studies, Oxford University.

References

Allsop, J. and Mulcahy, L. (1996) *Regulating Medical Work: Formal and Informal Controls.* Buckingham: Open University Press.

Antaki, C. (1988) *Analyzing Everyday Explanation: A Casebook of Methods.* London: Sage.

Brennan, T., Leape, L., Laird, N. *et al.* (1991) Incidence of adverse events and negligence in hospitalized patients: The results from the Harvard Medical Practice Study, *New England Journal of Medicine* 324: 370–6.

Genn, H. and Lloyd-Bostock, S. (1995) Medical Negligence Research Project: The operation of the tort system in medical negligence cases. Report to the Nuffield Foundation.

Goffman, E. (1971) *Relations in Public.* Harmondsworth: Penguin.

Hewstone, M. (1989) *Causal Attribution: From Cognitive Processes to Collective Beliefs.* Oxford: Basil Blackwell.

Kelley, H.H. (1967) *Attribution Theory in Social Psychology*, Nebraska Symposium on Motivation, Vol. 15. Lincoln, NE: University of Nebraska Press.

Lloyd-Bostock, S. (1992) Attributions and apologies in letters of complaint to hospitals and letters of response, in J.H. Harvey, T. Orbuch and A.L. Weber (eds) *Attributions, Accounts and Close Relationships.* New York: Springer-Verlag.

Lloyd-Bostock, S. and Mulcahy, L. (1992) Formal complaints to acute NHS hospitals: The complainant's perspective and the organizational perspective. End-of-Award Report to ESRC.

Lloyd-Bostock, S. and Mulcahy, L. (1994) The social psychology of making and responding to hospital complaints: An account model of complaint processes, *Law and Policy*, 16(2): 123–47.

Lord Chancellor's Department (1996) *Access to Justice*, Report of Lord Woolf's Inquiry. London: HMSO.

Mulcahy, L. (1996) From fear to fraternity: Doctors' construction of rational accounts of complaining behaviour, *Journal of Social Welfare and Family Law*, 18(4): 397–418.

Mulcahy, L., Allsop, J. and Shirley, C. (1996) *The Voices of Complainants and GPs in Complaints about Health Care*, Social Science Research Papers No. 3. London: School of Education, Politics and Social Science, South Bank University.

Mulcahy, L. and Lloyd-Bostock, S. (1992) Complaining – what's the use?, in R. Dingwall and P. Fenn (eds) *Quality and Regulation in Health Care*. London: Routledge.

Schonbach, P. (1990) *Account Episodes: The Management or Escalation of Conflict*. Cambridge: Cambridge University Press.

Scott, M. and Lyman, S. (1968) Accounts, *American Sociological Review*, 33(1): 46–62.

Vincent, P.A., Pincus, T. and Scurr, J.H. (1993) Patients' experience of surgical accidents, *Quality in Health Care*, 2: 77–82.

9 | Doctors' responses to patient complaints

Judith Allsop and
Linda Mulcahy

Introduction and background to the research

In this chapter, we report on two studies which collected data on how doctors responded to complaints from patients and/or their carers. The issue is an important one for two reasons. First, making a complaint, or 'voicing', can be seen as one way in which the people who use health services can hold those who provide them to account. Complaints can serve to regulate the work of a profession which in other respects is largely self-regulating. Like medical negligence claims, complaints are a very blunt tool in the regulation of medical work, and it is unlikely that they are representative of the incidence or subject matter of medical mishaps. However, they do represent the main form of patient-initiated indications of poor quality. Second, policy-makers have seen more responsive complaint systems as part of achieving improvements in the quality of public services. Managers and professionals can use data from complaints to pinpoint shortcomings and alter service provision. Furthermore, a quick and sympathetic response to a complaint can often resolve an issue so that matters are not pursued through the more formal complaints systems, where costs rise. To this end, following widespread criticism of existing NHS complaints procedures, new systems were introduced in the NHS on 1 April 1996 (Department of Health 1995; NHS Executive 1996). Despite this policy emphasis, we do not know how doctors, one of the key groups in healthcare delivery, respond to complaints. Do they accept them as 'jewels to be treasured' or do they react defensively?

From previous research we know something about complainants' behaviour and expectations. What people consider as complaint-worthy varies considerably (Allsop 1994; Lloyd-Bostock and Mulcahy 1994). Research has shown that the subject matter of written complaints can vary from very minor issues to major catastrophes (Lloyd-Bostock and Mulcahy 1994). We also know that complainants say they want explanations for events and, in certain circumstances, apologies rather than punishment or compensation. A commonly accepted definition of a complaint as an expression of dissatisfaction on the part of a patient or carer indicates that a complaint represents a particular perception of events. A complaint may or may not reveal that a mistake or error has occurred. It has been shown that using written complaints as grievance indicators encourages significant underestimation of patient dissatisfaction (NHS Executive 1994; Citizen's Charter Complaints Task Force 1995; and for a general literature review, see Mulcahy *et al.* 1996c).

Against this background, the research reported here aimed to find out how doctors at the receiving end reacted to being complained about. One study focused on hospital consultants and the second on general practitioners. The studies were commissioned by two different health authorities within the same region. In developing the research questions, we thought it likely that doctors would perceive things differently than patients and carers as a result of their sense of identity as expert professionals. For doctors, treating patients is an everyday task and each patient interaction is one among many. So on receiving a complaint, how did they respond? What was the emotional impact of the complaint? To whom did doctors talk? How did they account for complaints and what action did they take following a complaint? This chapter provides data relevant to some of these questions. However, in order to set the findings in context, we first discuss the concept of identity and identity maintenance, drawing on selected sociological literature on professional identities within medicine.

Professional identities in medicine

Social interactionists have argued that most people seek to maintain their sense of self as competent social actors. For example, Goffman saw personal identity as an intentional construct designed to secure the greatest advantage for its bearer. He analysed behaviour as if it were composed of tactical moves in a strategic game. Thus, in *On Face Work* (Goffman 1967), he discusses the maintenance of identity in circumstances where there has been a challenge or threat of some sort. He suggests that the individual will work to maintain 'face' or a positive social value. In addition to the ongoing process of face-work, social actors also engage in character-work. In character-work, people make judgements about each other which may result in threats to the self and the sense of identity. Among professionals, the sense of identity is likely to be closely linked to the claim to expertise. As Lloyd-Bostock suggested in the previous chapter, a complaint which is a challenge to that expertise is likely to be resisted.

Within medicine, clinical autonomy for the individual practitioner is a well-established cultural norm. As Freidson (1970) has pointed out in a classic formulation, the doctor's individual clinical autonomy means that he or she has the responsibility for decisions taken in treating the patient. This depends on experiential as well as technical knowledge. Freidson (1970: 170) comments:

> In having to rely so heavily upon his personal, clinical judgement with concrete individual cases, the practitioner comes essentially to rely on the authority of his own senses. After all, he can only act on the basis of what he experiences, and if his own activity seems to get results . . . he is likely to need to see or to feel the case for himself.

This leads to the belief in observation and judgement as the proper basis for decision-making. The doctor has a personal responsibility for the quality of medical work and thus regulates his or her own work. The notion of clinical autonomy is closely linked to the principle of professional self-regulation. According to this, only a doctor's peers can comment on his or her actions as only they are able to judge whether norms have been breached or technical performance has been poor. As a consequence of this, another cultural norm has developed which encourages doctors to be reluctant to criticize each other (see Rosenthal, Chapter 10).

Although the profession is made up of different specialties, strata and thought collectives, each with its own values and set of techniques, a variety of factors could be said to provide the basis of a shared culture. Among these are the commonality of entry criteria and the long socialization process, which includes the acquisition of book knowledge, the practice of skills and techniques and the absorption of norms and values. Sociological studies, based on empirical work in the USA undertaken in the 1950s and 1960s, showed how doctors are socialized into the norms of a biomedical culture which provides shared understandings of the limits of expertise, the uncertainty of medical work and personal responsibility (Fox 1957; Becker *et al.* 1961; Bucher and Strauss 1961; Stelling and Bucher 1973). Fox (1957) and Stelling and Bucher (1973) used the term 'vocabularies of realism' to describe the ways in which medical students came to terms with different forms of uncertainty and the inevitable failures which are part of medical practice. There were uncertainties about the course of a disease in a particular individual. There were limits to clinical knowledge and there was uncertainty on the part of the practitioner about his or her own grasp of available knowledge. However, Atkinson (1981; 1984; 1995) has pointed to a paradox. He argued that the training process is designed to inculcate certainty in decision-making in the face of uncertainty. Fully qualified doctors learn to take responsibility for making decisions, trusting their own judgement and being confident of their expertise.

A few studies have been undertaken to determine how doctors deal with mistakes and errors. For example, Bosk (1979) showed that, in dealing with juniors, senior surgeons were likely to condone failures in technique as part of learning the job. In a study of medical interns undertaking specialty training in the USA, Mizrahi (1984) found common strategies for distancing and denial in response to possible 'mistakes' by doctors themselves or their peers. Typically, untoward events were redefined not as mistakes, for which they were culpable, but as merely part of the uncertainty of the disease process and of medical practice. Mizrahi argued that these strategies provided a framework for dealing with threats to competence and reflected a common socialization process. More recently, Donaldson (1994) and Rosenthal (1995) have concluded that both informal and formal internal controls for dealing with poor practice are weakly developed within the medical profession. Only the grossest misdemeanours reach the disciplinary procedures.

If doctors are reluctant to criticize each other, it is even more likely that criticisms by lay people will be resisted. As Schutz (1964: 123) commented: 'the expert . . . knows very well that only a fellow expert will understand all the technicalities and implications of a problem in his field, and he will never accept a layman or dilettante as the competent judge of his performance'. Indeed, in a large-scale study of doctor–patient encounters in a paediatric setting, Strong (1979) found that challenges to professional authority were rare. Typically the etiquette of politeness was maintained. He argued that it is in patients' interests to accept the doctor's expertise, at least overtly, and to be bound by their authority within the encounter. Service users lacked knowledge, and to enter into a dispute with the doctor was to engage in an argument they could not win. 'Quiet obedience was the easiest path and where patients did revolt they were soon quietened' (Strong and Davis 1977: 793). However, almost 20 years on from this study, research shows that patients are complaining more and that challenges to medicine in general are increasing (Gabe *et al.* 1994). Expectations of biomedicine are high, but also increasingly diverse. So, how do doctors respond when they receive a written complaint?

Doctors' responses to complaints

The scope and methods of the studies

In the two studies, data were collected using questionnaires and interviews with hospital consultants and GPs. Here, the focus is on four main issues: first, the initial impact of the complaint on the doctor; second, the support networks which doctors used when they received a complaint; third, the explanations they gave for complaints; and fourth, the actions which doctors said they took in response to complaints. Although the design of each project differed due to the different medical settings, broadly the same questions were addressed in each.

In the first study, referred to as the consultants' study (Mulcahy and Selwood 1995; Mulcahy 1996), data were collected in two stages. First, a detailed questionnaire was sent out to all hospital consultants practising in an English health region (848), 54 per cent of whom responded. Second,

70 in-depth interviews were conducted with health service managers (25), hospital consultants (35) and with pressure groups and national organizations which supported doctors and patients (10).

In the second study, the GP study, general medical practitioners' responses to complaints were investigated (Mulcahy *et al.* 1996a; 1996b). This study was intended to be parallel to the consultants' study, but the methods employed had to be varied to meet funding constraints. A postal questionnaire was sent to all 363 GPs in a family health service authority (FHSA) located in the same region. There was a response rate of 56 per cent. In addition, in-depth interviews were carried out with the four local medical committee (LMC) secretaries in the region. These secretaries represent medical interests and provide advice and help for doctors who have received a complaint. Collectively, they provided help for about 900 GPs.

The incidence and substance of complaints

National statistics show that the number of complaints is increasing. In both the consultants' and the GP study, there was widespread experience of complaints (NHS Executive 1994). In the consultants' study, 56 per cent of the respondents reported that they had received at least one complaint about medical care during their career (which averaged 23 years). In the GP study, 34 per cent of doctors had received a complaint within the previous five years.

Respondents in both studies were asked what they considered complaints against them to be about. Their answers were classified by the research team using a coding framework based on that used in the Harvard Medical Practice Study (Brennan *et al.* 1991) and developed by Lloyd-Bostock and Mulcahy (1994). The complaints they mentioned varied widely from relatively minor matters, such as complaints about rudeness, to more serious issues of alleged incompetence causing serious physical harm to a patient.

Table 9.1 shows data from both studies, although these are not always strictly comparable, as different types of medical care are provided by hospital consultants and the community-based GPs. General practitioners are under contract to provide general medical services to their practice population during surgery hours and, if the condition of patients warrants it, to visit them at home. They also have a duty to refer patients for specialist care if this is necessary. Consultants are not expected to visit patients at home, nor do they have an obligation to refer unless the patient asks for a second opinion. In addition, at the time the study was undertaken, the GP complaints procedure was much more prescriptive than the hospital procedure as to what allegations came within its jurisdiction. This is likely to have affected consultants' and GPs' perceptions of what they defined as complaints. In particular, both GPs and consultants considered a large proportion of complaints to be about communication and attitude, general treatment problems and diagnostic procedures.

Table 9.1   Allegations made in complaints

Subject of the complaint	Consultants' study: % of respondents	GP study: % of respondents
Communications and attitude	26	17
Visiting patients at home and other access issues	Not applicable	18
Failure to refer to a specialist	Not applicable	18
Treatment problems	17	13
Diagnosis, tests and examination	16	17
Problems with surgery	11	Not applicable
General patient care	10	0
Waiting times	9	2
Medication and prescribing	8	8
Other	6	7
Total	100	100

The initial impact of complaints

The data suggest that receiving a complaint has a powerful impact on a doctor. In both the consultants' and the GP studies, virtually all the doctors talked about the huge emotional effect which complaints had. The ten emotions most frequently mentioned by consultants were all negative: irritation (52 per cent), worry (42 per cent), concern (38 per cent), surprise (38 per cent), annoyance (37 per cent), anger (33 per cent), distress (32 per cent), disappointment (31 per cent), anxiety (28 per cent) and vulnerability (28 per cent). One consultant commented that on receiving a complaint:

> I had sleepless nights – I was devastated. Colleagues told me not to worry, but my reputation was being questioned.

Another said:

> Complaints are very hurtful. One gets emotionally involved because they strike at one's perception of one's self as a doctor. That perception may be idealistic but it's important.

Complaints were also seen as disempowering:

> The greatest sense is of futility – why bother to try when resources are inadequate and patients are complaining.

Significantly, these emotions were experienced whether doctors believed the complaint to be justified or not.

In the GP study, all four LMC secretaries interviewed commented in a similar vein. Referring to the emotions aroused, one said:

> Anger is the first thing, nearly always they are extremely cross.

Another said:

> I've been on the receiving end of a complaint as well and I lost stones
> in weight with anxiety. It upset my life and altered my pattern of life.
> People are very distressed, somehow it's our whole value as a doctor
> that's on the line. I think it's very difficult to see the issues. All they
> can see is somebody being very critical of them and they're upset.

The sense of crisis and the process of adjustment to criticism were also
captured in the comment of one clinical director in the consultants' study,
who said:

> When doctors receive complaints they go through a series of emo-
> tions. First of all they are frightened, because it is the beginning of a
> process they don't understand. Then they feel injured, because the
> complainant does not understand what they have done. Where the
> complaint is unjustified, they feel irritation. Finally, they get round to
> asking the most important question of all – is the complaint actually
> about the standards of clinical care?

The findings of the consultants' study also showed that complaints had
long-term consequences. Consultants reported a sense of powerlessness
because some complainants were 'unsatisfiable' and because doctors did
not have control over all aspects of care. Complaints could also provoke
a sense of counter-grievance and a desire for redress. Some respondents
expressed the view that doctors too had a right to be heard.

Most consultants (85 per cent) and GPs (96 per cent) felt that the
complaints against them were partly, or completely, unjustified. These
findings confirm an earlier study where almost all GPs (98 per cent) denied
the allegations against them in cases which came to a service committee
hearing (Allsop 1994). It was interesting to note that in the consultants'
study, doctors' emotional reactions were likely to be more intense where
they felt a complaint was *unjustified*. In sum, complaints appear to prompt
a personal legitimation crisis among doctors to which they have to adjust
and respond (Mulcahy 1996). Complaints are interpreted as a challenge to
the expertise and authority which lies at the heart of doctors' sense of
themselves as professionals.

Professional networks for dealing with complaints

To whom do doctors turn when they have complaints made against them?
Both the consultants' study and the GP study asked questions about whether
respondents talked to anyone about the complaint and if so, to whom.
A large majority of consultants (92 per cent) and GPs (86 per cent) had
talked to at least one other person, and medical networks were extensively
used by both groups. Table 9.2 shows the results. Again, these data cannot
be directly compared for all categories due to different systems of care
delivery. General practices are much smaller organizations than hospitals.

Table 9.2 Who consultants and GPs spoke to about the complaint

Person approached	Consultants' study % of contacts	GPs' study % of contacts
Medical colleague	47	44
Medical defence societies	28	20
Legal claims department	11	Not applicable
LMC secretary	Not applicable	12
Senior manager	7	Not applicable
FHSA staff or medical adviser	Not applicable	5
Friends and relatives	5	14
Other person	1	5
Solicitor	1	0
Total	100	100

They are typically small partnerships which do not have a management stratum or legal claims departments. On the other hand, hospital consultants do not use the services of LMC secretaries when they receive a complaint.

Table 9.2 shows that both groups of doctors used similar support pathways. Medical networks were used to the exclusion of almost all others. Further analysis showed that both consultants and GPs turned most often to close medical colleagues *within* their organization. Among consultants, almost three-quarters discussed the complaint with medical colleagues from within the hospital. GPs were even more likely to talk to other GPs within their own practice. The data showed that other doctors were most often approached for advice (19 per cent), support (17 per cent), information (10 per cent) and to unburden feelings (10 per cent). Even for this last category, medical colleagues were approached as often as family and friends.

The consultant study also demonstrated that where respondents were able to conceal receipt of a complaint from a manager, they often did so. In theory, managers should be informed of all formal complaints within a hospital, but in 60 per cent of the complaints addressed to the responsible consultant, the doctor dealt with the complaint without contacting a manager. One of the main reasons which consultants gave for not referring complaints to managers was that they did not believe that managers had 'the right' to handle clinical complaints. In other words, they acted to protect their individual and group autonomy. Indeed, one said:

Clinical complaints about clinicians must be dealt with by clinicians. What do managers know about treating patients?

In all the studies, a small minority of doctors said they did not seek any help from others. From the GP study, we found that this was a matter of concern to all the LMC secretaries interviewed. They believed that doctors required support to deal with the anxiety of coping with a complaint, as well as advice on how to prepare their defence. An LMC secretary recalled a doctor he had helped, saying:

> He got up on the morning of the hearing and his wife said you don't normally put your suit on to go to the surgery and he broke down and wept and said he hadn't told her because he was worried that he'd be struck off and they'd lose the house. This was an intelligent, highly competent doctor who had set up his own practice against the odds, a very strong character, and that was how a complaint affected him.

The same LMC secretary said that he had told GP colleagues that complaints were now a fact of life and they had to share them. His concern was the doctors who did not, and he commented:

> The ones you really like to get at are those who freeze and panic. Some scribble the first thing that occurs to them and you discourage that as well. I try to get them to link their response to each part of the complaint.

Explaining complaints: explanations, rationalizations and defences

Tedeschi and Reiss (1981) suggest that when untoward events occur, people seek to attribute cause, responsibility and blame. Typically, they tend to attribute responsibility and blame to themselves, to others, to external circumstances or to fate. In an earlier study of GP responses to complaints which were adjudicated by a medical service committee, Allsop (1994) identified similar themes in GP letters of defence. She found that most doctors drew on biomedicine in explanation of the events which had occurred. Over three-quarters of the doctors referred to the difficulties of diagnosis, the inevitability of the course of the disease or the speed with which the condition of the patient could change. In just under half of the cases, the patient or lay carer was partly or wholly blamed. A few doctors blamed external circumstances, such as the weather or bed shortages, for the untoward event. Similarly, in their work on 339 hospital complaints, Lloyd-Bostock and Mulcahy (1994) found that letters of response from doctors were typically concerned to undermine complainants' competence by correcting or casting doubt on the details of their account.

In the two studies reported on here, it was found that doctors used similar types of explanation when reflecting on complaints. First, they drew on their knowledge of disease, science and medicine to focus on the features which were likely to prompt complaints. The uncertainties of the disease process and effect of treatments were used to explain why the doctor's view of what was appropriate action might differ from that of the lay person. Sometimes, complaints were seen as a consequence of illness itself. Second, some doctors in both studies attributed the complaint to the personality of the complainant. Finally, although less often, doctors attributed the causes of the complaint to external circumstances over which they had no control.

Biomedical explanations of complaining

In both studies, the complaint was commonly contexualized within the arena of biomedical expert knowledge. This explicitly or implicitly reaffirmed the doctor's position as an expert who was knowledgeable about the intrinsic limitations and risks of his or her area of practice, as compared to the complainant, who could not know about the likely course of disease and what could be done to treat it. In the consultants' study, one doctor explicitly voiced his view of the authority of the expert to give opinions thus:

> Practising medicine is about exercising judgement. . . . That is why we're so opinionated.

The occurrence of a complaint was explained in terms of inadequate lay knowledge, compared to the scientific knowledge of the doctor, and/or as a reflection of the character and motivations of the complainant. The complainant's lack of knowledge and irrationality were often contrasted to the rationality, knowledge, competence of the doctor. Patients were also said to have 'unrealistic expectations', either because of their social position or because they did not understand the disease process.

Many consultants identified features of their particular specialty which could attract or discourage complaints. The data collected on the incidence of complaints in different specialties supported consultants' perceptions. For example, the average number of complaints per consultant in specialties such as obstetrics and gynaecology, surgery and general medicine was more than double the level for psychiatry, radiology and pathology. Consultants argued that factors to be taken into account included: the potential for a good outcome from the procedure, the degree of uncertainty about the outcome of care, the length and intensity of the treatment episode, the risks involved in treatment, the potential for treatment to cause serious harm and the level of emotional investment in success or failure. Thus, the causes of complaints were 'objectified' by reference to factors associated with medical practice despite the fact that around 60 per cent of complaints about hospitals were made by relatives of the patient (Lloyd-Bostock and Mulcahy 1994). It was these factors, rather than poor care, which could explain the occurrence of a complaint in a particular specialism.

Oncology, gynaecology and areas of general medicine, such as terminal care, were said to be at particular risk of receiving complaints and were seen as 'bad news' specialties. One consultant said:

> We are definitely a bad news specialty. Young patients often die unexpectedly and there is a lot of guilt at the death. When it comes to it, people often do not know how to deal with it and their obvious reaction is to channel the emotions on to someone else. It's a case of shooting the messenger. It is very difficult to do anything about those complaints because probably you couldn't have done any better.

And another commented:

> You get problems in gynaecology. In particular, there's the problem of miscarriage which needs to be handled sensitively because people see themselves as having lost a child.

Conversely, orthodontics was described in terms of being a 'good news' specialty and therefore not vulnerable to complaints. One orthodontic consultant commented:

> There are very few down-sides to treatment. It does not involve excessive discomfort and there is an inbuilt system for explaining the treatment. . . . In addition, I only take on patients who really want to have the treatment done. We will only take on a patient if we think we can improve them significantly. In other words, we design the system so that they will be happy.

The personality of the complainant

Another major way in which doctors explained complaints was by attributing them in some way to the complainant or another lay person. Complainants were described by a number of consultants in negative or dismissive terms such as 'moaners' or 'nasty', or as 'abusers' and 'malcontents'. Out of 141 commentaries by consultants on this theme, 21 (only 12 of whom were specialists in psychiatric medicine) described complainants as exhibiting signs of psychiatric illness. Twenty-eight consultants referred to the assertive, rights-conscious patient while only six made positive or empathetic comments about the person who had made a complaint. One doctor commented:

> You could do a psychological profile of patients coming into the hospital and select those who were likely to complain before giving them any clinical care.

Sometimes complainants could be seen as vindictive. Another suggested:

> There is the complaining type. They live in——and they are on the dinner party circuit. Tarquin is at The Clarendon [a private school]. They shake hands with you but they are vicious. Basically, they want you to know they are in charge.

Similarly, in the GP study, one GP commented:

> Many complain because they find the process entertains them.

Another suggested that the complainant wanted

> blood (mine) on the floor.

Doctors also saw relatives or carers as frequent initiators of complaints for a variety of psychological, emotional or self-interested reasons. The view of one hospital consultant was that:

There are lots of problems with relatives. They have lots of trouble coming to terms with the diagnosis and there's lots of guilt around. They deal with this by being aggressive to me. Some relatives even have psychiatric problems themselves.

The external context to explaining complaints

In both studies, some doctors referred to external circumstances such as diminishing resources and a loss of control over the medical process to explain complaints. For example, one consultant anaesthetist said that the shortage of resources no longer gave him time to explain the treatment and risks to patients. He said:

We used to see patients regularly before the operation. We would see them the evening before, when they were relatively calm and relaxed. That has changed now and we are rushed . . . People often come in after the list of patients for surgery that day has started. They often get cursory treatment from staff.

Another made reference to the shortage of resources in the following way:

I feel what we do is unsafe. You should not really run a unit like ours unless you have adequate staff, but what do you do? Turn sick people away? I'm not just concerned that we are getting more and more complaints. I am concerned that we will get shut down.

Some doctors also talked about the emergence of the 'demanding patient' and a complaints culture which was encouraged by the Patient's Charter drawn up in 1992 for the NHS. One GP commented:

The attitude of patients, especially in the present climate of the Patient's Charter, is that we (the doctors) should drop everything and attend to their needs.

The impact of complaints on clinical practice

Both the consultants' and the GP studies provided data on the ways in which doctors changed their clinical practice in response to complaints. Doctors were asked whether their practice of medicine was influenced by the complaints they received. A similar proportion in each study, about two-thirds of the doctors who had received a complaint, said they had an impact on the way they practised. In the GP study, most of the changes (79 per cent) related to medical care, the rest related to the administration of the practice. Table 9.3 shows the types of changes to medical care indicated in both studies.

The categories in this table reflect both general and specific examples of changes in practice and all of them reflect increased caution. In the GP

Table 9.3 The impact of complaints on the practice of medicine

Action taken by doctors as a result of complaints	Consultants' study (N=304)	GP study (N=34)
More detailed record-keeping	100	24
Increased number of referrals to hospital	Not applicable	18
More home visits out of hours	Not applicable	14
General increased clinical vigilance or wariness	75	15
Fuller consultation with patients and relatives	69	5
Giving more responsibility for decision-making to patients	28	8
Adjustment of bedside manner	24	Not asked
Avoidance of certain patient types	23	7
Ordering more diagnostic tests	18	12
Tendency to seek more advice	17	11
Reducing the size of lists or clinics	10	1
Other	27	0

study, respondents were also asked about their motivation for making the change in order to distinguish negative actions taken to avert complaints from positive actions taken to improve practice.

There has been extensive discussion of the problems of 'defensive medicine' in both medical and legal journals. This is said to occur when specific procedures, tests or treatments are employed or withheld to avert a possible lawsuit (Ennis and Vincent 1994). Summerton (1995) found that GPs in his survey had made significant changes in their practice to avert the possibility of a patient complaining in the future. Of the defensive medical practices found in this survey, the most common strategies were an increase in diagnostic testing, an increased referral and follow-up rate, more detailed patient explanations and more detailed note-taking. These changes reflected practitioners' concern with avoiding risk. It could be argued that, despite the negative motivation, some of the changes made could have beneficial effects on patient care.

The GP study found that, whether undertaken to improve care or avert complaints, more detailed record-keeping and more out-of-hours visits were common responses to complaints. However, those seeking to improve the quality of care were much more likely say that they increased their clinical vigilance (23 per cent) than those seeking to avert complaints (10 per cent). Conversely, those in the latter group were more likely to say that they would increase the number of referrals to hospital (17 per cent) compared to the former (8 per cent). In other words, those who were more positive in their approach made changes within their own practice rather than referring patients on to other professionals.

The implications of doctors' responses for complaint handling

In today's health service an emphasis is placed on improving quality and managing the risks incurred by healthcare interventions. One aspect of this has been the introduction of more informal complaints procedures which seek to improve complaint handling services and are linked to quality management. The aim is to resolve dissatisfaction as quickly as possible. Disciplinary procedures have been separated from complaint handling so that there has been a shift away from attributing blame to a single individual towards a learning model which places greater emphasis on systemic failures (Allsop and Mulcahy 1996; see also Vincent and Reason, Chapter 3). The objective is to encourage doctors and other NHS staff to be more conciliatory towards patients' concerns and to approach complaints in a positive rather than a negative way. But will doctors' responses need to change in order to achieve this objective? The study findings suggest that they will.

If this is to occur, it is important to understand the doctors' perspective. The findings suggest that a doctor's sense of self is closely tied to professional identity. As a person with a claim to competence and expertise, his or her security is threatened by complaints and there is a strong emotional reaction. In the longer term, doctors may even adopt a more aggressive attitude towards patients when they undertake procedures merely to avert complaints. Not only are complaints taken as a challenge to competence, they can also have further serious consequences. There is a fear among doctors that a complaint may blemish their reputation, leading to disciplinary action and possibly being struck off the register.

Given the personal threat posed by complaints, it is perhaps not surprising to find that most doctors prefer to seek the help and support of medical colleagues in their place of work. This confirms earlier studies of the close identification with colleagues which results from the process of medical socialization. This strategy has both strengths and weaknesses. On the one hand, close medical colleagues can provide emotional and practical support with an appreciation of the context in which the complaint occurred. Stress levels in medicine are high and there is usually a variety of factors involved when untoward events occur. Therefore, colleague support can be an aid to a positive approach to following up a complaint. This finding is encouraging if only because it suggests that specialties and departments may be working as teams rather than as individuals. On the other hand, from the perspective of others, a reliance on close medical colleagues can reinforce stereotypes of a group identity which excludes others and may deny that the complainant has a valid point to make, albeit from a different perspective. It may also lead the doctor to ignore the distress of the complainant.

Recourse to the peer group for support may reinforce the tendency to seek explanations for complaints in biomedicine or in the personality of the complainant. Such explanations emphasize the divide between the patient, the doctor and the manager. If knowledge of complaints and their effects stays within a close-knit medical fraternity, there are three possible consequences. First, there is a lack of appreciation of patients' concerns and their right to be heard. Second, rationalizations of complaints on the basis of biomedical explanations fail to address the possibility of poor practice and/or error. Collective understandings are articulated, reinforced and constantly renewed within the medical community without input from competing discourses, meaning that the system remains closed. Third, some doctors deliberately exclude managers from their information network. At best, this may mean that the separate interests in healthcare delivery continue to coexist; at worst, the complex pathway of factors leading to poor care is never examined. This may inhibit learning from complaints in the interest of quality and risk management.

Many of the issues which we have addressed in this chapter, as well as our findings, have highlighted the tensions which can exist between the benefits of group solidarity and the accountability of groups to the wider society. These tensions have been heightened as patients become more assertive and organizations within which medical professionals work promote corporate approaches to service delivery. The rhetoric doctors employ to explain complaints is not the only one. The consumerist model provides an alternative account and can appear equally closed. New complaints systems have to be sensitive to this. They cannot remove the challenge to medical expertise but conciliatory approaches could be developed which allow both patients' and doctors' concerns to be considered with the assistance of a third party. Greater openness and trust will be required by all such parties if the separate objectives of healthcare users and healthcare providers are to be met.

References

Allsop, J. (1994) Two sides to every story: Complainants' and doctors' perspectives in disputes about medical care in a general practice setting, *Law and Policy*, 16(2): 148–83.

Allsop, J. and Mulcahy, L. (1996) *Regulating Medical Work: Formal and Informal Controls*. Buckingham: Open University Press.

Atkinson, P. (1981) *The Clinical Experience: The Construction and Reconstruction of Medical Reality*. Farnborough: Gower.

Atkinson, P. (1984) Training for certainty, *Social Science and Medicine*, 19: 949–56.

Atkinson, P. (1995) *Medical Talk and Medical Work*. London: Sage.

Becker, H., Geer, B., Hughes, E. and Strauss, A. (1961) *Boys in White: Student Culture in Medical School*. Chicago: University of Chicago Press.

Bosk, C. (1979) *Forgive and Remember: Managing Medical Failure*. Chicago: Chicago University Press.

Brennan, T., Leape, L., Laird, N. *et al.* (1991) Incidence of adverse events and negligence in hospitalized patients: The results from the Harvard Medical Practice Study I, *New England Journal of Medicine*, 324: 370–6.

Bucher, R. and Strauss, A. (1961) Professions in process, *American Journal of Sociology*, 66: 325–54.

Citizen's Charter Complaints Task Force (1995) *Complaints Handling in the Public Sector*. A research study conducted by MORI. London: HMSO.

Department of Health (1995) *Acting on Complaints: The Government's Prospectus*. London: HMSO.

Donaldson, L. (1994) Doctors with problems in the NHS workforce, *British Medical Journal* 308: 1277–82.

Ennis, M. and Vincent, C. (1994) The effects of medical accidents and litigation on doctors and patients, *Law and Policy* – Special Issue, 16(2): 97–122.

Fox, R. (1957) Training for uncertainty, in R. Merton, G. Reader and P. Kendall (eds) *The Student Physician: Introductory Studies in the Sociology of Medical Education*. Cambridge, MA: Harvard University Press.

Freidson, E. (1970) *Profession of Medicine*. New York: Harper & Row.

Gabe, J., Kelleher, D. and Williams, G. (eds) (1994) *Challenging Medicine*. London: Routledge.

Goffman, I. (1967) *On Face Work*. New York: Doubleday.

Lloyd-Bostock, S. and Mulcahy, L. (1994) The social psychology of making and responding to hospital complaints: An account model of the complaint processes, *Law and Policy*, 16(2): 123–47.

Mizrahi, T. (1984) Managing medical mistakes: Ideology, insularity and accountability among internists in training, *Social Science and Medicine*, 19: 135–46.

Mulcahy, L. (1996) From fear to fraternity: Doctors' construction of rational accounts of complaining behaviour, *Journal of Social Welfare Law*, 18(4): 397–418.

Mulcahy, L. and Selwood, M. (1995) Being heard: Consultants' voices, final report, unpublished report. Oxford Regional Health Authority Clinical Complaints Project.

Mulcahy, L., Allsop, J. and Shirley, C. (1996a) *Different Voices: A Study of Complaints to Family Health Service Authorities*, Social Science Research Papers Series. London: School of Education, Politics and Social Sciences, South Bank University.

Mulcahy, L. Allsop, J. and Shirley, C. (1996b) Diplomatic service: Developing practice-based complaint systems, *Health Services Journal*, 11 January: 26–7.

Mulcahy, L., Lickiss, R., Allsop, J. and Karn, V. (1996c) *Small Voices, Big Issues: An Annotated Bibliography of the Literature on Public Sector Complaints*. London: University of North London Press.

National Health Service Executive (1994) *Being Heard: The Report of the Review Committee on NHS Complaints Procedures* (Chair Professor Alan Wilson). London: Department of Health.

National Health Service Executive (1996) *Complaints – Listening . . . Acting . . . Improving: Evidence on Implementation of the NHS Complaints Procedure*. London: Department of Health.

Rosenthal, M. (1995) *The Incompetent Doctor: Behind Closed Doors*. Buckingham: Open University Press.

Schutz, A. (1964) The well-informed citizen: An essay on the social distribution of knowledge, in A. Brotherson (ed.) *Collected Papers, Vol. 2*. The Hague: Martinus Nijhoff.

Stelling, J. and Bucher, R. (1973) Vocabularies of realism in professional socialisation, *Social Science and Medicine*, 7: 661–75.

Strong, P. (1979) *The Ceremonial Order of the Clinic*. London: Routledge.

Strong, P. and Davies, A. (1977) Roles, role formats and medical encounters, *Sociological Review*, 25(4): 775–800.

Summerton, N. (1995) Positive and negative factors in defensive medicine: A questionnaire study of general practitioners, *British Medical Journal*, 310: 27–29.

Tedeschi, J. and Reiss, M. (1981) Verbal strategies in impression management, in C. Antaki and N. Fielding (eds) *The Psychology of Ordinary Explanations in Social Behaviour*. London: Academic Press.

How doctors think about
medical mishaps

Marilynn M. Rosenthal

Introduction: exploring the culture of medicine

Understanding how doctors think about medical mishaps is a complex and
formidable task, yet it is invaluable in the construction of the puzzle that
we are calling 'perspectives on medical mishaps'. Medical thinking about
mishaps is deeply embedded in medical culture. A small number of social
scientists have been studying and analysing medical culture for decades.
By putting their work together with more recent research, it is possible
to construct a portrait of medical culture. It will be seen that the core
characteristics of that culture are medical uncertainty, the intense medical
collegiality that flows from uncertainty, and particular attitudes towards
clinical work including the potential for mishaps. Medical education, medical
thinking, the context of collegiality, socialization to appropriate behaviour
and perceptions of problem colleagues and error are the stuff of the following studies.

Education for uncertainty: Renee Fox

The ground-breaking work on medical uncertainty was published in the
late 1950s by the medical sociologist Renee C. Fox (1957). Her study of
students at Cornell Medical School led to the first, and still dominant,
description and analysis of 'training for uncertainty' in medical practice.
Her oft-quoted three categories of uncertainty that medical students encounter include: the limitations and gaps in medical knowledge and practice; incomplete or imperfect mastery of available knowledge; and difficulty

in differentiating between personal ignorance or ineptitude and the limitations in medical knowledge.

She traces the steps which students take through the pre-clinical and clinical years. During the former, medical students have to decide what portion of the huge body of knowledge presented should be mastered. They must accept that one can never know all medical knowledge. They slowly recognize, however, that there are gaps of knowledge in each of the subjects studied and that there is an 'irreducible' minimum of uncertainty inherent in medicine. They also begin to learn the inherent 'experimental' point of view in medical practice, that a great deal of practice is provisional. They are encouraged to acknowledge uncertainty. But lack of experience leaves them unable to distinguish between individual limited knowledge and the limits of the field.

Experiences with autopsy underscore the difficulties in ascertaining exact causes of death and demonstrate awareness of limitations in medical knowledge. This experience also reveals that instructors have an imperfect mastery of medical knowledge. The student is not alone. This is reinforced by exchange of experience with fellow students. Experience leads the student to a new revelation: uncertainty is a product of both ignorance and the nature of the work. In the face of this, all students learn that some humility is the most appropriate stance, even as knowledge and experience increase.

During the clinical years, with exposure to patients, comes the addition of patient factors. How much of the continuing uncertainty is attributable to variations among patients? The degree of uncertainty is now intensified. In the struggle to think like a doctor, the uncertainty is in some ways more powerful. Following a patient over several months may emphasize the mysteries and the fact that the patient's physical problems are compounded by emotional and environmental ones as well. Yet, at the same time, the student is now acquiring a manner of certitude as more and more patient encounters ensue. Closer contact with clinical faculty and observation of their uncertainties is fortifying, as is the need to act more certain and, indeed, to act more decisively on behalf of patients. During the clinical years, the student begins the pattern of laying blame for the inability to cure. Blame is placed usually on oneself, but sometimes on the patient (see Allsop and Mulcahy, Chapter 9). The student may begin to realize, with growing clarity, that medical education is training for uncertainty.

Bucher and Stelling's (1977) studies of medical students build on Fox's work and describe the need, therefore, to emphasize the process of work:

> Given the tenuous nature of much professional knowledge, it is perhaps not surprising that the trainees, in evaluating themselves and others, come to give greater emphasis to the actual process of doing their work than to the results of the process. If one is doing the right thing, one is practising competently.
>
> (Bucher and Stelling 1977: 23)

The special nature of medical thinking: Marianne Paget

An excellent but relatively ignored work by Paget (1988) further considers the phenomenology of medical uncertainty and thinking specifically about mistakes. It examines the specific language of medical mistakes. Instead of looking at medical mistakes as incidents or events at a single point in time, Paget sees them as a progression of incidents that unfold and emerge though time. Paget is particularly interested in the experience and expression of the person who makes the mistake and suggests that quantification and categorization of mistakes fail dismally to capture the reality. She rejects the meanings of medical mistake that suggest something that is 'wrong' or 'blameworthy'. The ease with which we connect making a mistake with being blameworthy and at fault is a result of a conventional way of thinking to which we have become accustomed.

For Paget, medical work is seen as a process of discovery. The doctor enters the scene when something is already wrong: the patient has become ill. The disease process and the clinical process now go along simultaneously, the one trying to affect the other. Medical work is a process of discovery, making inferences based on signs and symptoms, conducting experiments in various forms of treatment. It is often a trial and error process. The diagnostic and treatment process intersects the movement of an illness and unfolds in response to it. Paget describes this clinical work as an intrinsically error-ridden activity.

When you take action, you run the risk of doing something wrong, particularly in medicine which is practised with considerable unpredictability. Clinical judgement is 'acting as if' but without complete certainty. Most practitioners are technically competent and knowledgeable, but this is always circumscribed by uncertainty and emerging, sometimes unpredictable, events.

Physicians work with probabilities which do not predict a specific instance. The commonality of the experience of making mistakes should not be the important issue, although it is making mistakes that is at the core of many of the forms that organize medical work: morbidity and mortality conferences, autopsies, teaching rounds and medical audits. But blame is a social process that vilifies the person who errs. An error-ridden activity like medicine requires something different: understanding, correcting and avoiding repetition. Many mistakes are not clearly right or wrong. There are a multiplicity of rights and wrongs.

Public tension arises because of the image of the profession that both the patient and the doctor want: competence, knowledge, authority, autonomy. The 'crises' in healthcare costs and in malpractice have overwhelmed the discussion of mistakes, obscuring the complexity of their nature. Most mistakes do not involve negligence, but the two terms are increasingly confused and intermingled.

Paget's work is from the 1980s but the themes are persistent. A recently conducted focus group of chief residents in surgery reflects similar ideas (Rosenthal 1996). One chief resident spoke as follows:

Doctors and uncertainty means we think in terms of percentages, risks, best judgment; poor results from good procedures; bad procedures and good results; so we always try putting the best face on results; very little out-and-out negligence; there are very few 'mistakes' – how can there be mistakes when there is so much uncertainty? Although maybe there is poor supervision of young doctors.

Collegial culture: Eliot Freidson

Among scholars who study the professions, including medicine, there is general agreement that occupations attaining the status of 'profession' have the following characteristics: a systematic body of highly developed technical knowledge that is widely valued; strong standards of autonomy that emphasize self-regulation and altruism that submerges self-interest and emphasizes service; the need for extensive authority over clients; a distinct occupational culture and collegial etiquette; and recognition of this professional status by political, social and economic leadership. An ethical ideal of service, monopoly over important knowledge and skills, and high social regard coalesce to establish a high degree of autonomy over work. The medical profession is an excellent example of a profession that has brought all these traits together (see, for instance, Goode 1957).

The most sustained and comprehensive study of the medical profession is found in the work of the American sociologist Eliot Freidson (1970a; 1970b; 1977; 1980). The focal point of his work is the intricate dynamics of professional power and autonomy. As noted above, autonomy is the central characteristic of the profession. It is granted by the ultimate source of power in Western societies: the state. The state grants the profession the legal right to regulate itself. It carries out this important task in a variety of ways.

Medical education is considered by the profession to be the single most important factor influencing standards of medical performance. Students assimilate two important values during education: a deep sense of medical responsibility for patients and the importance of clinical experience.

The profession asserts that it will regulate itself rigorously and work by a code of strict ethics, what Freidson calls a claim of dedication, which is advanced to protect an interest (Freidson 1977). Instilling an ethic of work commitment is used to motivate members of the profession who also learn a strong commitment to colleagues and a strong sense of solidarity. Professional ethics has great importance in controlling and motivating the behaviour of individual doctors and maintaining a public professional image. The service orientation of the profession and the promise of self-regulation underpin the granting of autonomy by the state.

In his research, Freidson studied groups of American doctors in various organizational settings to observe the actual processes of self-regulation that took place. The only mechanism of collegial control that he observed was the 'boycott' or the avoidance of a colleague with questionable standards or behaviour. Where some form of supervision was observed, it was in the form of advice. Freidson concluded that self-regulation was weak and dependent on observability, vulnerability and willingness to be supervised.

When the boycott is used it has the disadvantage of pushing the practitioner out of surveillance range. Hence avoidance, not change, is the only mechanism operative. While there may be self-regulation, says Freidson, it is not observably effective. If boycott and exclusion are the only mechanism of regulation, then practitioners end up in networks that represent their level of standards and values. These networks have little to do with each other so offenders are beyond the control of those who disapprove of their behaviour (Freidson 1980).

Therefore the organization of work 'regulates' by encouraging different technical standards. Selective recruitment to medical school, the basic training core for licensing and the writings of medical leaders are then superficial mechanisms for imposing some minimal standards on the profession.

Socialization for appropriate behaviour: Charles Bosk

Forgive and Remember, Bosk's (1982) now classic study of how young residents learn to be surgeons, examines in close detail the inculcation of responsibility and devotion to the patient and the need to get along with the family and the nursing staff. He describes three categories of errors that are recognized: technical errors, judgemental errors and normative errors. Technical errors are forgiven if they are reported immediately, if they are remembered and not repeated. Judgemental errors, the responsibility of the senior doctor, are examined in mortality and morbidity committees and essentially forgiven through admission of mistakes. Normative errors are the most important. If the young doctor did not behave properly, did not take responsibility, did not try harder then average, let the patient and family down in some way, or did not perform according to the standards and protocols of the senior doctor, this is the least forgiven. Emphasis, then, is on proper behaviour during the process of care. Technical skill and knowledge are of primary importance, but it is proper behaviour that is paramount.

For the senior doctor, well past residency and established in practice, there is no surveillance. Bosk suggests that what was proper surveillance of a resident is seen as illegitimate meddling in the affairs of a peer. Senior doctors are not criticized by their peers but judged in terms of style, philosophy and personality. If a doctor has internalized the norms of proper behaviour, actual mistakes are generally ignored. Bosk deplores the lack of corporate (overall professional) responsibility for errors and competence. Light (1980: 186) has pointed out:

> In the medical professional world, one can make a mistake in technique without it affecting outcome or one can have perfect technique

with poor result. Only when poor results can be directly attributed to technique does outcome contribute to the definition of a mistake and often this is not the case. Residents . . . could not define mistakes in their work because the layman's ideas of mistake had become foreign to them through professional training. When something happens that might look like a mistake, professionals enact specific rituals (like mortality review) which have features designed to deflect or mollify charges of bad practice.

Uncertainty, collegiality and 'problem' colleagues

There are a variety of ways in which a profession like medicine tries to guarantee high standards and formally regulates itself. In the UK, this includes the General Medical Council's responsibility for licensing, ethical codes of appropriate professional behaviour, discipline and sick doctors; the Royal Colleges which establish and maintain medical educational standards; the British Medical Association and its local medical committees. These professional organizations share some areas of responsibility with managers and bureaucrats: chief medical officers, NHS trust chief executives, health authorities and managers of contracts, risk and quality. These are all important formal, and indeed legal, standard-setters. They define the boundaries of what is acceptable and unacceptable in medical practice and behaviour. How well these formal regulatory entities function has been systematically studied and reported (Rosenthal 1987; Stacey 1992).

However, every profession and occupation develops informal ways of setting standards and expediting work directly in the work environment. More casual techniques are established for self-regulation, promoting a positive work setting and dealing with problems, including 'problem' colleagues. These have rarely been studied in the medical profession. We know, from other occupations, that these informal techniques are more important than the formal ones which exist only as 'fall-backs' when nothing else works.

Therefore, this is an important aspect of medical professional self-regulation which is shaped by how doctors think about their work, particularly the boundaries between avoidable and unavoidable complications; how doctors treat each other as colleagues; and characteristics of their work environments as well as general societal culture.

My research on informal self-regulation, which was conducted in the UK, explored how British doctors think about their work and their experience with identifying and coping with 'problem' colleagues (Rosenthal 1995). This study, conducted in 1990 and published in 1995, involved over 60 interviews about how doctors think about being a clinician, the boundaries between avoidable and unavoidable complications and colleagues who pose some sort of challenge. The study collected over 200 anecdotal case studies involving medical mishaps or suspected mishaps and doctors who were identified as 'problems'.

An analysis of the cases revealed that seven overarching themes permeate medical thinking. The two basic themes are permanent uncertainty and necessary fallibility. From these grow a deep sense of shared personal vulnerability with one's colleagues, and therefore understanding and forgiveness for mishaps and a strong norm of non-criticism. Doctors did recognize and condemn egregious errors – outrageous violations of standard skills and knowledge – but insisted on exclusivity of professional judgement. Only fellow doctors are able to judge other doctors' work.

A number of people interviewed stressed the vulnerability of doctors. In the words of a senior GP with 25 years' experience:

> We're all entitled to mistakes aren't we? We're all vulnerable. 'There but for the grace of God go I . . . I remember making that mistake myself.' Only doctors can judge doctors because we can immediately empathize. We are all human. There are problems in all our lives that are not our fault. . . . As long as you can say: 'That could happen to me', you're going to be sympathetic.
>
> (Rosenthal 1995: 15)

A regional GP adviser commented:

> Mistakes anyone can make; those are acceptable. We all misdiagnose a simple complaint sometimes. We fail to refer at an early stage. Anyone can make this mistake . . . It becomes unacceptable when it's too gross – to miss breast cancer, for example. Doctors should be reprimanded but no one likes to do this . . . we're protective, perhaps too protective.
>
> (Rosenthal 1995: 29)

A number of respondents explained the problems which exist in recognizing the boundaries of culpable behaviour. A consultant surgeon with 22 years' experience in a teaching hospital argued:

> It is very difficult to define the boundary between the avoidable and unavoidable mistake. Surgeons are ordinary people really. It is a question of how far one can deviate from the average before it becomes so bad that action has to be taken. Grossness . . . frequency . . . but it is very difficult to estimate. Vast numbers of things go wrong and are not reported. If something goes wrong, I want to know right away. [But] I get more and more forgiving as I get older.
>
> (Rosenthal 1995: 15)

Understanding and appreciating this thinking, we can understand better how difficult it is to gather reliable information about an errant colleague and then to confront and cope with such a colleague. It is also important in understanding who and what kind of behaviour is identified as a problem and the extent to which a 'problem' is considered serious. The data collected fell into five categories: clear mistakes committed by competent doctors; clear mistakes committed by incompetent doctors; inappropriate behaviour which suggests incompetence; unprofessional behaviour; and impaired doctors.

One widely respected, highly experienced GP, then in a national position of considerable status, explained that all doctors, including competent ones, will occasionally make mistakes:

> I was a good and a respected doctor. But I can remember the mistakes I made. I will carry them to my grave. I can understand why I made them; I can live with them, although in two cases they were fatal. The first was in the 1950s when I was a junior doctor. I misprescribed for a patient and he died. The other was a woman I had examined on half a dozen occasions. I didn't detect anything unusual. She died of a brain tumour. I can understand how I failed to detect that. These are scars I carry always; all doctors carry these scars.
>
> (Rosenthal 1995: 19)

But these were distinguished from mistakes where there was incompetence that required action to be taken. As a consultant surgeon and national expert opined:

> Sometimes just one case requires discipline. A patient was transferred to the——from another hospital. The case started with termination of a pregnancy and ended with surgical mayhem. It was very bad. This requires discipline; it will get turned over to the courts. There will be a substantial settlement.
>
> (Rosenthal 1995: 23–4)

Other doctors caused suspicion amongst their colleagues. A District Director of Public Health explained how this could lead to a distancing of colleagues:

> There is a radiologist here who is quite difficult. Maybe there are some errors of judgement but he is a difficult personality. In the past, we were careful to scrutinize reports from his department. If something is seriously wrong, you can move. But at the end of the day, [suspension] is really impossible and nasty. . . . And it is difficult to control the flow of patients if there are a limited number of consultants . . . This radiologist gives good service to GPs. He calls immediately so he gets a lot of work from them but not . . . from hospital consultants.
>
> (Rosenthal 1995: 81)

Other behaviour was viewed as unprofessional rather than technically incompetent. This included crimes, fraud, selling drugs and sexual harassment. As one senior GP explained:

> A GP was thought to be handing out tablets too freely. He had rented space in a health centre and the social worker noticed a fair run of

undesirable people. She contacted the manager who contacted the LMC. It was looked into and discovered that he was taking them, too. He was sent away for six months of treatment. It was probably a year before we got to him.

(Rosenthal 1995: 87)

Finally, respondents referred to the special case of the impaired doctor. This category included mental illness, physical illness, approaching senility, alcoholism and drug addiction. One former regional medical officer said:

A single-handed general practitioner gave terrific service for 25–30 years. He drank heavily for at least 20 years, showed all the signs of being an alcoholic for ten years, also signs of drug dependence. In World War II, under difficulty, he ran services for the community doing heroic things. This was a remote rural area. He did surgeries in different places. He stops for a whisky at the top of a particular hill. Patients would catch him, with their big problems, at the top of the hill (before he took his drink). Sometimes patients think it reflects on them. Is something lacking in them if the doctor has taken to the bottle?

(Rosenthal 1995: 85)

Estimates of all categories of problem doctors ranged from 2 to 5 per cent in the UK, according to the medical leaders and managers interviewed. Further research is needed with carefully constructed definitions of 'problem' to determine the accuracy of these guesses. It is likely that a certain percentage in any occupation, in any large group, will be problems and it is not clear that medicine has a larger proportion than other groups.

One of many questions emerging from this study is whether 'problem' doctors are 'incompetent'. Clearly the answer is 'no'. The cases, and the reactions to them, are illuminated by our understanding of the nature of medical thinking. Competent doctors make mistakes, serious and heartbreaking ones. They are judged neither as 'problem colleagues' nor as incompetent. They elicit understanding and forgiveness if they have behaved properly. The truly incompetent are a tiny minority, the ones who make gross mistakes, egregious errors, and don't appear to learn from them. The truly incompetent doctor needs to be firmly removed from patient care.

Doctors with distasteful personalities are often considered 'problem' colleagues. Such practitioners are often suspected of being incompetent. However, usually there is no more evidence of this than for the average doctor. The sick doctor is a challenge, and we simply need more research to understand when the sick doctor is incompetent. The sick doctor needs compassionate help; as do the distasteful personality and the unprofessional doctor. So does the competent doctor in order to reduce medical error and medical uncertainty.

Informal techniques of self-regulation occur. The interviews revealed a number of them. They include the quiet chat, protective support, work shifting, exporting the problem and being pushed out of a partnership, use of the hospital wise men committee and informal pressure imposed by a Royal College. These are the means by which the medical profession tries to deal with 'problem' colleagues, particularly the sick, the disturbing personality and the truly incompetent.

How effective are the informal techniques? According to those interviewed, under half the cases where informal techniques were used were considered to have concluded successfully. Again, we need some systematic analysis to be more precise about successes and failures of the informal techniques. If a group of colleagues have dealt with an incompetent colleague by 'exporting' the problem to another district or region, for example, this is hardly a success.

There are certain common patterns to the use of the informal techniques. A few of them reflect medical uncertainty and medical collegiality, the twin pillars of medical culture. They also reveal the great ambiguities that shade medical thinking about mishaps. They illustrate not only this recent study, but also the earlier findings of Fox, Paget, Freidson and Bosk.

First, it takes a long time to take first steps. It is difficult to assess the rumours and information that circulate. Action is delayed as long as possible. One regional general practice adviser argued:

> Problems go on for a very long time. Other GPs may be suspicious but they don't want to delve too deeply because if they know too much, they will have to take action. So the problem may go on for a very long time. It has to be absolutely catastrophic and threatening patient harm for someone to interfere.
>
> (Rosenthal 1995: 41)

Second, the norms of professional etiquette and equality among peers make it difficult to pass judgement on a fellow doctor. In the words of an emeritus professor of surgery:

> The moment you become a consultant in the UK, you are omnicompetent. You don't have to pay attention to your colleagues; you don't have to pay attention to anybody.
>
> (Rosenthal 1995: 41)

This reluctance to criticize grows, of course, out of the way doctors think about mistakes. Uncertainty, necessary fallibility and shared vulnerability buttress such reticence. Clinical freedom, particularly among senior doctors, is deeply cherished. All these, along with hesitation to interfere in another's livelihood, combine to delay taking action at all points along the continuum of informal mechanisms.

Third, the quality of interpersonal relations determines the kind of approach taken and certainly whether a problem colleague gets protective support. The nature and degree of collegiality and tolerance for deviance in the group, the 'problem' doctor's previous reputation, the nature of the aberrant behaviour and the quality of previous relations are important factors in whether a problem is identified, how a doctor is approached and how the doctor is dealt with.

Finally, the quality of management skills of the colleagues taking responsibility for initiative with 'problem' colleagues is important in their success. This is particularly true given the reality (or former reality) of life contracts for consultants in British hospitals and the independent nature of the British GP. There is usually no special training for this role. While the profession says 'only we can judge each other', and promises self-regulation, it has no particular expertise for this. Where some individuals in positions of responsibility (an LMC secretary, a regional director of public health) seem considerably more successful than their colleagues in dealing with 'problem' doctors, their interpersonal and management skill levels are higher.

Despite difficulty in using the informal techniques, they merit greater attention and support. Why? They are reasonable, more humane, less costly, less contentious and less harsh than the formal regulation. Those closest to the problems are in the best position to judge, if they are willing to do so.

But clearly the informal techniques need to be strengthened, to protect patients more quickly, to bring help to 'problem' doctors and to keep the work environment going smoothly. First, the informal techniques of self-regulation need to be recognized and understood more clearly and systematically. Then, colleagues need to sort out the categories of 'problem' doctors so that each is handled in the most appropriate way.

However, the overarching themes in how doctors think about their work suggest there are even larger issues. Do individual doctors distinguish between varying degrees of uncertainty in clinical practice? Is there too much understanding and forgiveness? Does medical education and socialization prepare doctors well enough for the resilience, flexibility and responsiveness needed in a work world of uncertainty? Has the profession taken on board, in systematic ways, the findings of evidence-based medicine, medical outcomes research and other empirical efforts to describe and understand medical mishaps? Has the profession scrutinized how it organizes its work to mitigate the uncertainties?

Discussion: putting it all together for a portrait of a profession

Renee Fox has given us insight into medical uncertainty and its three faces: the uncertainty in medical knowledge itself; the uncertainty of the doctor's mastery of that knowledge; and the uncertainty of distinguishing between the two. Paget describes the language of uncertainty and mistakes, emphasizing that medical work is a process of discovery and experimentation where the word 'mistake' and its connotation of blame are inappropriate.

Bosk provides a picture of how training is carried out in a work world of uncertainty and how that training puts the emphasis on behaviour and process, on a high sense of responsibility and very hard work as the desired norms of behaviour. Freidson provides a portrait of professional culture with its emphasis on autonomy, intense collegiality and self-regulation. My research provides details of how that self-regulation is carried out, with uncertainty making it difficult to identify 'mistakes' objectively, and collegiality making it difficult to restrain 'problem' colleagues of whatever type.

Putting all this work together, we have a clearer picture of medical work, the various facets of uncertainty, and the behaviour that compensates for uncertainty. This is a 'culture of uncertainty' with its own values, beliefs and behaviour. This culture promotes a unique way of understanding mishaps, obviously different, painfully different, than how the average patient and lay person think about mistakes. The profession is caught in a conundrum: an intricate and difficult problem that includes the perception of uncertainty, the realities of uncertainty, the norms of individual responsibility and hard work, the desire to be autonomous and self-regulating, and limitations on effective self-regulation because of collegiality. We find a powerful mix of blame – either self-blame or patient blame – and professional leniency because of shared uncertainty.

As described in a recent *British Medical Journal* article:

> Professional collegiality has many faces. A circle of esteem and mutual respect. A circle of support in the face of great responsibility for patient care. A circle of comfort in a stressful work environment. A protective retreat in the face of difficult cases, complications and inevitable fallibility. And then there is the other side of collegiality. Closing ranks against outsiders, including patients. Reticence to criticize and protection of the questionable. How to balance the absolutely legitimate need for collegiality with the need to help (and stop) faltering, fumbling and failing fellow doctors.
>
> (Rosenthal 1997: 1633)

It is against this backdrop that the profession searches for ways to improve patient care, understand medical mistakes and reduce or constrain their occurrence. It may be that the profession will have to reach outside its own ranks, to other experts, who have studied human error in other fields. In this way the profession may gain greater insight into the context of errors and more effective techniques for dealing with medical mishaps. The profession can rededicate itself to working hard for the individual patient, retaining that high sense of personal responsibility so widely respected among the public, with new understanding of those areas of experience where we know that uncertainty is the certainty. As it does this, the profession will be most successful if it understands the subtleties of its own culture, its own beliefs, its own thinking and its own behaviour with as much clarity and objectivity as possible.

References

Bosk, C. (1979) *Forgive and Remember: Managing Medical Failure*. Chicago: University of Chicago Press.

Bucher, R. and Stelling, J. (1977) *Becoming Professional*. Beverly Hills, CA: Sage.

Fox, R. (1957) Training for uncertainty, in R. Merton, G. Reader and P. Kendall (eds) *The Student Physician: Introductory Studies in the Sociology of Medical Education*. Cambridge, MA: Harvard University Press.

Freidson, E. (1970a) *Profession of Medicine*. New York: Harper & Row.

Freidson, E. (1970b) *Professional Dominance*. New York: Atherton Press.

Freidson, E. (1977) The future of professionalization, in M. Stacey, M. Reid, C. Heath and R. Dingwall (eds) *Health and the Division of Labour*. London: Croom Helm.

Freidson, E. (1980) *Doctoring Together*. Chicago: University of Chicago Press.

Goode, W. (1957) Community within a community: The professions, *American Sociological Review*, 25: 902–14.

Light, D. (1980) *Becoming Psychiatrists*. New York: Norton.

Paget, M. (1988) *The Unity of Mistakes: A Phenomenological Interpretation of Medical Work*. Philadelphia: Temple University Press.

Rosenthal, M. (1987) *Dealing with Medical Malpractice: The British and Swedish Experience*. London: Tavistock.

Rosenthal, M. (1995) *The Incompetent Doctor: Behind Closed Doors*. Buckingham: Open University Press.

Rosenthal, M. (1996) Focus group interview, surgery chief residents. Unpublished paper.

Rosenthal, M. (1997) Knowledge monopoly, uncertainty and regulation of the medical profession, *British Medical Journal*, 7094: 1633.

Stacey, M. (1992) *Regulating British Medicine: The General Medical Council*. Chichester: Wiley.

11 | Mediation of medical negligence actions: an option for the future?

Linda Mulcahy

Introduction

Medical negligence actions are one of many indicators that medical mishaps occur, but the primary aim of the litigation system is to consider whether the NHS should be required to pay compensation to injured patients. To date, debates about medical negligence have concentrated more on the issue of whether the high cost of compensation should be met than on issues of the regulation and accountability of the medical profession (Simanowitz 1987). Use of the law in the identification of medical mistakes is an extreme form of regulation of mishaps since it concentrates on the attribution of blame to individual medics and on compensating patients for discrete mistakes.

Not all adverse outcomes are the result of error and fewer still are the result of negligence. People pursue medical negligence actions for a variety of reasons, and not all such cases reveal poor standards. More importantly, many potential litigants who have suffered poor care do not take any action in response to it (Royal Commission 1978; Felstiner *et al.* 1980–81; Brennan *et al.* 1991; Leape *et al.* 1991; Mulcahy and Tritter 1998). Systems for handling medical negligence claims do not lend themselves to the systemic approach to medical mishaps identified by Vincent and Reason in Chapter 3 of this volume (see also Leape, Chapter 2; and Dickinson, Chapter 16) and the fear of being challenged in this way may well cause healthcare professionals to distance themselves from the proactive approach to mishaps suggested elsewhere in this volume (see Polywka and Chapman, Chapter 18; Robinson, Chapter 22; and Nathanson, Chapter 15).

However, medical negligence actions also occupy a strategic role in the various systems used together to contribute to the identification of medical mishaps. Unlike many of the other indicators discussed in this collection, such as review of patient records, surveys of doctors and patients, medical audit and confidential enquiries into clinical outcomes, medical negligence actions are dependent on patients or their carers identifying a mistake and acting on it. Because actions are instigated by patients rather than those responsible for the provision of healthcare, they play an important part in goading policy-makers, managers and health professionals into more proactive management of mishaps and provide an essential external check on managers' and clinicians' activity. Fears of a litigation 'crisis' have undoubtedly played an important part in the development of risk management strategies.

But medical negligence actions have also become an increasingly expensive form of regulation, and litigants have been extremely critical of the civil justice system's ability to provide compensation for those in need and to hold responsible service providers to account. In this chapter I consider how a new mediation pilot scheme launched by the Department of Health in 1995 and terminated in 1998 has sought to resolve many of the problems faced by litigants and encourage a more constructive approach to the handling of these claims. I present some of the preliminary findings of an evaluation of the scheme which I was commissioned to undertake by the Department of Health. The chapter is of relevance to this collection for three reasons. First, it considers what may happen in the aftermath of medical mishap to patients and doctors and how victims' needs are best met. Second, it considers whether a revised system for handling medical negligence claims would be able to provide more information for use in the effective identification of mishaps. Third, it considers whether a more conciliatory approach to resolution of medical negligence disputes would facilitate less defensive investigations and responses and mitigate some of the harmful consequences of becoming involved in these disputes which are experienced by the parties.

What is medical negligence?

The law of medical negligence operates on two principles: that the patient must agree to treatment and that treatment must be carried out with proper skill by the doctors involved (Brazier 1992). But it holds doctors and other healthcare professionals liable only for that subset of iatrogenic injury that occurs when there is a breach of the duty to use reasonable care and, as a consequence, the patient experiences an injury. Doctors are not meant to be miracle workers. In principle, adverse outcomes consistent with 'normal' risk must be borne by the patient (Danzon 1985).

The courts have defined the degree of competence expected of the ordinary skilful doctor as being that of the practitioner who follows the standard practice of his colleagues within the profession. This has led some to claim that the test is effectively set by doctors for doctors (Kennedy and Grubb, 1994), while others see this as inevitable given the regular technological advance of medicine (Irwin *et al.* 1996). A doctor's actions or omissions are acceptable in law if they at least follow practices that would not be disapproved of by a body of responsible opinion within the profession. Negligence cannot be inferred, therefore, just because another doctor, or body of doctors, would have taken a contrary view.

Problems with the current system

There has been widespread criticism of existing systems for handing medical negligence claims in the UK. Critics come from a number of different quarters, including the consumer lobby, the legal profession, the medical profession and health service managers (Ham *et al.* 1988; Capstick *et al.* 1991; Simanovitz 1989). These criticisms have focused on the aftermath of mishap and the impact of the legal process on both patients and health professionals.

Patients face a number of difficulties in mounting a claim and finding the significant resources needed to do this (Mildred 1989). The amount of legal aid devoted to the pursuit of medical negligence actions is being reduced and little is known, as yet, about the impact that the proposed introduction of contingency fees will have on plaintiffs' abilities to mount actions. A widespread review of the legal aid system has left legal aid for medical negligence actions untouched, but only temporarily. Patients' problems have been compounded by the inadequacy of much legal advice (Ham *et al.* 1988; Ham 1989; McIntosh 1989) although the Law Society has made some attempts to deal with this problem with the introduction of expert panels of medical negligence specialists. The problem of inexperienced solicitors accepting medical negligence work is such that the Legal Aid Board intends, in future, to accredit only a limited number of solicitors to undertake work in this field (Grosskurth 1996; but see Simanowitz, Chapter 19). Plaintiffs also have problems in getting medical experts to act for them, and even when they do succeed in this the standard of proof is high (Mildred 1989; Simanowitz 1989; Irwin *et al.* 1996). The problems of fault are such that in some countries the burden of proof is reversed and it rests on the defendant to prove that there was no negligence where a prima-facie case has been made.

Plaintiffs, defendants and policy-makers have all demonstrated concern about the adversarial nature of the litigation system. In his recent review of civil litigation systems, Lord Woolf argued that litigation practice in general has 'degenerated into an environment in which the civil litigation process is too often seen as a battlefield where no rules apply' (Lord Chancellor's Department 1996: para. 3.4). In addition, he was concerned that unmeritorious and indefensible claims are pursued for too long. It has been argued that much of the cost and delay in the existing systems is attributable to the competitiveness and rancour with which modern litigation is conducted (Menkel-Meadow 1996). Other critics have drawn attention to the impersonality, insensitivity and remoteness of the law, which is perceived as rigid and formal and as forcing the parties into defensive positions. As a result the system is ill equipped to deliver what research suggests risk managers and plaintiffs want most – an explanation and investigation of what has occurred (Vincent *et al.* 1994; see also Lloyd-Bostock, Chapter 8; and Polywka and Chapman, Chapter 18).

These features provide many disincentives to quality improvement. While it has been argued that legal claims can lead to improvements in patient care and to the accountability of doctors by encouraging doctors and institutions to review procedures and standards (Harper Mills and von Bolschwing 1995), others have suggested that the threat of claims has led to the introduction of litigation reduction strategies which can serve to mask errors in clinical practice (Annandale 1989) or to encourage defensive behaviour.

Doctors have also been concerned about the negative impact of claims on medical activity. In their review of the literature on the effect of medical accidents and litigation on doctors, Ennis and Vincent (1994) report that the most often cited effect of litigation on clinical practice is the adoption of defensive medicine (see also Ennis *et al.* 1991; Macfarlane and Chamberlain 1993; Summerton 1995), although in an important review of trends Ham *et al.* (1988) suggested that there is little hard evidence that defensive medicine was on the increase. Despite this, the courts appear to have acknowledged the existence of the phenomenon, and many commentators assume this effect. Brown and Simanovitz (1995: 488) suggest that the 'mere hint of negligence may lead to a knee jerk reaction of determined defence'. Similarly, in an American context, McQuade (1991) suggests that the perceived threat of litigation has almost as much impact on clinical practice as an actual lawsuit.

Medical negligence actions are also an extremely costly form of identifying and responding to medical mishaps. In the vast majority of actions, plaintiffs are funded by legal aid and defendants are public sector hospitals, with the result that such actions are almost exclusively paid for out of the public purse. The number of claims has risen considerably (Ham *et al.* 1988; Dingwall and Fenn 1995; Hoyte 1995). In their review of 142 district health authorities, Dingwall and Fenn (1995) surmise that the frequency of claims increased by about 500 per cent during the 1980s. Allowing for inflation, the cost of settling claims increased by about 250 per cent over the same period. The National Audit Office (1995–96) recently estimated that the cost of clinical negligence is £200 million per year, and the Clinical Negligence Scheme for Trusts, a mutual insurance scheme for NHS trusts, recently reported that it had 634 open claims on its books with an estimated value of £180 million (Hogan 1997). In

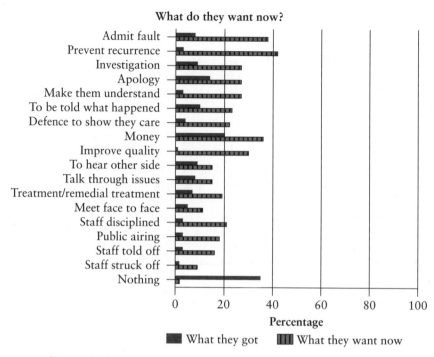

Figure 11.1   Residual dissatisfaction remaining after claims settlement

addition, the legal aid board spends in the region of £28 million a year on these actions.[1]

Perhaps most importantly, critics have been concerned that the civil litigation system is not giving plaintiffs what they want. In their study of the reasons why 227 patients and relatives had decided to take legal action, Vincent *et al.* (1994) found that claimants were motivated not only by the need for retribution and compensation, but also because they were concerned about standards of care. Both patients and relatives reported that an important aim was to prevent similar accidents happening to others in the future. In addition, they believed that both the staff involved and the organization should have to account for what had occurred (see also Lloyd-Bostock, Chapter 8). Research conducted for the mediation pilot scheme suggests that a residue of dissatisfaction remains after the claims have been settled by traditional methods. Figure 11.1 demonstrates this by showing what claimants achieved through the civil justice system and what they want now. It is clear from these data that claimants remain dissatisfied not only because they have not received compensation but also because of a lack of provision of 'softer' remedies such as a feeling that health providers care.

Reactions to these problems and the launch of the mediation pilot scheme

The publication of Lord Woolf's review of the civil justice system provided a focus for these concerns as well as a strategic incentive for change. The report pledged its support for more constructive methods of handling grievances which save time and money. An entire chapter was devoted to the particular problems posed by the medical negligence system and identified a number of features which suggested that it was ill disposed towards efficient resolution of disputes. It was argued that it was in the field of medical negligence that the civil justice system was most conspicuously failing to serve litigants. The report has been well received by government, and case management reforms are being introduced which increase court supervision of cases. The broader aims are to achieve earlier settlement of cases where practicable, divert cases to alternative dispute resolution where this is likely to be beneficial, encourage cooperation between litigants and, where settlement cannot be achieved, progress cases to trial as speedily as possible.

In the UK and elsewhere, a number of alternatives to the formal court system had already emerged or been suggested, including arbitration, pre-screening panels and schemes awarding certificates to claims worthy of consideration by the courts (Murray *et al.* 1989), expert determination, the setting up of a medical inspectorate and mediation (Brown and Simanovitz 1995). A number of private members' bills have been introduced into the British Parliament with a view to introducing arbitration or no-fault compensation schemes. The last Conservative government reacted to these by committing itself to looking at the possibility of introducing some form of alternative dispute resolution. The government consulted on the feasibility of a paper-based arbitration scheme (Department of Health 1991) but this was not received with enthusiasm (Brown and Simanovitz 1995). However, the government did set up a clinical negligence working group and shortly afterwards, at the instigation of its members, arranged in April 1995 for the launch of a mediation pilot scheme in two of England's eight health regions, together with an evaluation of the scheme. The scheme was coordinated by two regional NHS representatives who disseminated information about the scheme and encouraged referrals from claims managers within hospitals, plaintiff solicitors and defence solicitors.

In parallel with these developments, the judiciary have also demonstrated their enthusiasm for alternative methods of resolving legal claims. Since 1995 a practice direction has required the parties to medical negligence disputes to lodge a pre-trial checklist at the court which includes questions as to whether they have considered the possibility of using alternative dispute resolution (ADR) to resolve the dispute. Woolf further recommends that, in deciding on the future conduct of the case, the judge should be able to take into account a litigant's unreasonable refusal to attempt ADR. Judge-led mediation schemes of this kind clearly introduce a coercive shadow over what has traditionally been seen as a voluntary process. However, the level of enthusiasm for mediation is such that it is unlikely that it will emerge as a well used alternative to the current system.

What is mediation?

Mediation shares some of the characteristics of both court and out-of-court resolution of disputes (Black and Baumgartner 1983) and is a form of facilitated negotiation. It is generally seen as the main alternative to court-based adjudication, but its use pre-dates the formal creation and enforcement of law and it has been suggested that its use reflects a natural human instinct to seek the approval, help and guidance of others in settling differences. Unlike judges, mediators do not have the capacity to impose judgements upon the parties. Instead, they purport to help the parties to reach a settlement which is acceptable to them although academic studies of mediation have suggested various ways in which mediators influence outcomes (see for example Dingwall, 1994).

Proponents of mediation argue that mediators should be neutral third parties and this sense of neutrality is maintained by an emphasis on the management of the process of facilitated settlement rather than an evaluation of content. Mediation is generally a form of private ordering in which whatever is said to the mediator or agreed between the parties remains confidential. Mediators are generally expected to possess a number of attributes which are said to enhance the chances of successful negotiation. These include an ability to listen; sensitivity and creativity; integrity, flexibility and authority; and communication and management skills (Brown and Simanowitz 1995).

There is no single accepted definition of mediation, and ideologies, styles and practices can vary considerably according to the scheme being considered, the provider agency and the characteristics of the dispute. A range of models exist which vary according to a number of characteristics: sole or co-mediators; facilitative or evaluative approaches; qualifications which are prerequisites to training; the use of face-to-face meetings or private caucusing; and whether the schemes are compulsory or not. Despite these differences, the majority of commentators claim that there are two broad principles and frameworks with which most mediators concur (Black and Baumgartner 1983; Roberts 1986; Murray *et al.* 1989; Brown and Simanovitz, 1995). First, mediation is commonly described as an empowering process which enables the parties to explore their mutual interests as well as their differences and arrive at settlement which is in, and maximizes, their joint interests. Unlike the litigation system, the parties are encouraged to explore any issues which contribute to the sense of grievance and in this way the process can be seen to be complementary to that of more proactive claims management, as it carries with it the potential to provide vital information about mishaps and their causes (see Polywka and Chapman, Chapter 18). Fuller (1971) has argued that mediation is commonly directed towards the *creation* of relevant norms rather than conformity to those supported by the formal legal system. It follows from this that mediation is seen as a flexible process in terms of process and content. Second, proponents of mediation argue that it is a voluntary process and that, as a result, the parties are much more likely to adhere to the agreement reached.

The stages of mediation are said to follow those of the negotiation process, although different strategies may be called for at different stages. Contact is made between the parties and ground rules agreed upon. The parties are each given time to present the crux of their argument and these are then explored further in caucuses or in joint sessions. This initial phase concentrates on information giving, clarification and exploration of respective arguments and leads on to the substantive phase in which bartering begins. The mediator's main concern during these processes is to keep the flow of information going, keep extreme emotions and behaviour in check and encourage the parties to try to understand the other parties' perspectives and be creative about possible solutions. Mediators may play devil's advocate when shuttling from private caucus to private caucus, encourage movement away from positions stated in public meetings and encourage the constant reassessment of positions and alternatives by a series of 'what if' questions. A number of strategies are used when an impasse emerges, such as switching the discussion to another issue and exploring the parties' differing notions of what constitutes fairness (Roberts 1993).

The Woolf report suggested that mediation's greatest benefit is its capacity to reduce the culture of adversarialism and increase cooperation and collaboration between the parties to disputes (Lord Chancellor's Department 1996).

Similarly, Brown and Simanowitz (1995) argue that mediation of medical disputes offers an opportunity of incorporating fact finding, explanation and dialogue, assisted negotiation, neutral expert settlement guidance, accountability and any other factors the parties consider to be important. They claim that settlement terms can, and often need to, include not only financial aspects but also a form of words that parties find mutually acceptable in a way that conventional litigation cannot achieve.

Cases which are suitable for mediation

During the course of the pilot scheme 12 cases were mediated and all except one resulted in settlement. Interviews with 20 key claims managers, mediators and the regional coordinators conducted as part of the evaluation of the pilot reveal a number of characteristics of cases which are thought to make them particularly suitable for mediation. Six main categories of cases which are considered suitable for mediation have been identified.

The first category involves cases where there is a significant emotional overlay to the issues in dispute, leading to a need to explore the issues in full and provide sensitive explanations of cause. Cases said to fall into this category include baby bereavement cases, failed sterilization, miscarriages and the sudden death of a partner.

In the second category are cases where the claimant wants greater involvement in case management. In one mediated case the client felt that she had not been given an adequate personal explanation from her consultant. The benefit of mediation to her was that she got the opportunity to put her case in front of the consultant and hear his personal response. Another claims manager drew attention to a mediated case which was on the verge of settlement when the claimant heard of the mediation scheme and felt that it would serve their interests better to draw the dispute to a close personally.

Third, claims managers identified as being suitable for mediation cases where the expectations of the parties differ considerably. These were described as situations where there was a need for a 'reality check'. Examples of cases which were considered to fall into this category include those in which there are difficult causation or liability issues which it is difficult to explain to clients, or cases where the trust has a good defence but the plaintiff's lawyers are legally aided and set to continue. Some potential users of the scheme have expressed a concern that the mediation process inevitably involves compromise. In fact, the one case which did not settle was one in which the defence thought it had a very strong case but was unable to convince the plaintiff of this until they reached mediation. Such cases have become known as 'reality check' cases and mediation has been identified as an important tool by those expert solicitors unable to persuade less able colleagues that their client has a poor case.

A fourth category were cases where mediation made economic sense. These cases are not always easy to identify since the instability of disease and uncertainties of medical care can make any predictive activity in this field difficult. One claims manager gave the example of a mediated case they had been involved in where the settlement reached was larger than the trust had anticipated but was lower than the joint expense of costs and quantum would have been if they had continued to defend the case and allowed resources to be channelled from payment of legal fees to the plaintiff.

Claims managers also felt that mediation could achieve speedier resolution. Mediation can occur at any stage in the civil litigation or complaints process and during the course of the pilot scheme it has taken place before and after the issue of a writ, as well as before and after the commissioning of expert medical and legal advice. What makes the process different is that mediation can occur within just a few weeks of referral to a mediation agency. This was essential in one case in the pilot scheme where the plaintiff's death was imminent. Earlier settlement might also be encouraged by the fact that mediation, like litigation, can force the parties to focus on the issues at stake and the details of case management. Claims managers admit to allowing case management to be driven by court timetables, and some suggested that mediation provided them with an opportunity to think proactively at an earlier stage.

Another category of cases identified as being suitable for mediation were those where a patient has a long-term relationship with their healthcare provider. Medical negligence actions tend to cause the termination of doctor–patient relationships, but this option is not always available if a medical condition is rare or the parties live in a remote or rural location. In one of the cases mediated a dying patient was able to use the mediation session to secure agreement about their partner's future career prospects at the hospital where they worked which had coincidentally also been defending the medical negligence action in question. Finally, it was argued that mediation could facilitate a ritualistic closure of the dispute and face-saving exercise. This was a view expounded by one mediator involved in a case which had received substantial media coverage in the national and local press.

These views are only a starting point in trying to understand the contribution which mediation can make to effective resolution of medical negligence claims. The evaluation of the mediation pilot has many other facets, and future work will report on the mediatory models used, the satisfaction of all the major parties to the mediations, the costs of the scheme and the reasons why certain key players consider mediation to be inappropriate. Client satisfaction with the scheme is strong and plaintiffs, in particular, have been unanimous in their praise of mediation. For many, mediation provided an opportunity to participate in the settlement discussions in a way which is not anticipated in bi-lateral negotiated settlements which commonly takes place over the phone or in letters between solicitors. The mediation alternative has clearly facilitated catharsis and more creative solutions to disputes, such as apologies, tours around the departments complained about to inspect improved systems, face-to-face apologies, technical and personalized explanations and the opportunity to put their case. A strong theme to emerge is the degree to which these processes become an outcome.

Conclusion

There is considerable evidence of dissatisfaction with current systems for the handling of medical negligence claims, and this impacts on identification and management of medical mishaps in a number of ways. The adversarial system encourages the issues in dispute to be framed narrowly in terms of what is considered legally relevant. Full exploration of the issues considered to be at stake by the parties is discouraged and with it the full investigation which would aid the identification of risk. The litigation system also serves to individualize blame. Culpability, when proven, is attached to an individual and little, if no, account is taken of systemic failures of the kind identified by Vincent and Reason (Chapter 3). These factors would not be so significant if proactive risk management proced-ures were in place which could identify a mishap or near-miss whether or not it became a legal claim, but in this volume Polywka and Chapman (Chapter 18) provide us with a salutary reminder that this does not always happen.

The inaccessibility of the litigation system and the particular difficulties of proving medical negligence deter many potential litigants from pursuing their claim. This means that those cases which are pursued are unrepre-sentative of the number and type of medical mishaps which occur or are thought to have occurred. One reaction to these problems might be to call for more systems for the identification of mishaps and near-misses which more closely represent their level of occurrence. But this argument misses an essential point about incentives to identify mishaps. Various contribu-tors to this volume have made reference to the difficulty in encouraging healthcare professionals to provide full and frank information about mis-haps which they have witnessed or been responsible for. Ethical concerns compete with fear of being disciplined. Given these considerations, the medical negligence action is one of the few external checks on the success of internal management systems for the identification of risk and mishaps. Of all system actors, the plaintiff has the greatest personal incentive to expose substandard care.

But many plaintiffs are also victims. Dissatisfaction with the current system for handling claims is also fuelled by concerns that they should be treated with honesty and compassion. Concerns about what happens in the aftermath should also extend to clinicians. The current litigation pro-cess clearly has a settlement orientation but not necessarily a dispute resolu-tion orientation. Research has demonstrated that the parties often feel a residue of dissatisfaction if the process of settlement has undermined their ability to put across their own account of what happened.

The reforms recommended by Lord Woolf would do much to improve certain aspects of the process, such as time and cost, but the settlement orientation of his proposed new case management system may get no closer to a quality resolution (Lord Chancellor's Department 1996). The use of mediation in the resolution of medical negligence cases would seem to be more fertile ground, but at present it is too early to be sure. There has been intense debate in other areas about the extent to which mediation fulfils its promise in practice, and particular concerns have been expressed about the ways in which the coercive powers of the mediator can be disguised by the rhetoric of informalism.

Whatever the outcome of the evaluation of the pilot scheme, the key question for readers of this book remains how the management of medical negligence actions can better facilitate the identification and handling of mishaps. Mediation clearly provides an opportunity to explore all aspects of the claim rather than just those elements on which the legal system focuses. It facilitates settlements which involve more than financial compensation, including explanations, review of protocols and a promise of full discussion of issues at board level. It can provide a more conciliatory and less inhibiting environment for clinical staff which is less likely to prompt defensive responses. But it also remains a private forum with no external check on the fairness of process and outcome. In the final analysis, the success of the scheme may well depend on our willingness to be pragmatists or idealists, and on our acceptance of the fact that mediation is an alternative not to court-based adjudication, but to out-of-court settlements conducted over the phone. The Department of Health and others have high expectations of the pilot scheme and there has perhaps been a tendency to see mediation as something of a panacea. The mediations conducted to date suggest, by way of alternative, that mediation is an extra tool in the toolkit of litigators and defendants.

Note

1 It has been noted, however, that this is less than the annual subsidy which the government pays to the Royal Opera House.

References

Abel, R. (1982) The politics of informal justice, in R. Abel (ed.) *The Politics of Informal Justice*. New York: Academic Press.

Annandale, E.C. (1989) The malpractice crisis and the doctor–patient relationship, *Sociology of Health and Illness*, 11(1): 1–23.

Atiyah, P. (1997) *The Damages Lottery*. Oxford: Hart Publishing.

Black, D. and Baumgartner, M. (1983) Towards a theory of the third party, in K. Boyum and L. Mather (eds) *Empirical Theories about Courts*. New York: Longman.

Brazier, M. (1992) *Medicine, Patients and the Law*, 2nd edn. Harmondsworth: Penguin.

Brennan, T., Leape, L., Laird, N. *et al.* (1991) Incidence of adverse events and negligence in hospitalized patients: The results from the Harvard Medical Practice Study I, *New England Journal of Medicine*, 324: 370–6.

Brown, H. and Marriot, A. (1993) *ADR Principles and Practice*. London: Sweet and Maxwell.

Brown, H. and Simanovitz, A. (1995) Alternative dispute resolution and mediation, in C.A. Vincent (ed.) *Clinical Risk Management*. London: BMJ Publishing Group.

Capstick, B., Edwards, P. and Mason, D. (1991) Compensation for medical accidents, *British Medical Journal*, 302: 230–2.

Clements, R. (1995) Essentials of clinical risk management, *Quality in Health Care*, 4(2): 129–34.

Danzon, P.M. (1985) *Medical Malpractice – Theory, Evidence, and Public Policy.* Cambridge, MA: Harvard University Press.

Department of Health (1991) *Arbitration in Respect of Claims for Medical Negligence against the NHS.* London: Department of Health.

Dingwall, R. (1994) Litigation and the threat to medicine, in J. Gabe, D. Kelleher and G. Williams (eds) *Challenging Medicine.* London: Routledge.

Dingwall, R. and Fenn, P. (1995) Risk management: financial implications, in C. Vincent (ed.) *Clinical Risk Management.* London: BMJ Publishing Group.

Ennis, M. and Vincent, C. (1994) The effects of medical accidents and litigation on doctors and patients, *Law and Policy,* 16(2): 97–122.

Ennis, M., Clark, A. and Grudzinkas, J.G. (1991) Change in obstetric practice in response to fear of litigation in the British Isles, *Lancet,* 338: 616–18.

Felstiner, W., Abel, R. and Sarat, A. (1980–81) The emergence and transformation of disputes: Naming, blaming, claiming . . . , *Law and Society Review,* 15(3–4): 631–54.

Fiss, O. (1984) Against settlement, *Yale Law Journal,* April/July, 1073–90.

Fuller, L. (1971) Mediation – its forms and functions, *California Law Review,* 44: 305–26.

Galanter, M. (1983) The radiating effects of the courts, in K. Boyum and L. Mather (eds) *Empirical Theories about Courts.* New York: Longman.

Grosskurth, A (1996) Mediation: Forming a view, in R. Smith (ed.) *Achieving Civil Justice – Appropriate Dispute Resolution for the 1990s.* London: Legal Action Group.

Ham, C. (1989) Should a no-fault compensation scheme be introduced and what would it cost?, in R. Mann and J. Harvard (eds) *No-Fault Compensation in Medicine.* London: Royal Society of Medicine Services Limited.

Ham, C., Dingwall, R., Fenn, P. and Harris, D. (1988) *Medical Negligence: Compensation and Accountability,* Briefing Paper 6. Oxford: Centre for Socio-Legal Studies, and London: King's Fund Institute.

Harper Mills, D. and von Bolschwing, G. (1995) Clinical risk management: Experiments from the US, *Quality in Health Care,* 4(2): 90–101.

Hogan, P. (1997) Claims data reveal true costs of negligence cases against trusts, *CNST Review,* 1997, Summer: 9.

Hoyte, P. (1995) Unsound practice: The epidemiology of medical negligence, *Medical Law Review,* 3: 53–73.

Irwin, S., Fazan, C. and Allfrey, R. (1996) *Medical Negligence Litigation – A Practitioner's Guide.* London: Legal Action Group.

Kennedy, I. and Grubb, A. (1994) *Medical Law,* 2nd edn. London: Butterworths.

Leape, L., Brennan, T., Laird, N. *et al.* (1991) Incidence of adverse events and negligence in hospitalised patients: Results of the Harvard Medical Practice Study II, *New England Journal of Medicine,* 324: 377–84.

Lord Chancellor's Department (1996) *Access to Justice.* London: HMSO.

Macfarlane, A. and Chamberlain, G. (1993) What is happening to caesarean section rates?, *Lancet,* 342 (23 October): 1005–6.

McIntosh, D. (1989) A prescription for medical negligence, in R. Mann and J. Harvard (eds) *No-Fault Compensation in Medicine.* London: Royal Society of Medicine Services Limited.

McQuade, J.S. (1991) The medical malpractice crisis – Reflections on the alleged causes and proposed cures: Discussion paper, *Journal of the Royal Society of Medicine,* 84 (July): 408–11.

Menkel-Meadow, C. (1996) Will managed care give us access to justice?, in R. Smith (ed.) *Achieving Civil Justice: Appropriate Dispute Resolution for the 1990s*. London: Legal Action Group.

Mildred, M. (1989) The view of the plaintiff's lawyer, in R. Mann and J. Harvard (eds) *No-Fault Compensation in Medicine*. London: Royal Society of Medicine Services Limited.

Mulcahy, L. and Tritter, J. (1998) Pyramids, pathways and icebergs – Mapping the links between dissatisfaction and complaints, *Sociology of Health and Illness*, 20(6): 825–47.

Murray, J., Rau, A. and Sherman, E. (1989) *Processes of Dispute Resolution – The Role of Lawyers*, University Casebook Series. New York: Foundation Press.

National Audit Office (1995–96) *The NHS (England) Summarised Accounts*, HC 127. London: HMSO.

Roberts, M. (1993) Who is in charge? Reflections on recent research on the role of the mediator, *Journal of Social Welfare and Family Law*, 372–387.

Roberts, S. (1986) Towards a minimal form of alternative intervention, *Mediation Quarterly*, 11: 25–41.

Royal Commission on Civil Liability and Compensation for Personal Injury (1978) *Report* (Chair: Lord Pearson), Cmd 7054. London: HMSO.

Silbey, S. and Merry, S. (1986) Mediator settlement strategies, *Law and Policy*, 8(7): 12–34.

Simanowitz, A. (1987) Medical accidents: The problem and the challenge, in P. Byrne (ed.) *Medicine in Contemporary Society*. London: King Edward's Hospital Fund, Oxford: Oxford University Press.

Simanowitz, A. (1989) No-fault compensation – Short term panacea or long term goal?, in R. Mann and J. Harvard (eds) *No-Fault Compensation in Medicine*. London: Royal Society of Medicine Services Limited.

Summerton, N. (1995) Positive and negative factors in defensive medicine: A questionnaire study of general practitioners, *British Medical Journal*, 310: 27–9.

Vincent, C., Young, M. and Phillips, A. (1994) Why do people sue doctors? A study of patients and relatives taking legal action, *Lancet*, 343: 1609–13.

12 Medical education: tomorrow's doctors today

Maeve Ennis

Improving communication between doctors and their patients, and between fellow NHS workers, is a vital component in the management of medical mishaps. The literature on mishaps, complaints and legal claims is riddled with instances of poor or non-existent communication skills. Poor communication affects patient satisfaction with care, but research suggests that it also has an impact on the ability of doctors to make effective clinical judgements. In this chapter I explore the relationship between medical mishaps and communication skills and consider the impact on tomorrow's doctors of the General Medical Council (GMC) recommendations concerning changes in the way doctors are trained.

Medical education in the UK has developed largely on an apprenticeship system. The need for a foundation in the basic sciences relevant to medicine was recognized and courses in anatomy, physiology and biochemistry were seen as a preliminary to clinical studies. The focus was largely on an understanding of disease processes and their diagnosis and management. The majority of services were hospital-based, with the more specialist services being at the large teaching hospitals (General Medical Council 1993).

This is changing and will change even further. There has been a shift from mainly hospital-based services to a situation where many services are provided in general practice and in the community. There has also been a shift towards a teamwork approach which takes some of the tasks traditionally undertaken by the doctor out of his or her hands and places them in the hands of other professionals such as practice nurses and psychologists. This has, in fact, been in response to an ageing population and an increasingly multicultural society; these factors have meant that patterns of disease and disability are changing, with an increasing complexity of care.

The impact of the patients' suffering on family and friends is also now more widely recognized, as is the understanding of the effects of chronicity and its psychological sequelae. An increasingly knowledgeable public has also been responsible for some change. Patients, through a variety of media, are now more aware of what can and cannot be done for their conditions. Their expectations are higher than ever before and they want a better understanding of the nature of their problems and the consequences of their treatments. This has led to a change in the relationship between patient and doctor, and in many cases it has shown up the deficiency of doctors' communication skills, which are responsible for many misunderstandings which lead to complaints. The advent of new technologies and the advances of science have also been a considerable force for change, and the future for tomorrow's doctors is indeed a daunting one.

Educating for these changes, while also 'recognising that the doctors of tomorrow and the societies in which they live will be confronted with as yet unforeseen moral and ethical issues arising from the scientific advances that are to be anticipated' (General Medical Council 1993), is also a daunting task. Many medical schools have already started this process and some of the GMC recommendations, such as the formal teaching of communication skills, have been a feature of the undergraduate curriculum for some years. Little is known, however, about the consistency of courses.

The new curriculum

The goals of the GMC's new curriculum are that the student should acquire a knowledge and understanding of health and its promotion; disease and its prevention; and management in the context of the individual and his or her place in the family and society. The student should acquire and become proficient in basic clinical skills and should also acquire and demonstrate attitudes necessary for the achievement of high standards of medical practice both for patient care and personal development (General Medical Council 1993).

The GMC did not, by design, lay down precise details for a new curriculum. Instead it suggested a framework, with the undergraduate course as the first step in the student's professional life. One of the problems of the present course is an excessively overloaded curriculum, with its attendant stress for students and frustration for teachers. There is an overburdening of information which leads students to learn only to pass exams and not for the acquisition of knowledge. Part of this overburdening comes from the historical pre-clinical–clinical divide with duplication of factual content. What the GMC is suggesting within its framework is a course that is modular, system-based and integrated both horizontally and vertically, with interdisciplinary synthesis (Figure 12.1). This, it is hoped, will lead to learning through curiosity, critical evaluation of evidence and the exploration of knowledge.

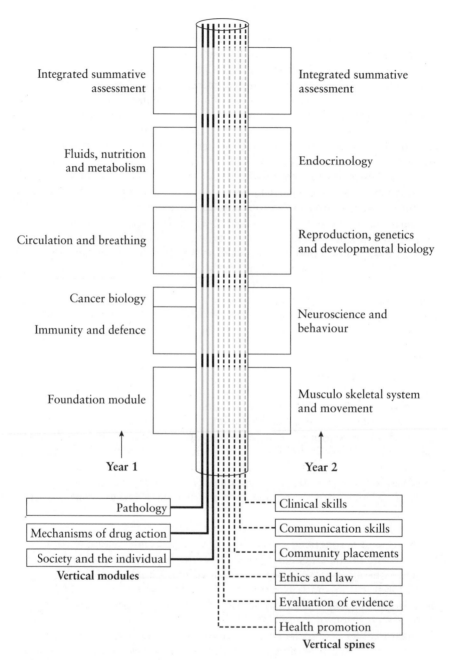

Figure 12.1   The GMC's new curriculum

The GMC has suggested that a core curriculum should be defined, although it has not itself defined core content, through the development of 'model core' curricula which will be adapted and modified by individual medical schools. It is recommended that this core curriculum will be augmented by special study modules which will allow students to study in depth topics or areas of special interest to them. It is hoped that this will instil in students a questioning approach and provide them with insights into the scientific method. These special study modules will run throughout the five years of the undergraduate course. During this period there will be a constant emphasis on acquiring sound communication skills. This will involve not just learning the basis of communicating with patients, but also the very necessary skill of communicating with other healthcare professionals and working as part of a multidisciplinary team. Interwoven into all of this will be evaluation of evidence, health promotion, ethics and law modules to develop students' understanding of the influences of the social environment and psychological factors on illness and the influence of organic disease on patients' well-being. This will include the principles and practice of preventive medicine and the role of health education (General Medical Council 1993).

Clinical firm teaching arranged as a rotation of specialty attachments has much to recommend it as an effective means of teaching/learning for small student groups. (Two consultants and three or four doctors on training posts are normally known as 'firms'.) Its benefits and strengths suggest it should be retained within the framework of a modular, systems-based, integrated programme, but the traditional reliance on hospital clinical firms needs widening to include community-based teaching and the inclusion of some teaching by other care professionals, such as senior midwives.

Delivering the new curriculum

A variety of systems, such as problem-based learning, computer-assisted learning and peer-assisted learning, as well as the more conventional lecture and tutorial systems, have been proposed as means of delivering the new curriculum. Different schools will, no doubt, use some of these systems and different combinations. Behind all of them lie modern theories in the science of learning and cognition which emphasize the importance of active learning. One of the pertinent findings of research is that prior knowledge strongly influences the nature and the amount of new information that can be processed (Anderson 1990). Based on their previous knowledge of the topic in hand, students actively construct explanatory models, which help them process and understand new information. This should be particularly relevant to a curriculum that is vertically as well as horizontally integrated, where each new module builds on what has gone before. It is also particularly helpful in small-group teaching where there is the facility for preliminary discussion which enables the students to access whatever knowledge they already have. Anderson (1990) also notes that new know-ledge is better understood and recalled if students are stimulated to elabor-ate on it. According to this argument, elaboration can take several forms, such as discussions, answering questions and giving explanations. This will increase the number of relations between concepts and the number of details in students' semantic networks and will lead to sophisticated knowledge structures. Studies have shown that this results in richer cognitive models which will lead to additional retrieval paths along which to recall the know-ledge acquired.

Research on memory shows that the role of the environment in which learning and recall take place has long been recognized as potentially important (Godden and Baddeley 1975). Situated knowledge is assumed to be easier to retrieve because the cues that activate the knowledge are stored within the same cognitive structures. This would suggest that stu-dents should be exposed to professionally meaningful problems or situ-ations that resemble the problems they will be confronted with later in real clinical situations. Dalmans *et al.* (1997) propose that problem-based learn-ing, using paper cases that rely on prior knowledge and relevant context cues to stimulate elaboration, will foster active learning. They suggest that competence is fostered not principally by teaching to deliver knowledge (teacher-centred approaches), but through teaching to engender specific kinds of cognitive activity. By using effectively designed cases, students can be encouraged to engage actively in acquiring knowledge and can be taught to define for themselves, to a large extent, the content to be mastered. With problem-based learning, students conduct literature searches and learn to find necessary materials independently. This should engender in students a learning style conducive to the independent lifelong learning approach set out in *Tomorrow's Doctors*.

It has been shown that the integration of basic science knowledge and clinical knowledge results in better diagnostic performance (Williams *et al.* 1997). If basic science concepts are learned in the context of a clinical problem within a clinical setting, those problems will be better integrated. The systems-based integrated curriculum proposed by the GMC asks for just this, and problem-based learning can lend itself well to this aim, as cases can be constructed not just from experience-based knowledge but also from evidence-based knowledge.

Communication skills

The literature on complaints is replete with instances of poor or non-existent communication skills. Dickson *et al.* (1989), in a survey of com-plaints to the HSC claim that most involved communication problems – at least as one factor in the matter complained of. Patients frequently express dissatisfaction with the amount of information they receive from doctors and the lack of or quality of expression of caring and respect (Evans *et al.*

1987). A *Which* report in 1989 found that 89 per cent of patients wanted their GP to listen to them more and 91 per cent wanted the doctor to spend more time explaining their illness (Consumer Association 1989).

Patient satisfaction, however, is not all that is affected by communication skills. If a doctor fails to listen adequately or ask the right questions, it follows that diagnosis and treatment may rest on inaccurate or incomplete information about the patient's problem. Evans *et al.* (1991) found that students trained in communication skills were significantly more 'diagnostically efficient' than untrained controls. In some cases, physical and psychological problems may be missed all together. These are situations that can lead to complaints, litigation and a poor service to patients.

In addition to questions of accurate diagnosis, communication skills affect compliance with treatment. The failure of many patients to follow medical advice (Ley 1988) is clearly a serious problem, not just in terms of the implications for their health but also because of the high cost to the NHS of medication prescribed but unused, as well as of missed appointments. Freeman *et al.* (1971) found that compliance was mediated by two factors, patient satisfaction and recall, and that doctors' interpersonal skills affected compliance. Further benefits of good communication skills may include a reduction in the distress experienced by patients in relation to medical procedures, and an improvement in outcome measures such as postoperative discomfort, length of hospital stay and amount of medication required (Johnson *et al.* 1978). However, the relevance of communication skills to outcome is much broader. Inaccuracy of detection and diagnosis, and failures in treatment compliance, must also have a deleterious effect on treatment outcome. In cases where the problem is primarily psychological, good communication skills may lead directly to amelioration of symptoms. Cape (1996), for example, studied interactions between GPs and patients and found significant relationships between listening interactions and consultation outcomes. It has been suggested that poor communication skills can cause such problems. According to Laurance (1997), a recent report issued by the Royal College of General Practitioners says that one-fifth of patients in cancer units develop full-blown psychiatric disorders, and the main cause is the way in which bad news is broken.

Can communication skills be taught?

Tomorrow's Doctors comments that, although there has been more effort made in recent years in the area of communication skills education, deficiencies in this area are still responsible for a high proportion of complaints and misunderstanding. Their recommendations are that doctors must learn to be good listeners, be able to provide advice and explanations that are comprehensible to patients, learn effective teamwork, be able to demonstrate proficiency in maintaining proper records and have the ability to present a good-quality written report (General Medical Council 1993).

Box 12.1   Communication problems?

A 10-year-old child was admitted to a large children's hospital having exhibited flu-like symptoms for a week and severe stomach pain and vomiting for 12 hours. The GP was concerned about the possibility of appendicitis. The hospital ruled this out but admitted the child for observation. Two days later as pain and vomiting persisted she was moved to an isolation ward for testing for food poisoning. Five days later the registrar told the mother that as the tests were all negative she could take her child home. As none of the child's symptoms had improved and in fact some such as diarrhoea and intensity of stomach pain were worse, the mother asked what was wrong with the child. She was told 'she has a tummy ache'. She tried to elicit more information and was asked 'why do parents always have to have a name for their children's illnesses?' The mother then proceeded to make arrangements to take the child home, although her daughter was still attached to a total nutrition drip. Two hours later a more senior registrar entered the room surrounded by a group of people, that the mother took to be students, although in the absence of any introduction she could not be sure. This registrar told the students, not the mother, that the child could not go home as 'she is a very poorly child and we could make ourselves look very silly indeed'. He then ordered more tests including a visit to radiology for a scan. There her daughter was told several times that the scan would not hurt but would just tickle. In fact the child screamed and insisted it caused quite a lot of pain. The radiologist continued to insist the procedure did not hurt and the child continued to scream as if in agony. The professional told the mother that the child's reaction was perfectly normal. However, later, another radiologist admitted to the mother that she had seldom heard a child scream so much. The scan showed a problem and the radiologist told the mother there was 'gunge that should not be there'. One of the registrars told the mother that her daughter needed an appendectomy, which was a straightforward operation. However, she was then told that the actual decision to operate must be made by the consultant surgeon. He examined the child and told the mother her daughter was 'fine'. The mother was angry and upset and instead of explaining or discussing what was going on the consultant told her she was making a 'fuss', that 'the trouble with parents is that you think we are God'. The mother says this was the furthest thought from her mind at that moment. Two days later her daughter had to have an emergency life-saving operation. She was in hospital for over six weeks. At no time did any professional make any attempt to explain or discuss with the mother her daughter's condition, although for many weeks she was at the hospital almost 24 hours a day. When she tried to communicate her anxieties she was brushed off and made to feel she was a difficult and over-anxious mother. The closing words of her report of the incident are, 'when is the message of the crucial importance of good communication – which includes listening as well as talking – ever going to get through to those people?'

(Goudge 1998)

Given the far-reaching consequences of inadequate communication skills on the part of doctors, the question arises whether such skills can be taught. Cushing (1996) found that there were many myths surrounding communication skills: for instance, that students will automatically acquire the skills through continuing experience with patients or the assumption that 'you either have it or you don't' and they are not learnable. The case presented in Box 12.1 suggests that there are doctors at all levels who do not have good communication skills, so it is unlikely that all students will be in a position to learn them in clinical settings.

A large number of studies have looked at the teaching of communication skills. For example, Bacon *et al.* (1997) found that a course, comprising 11 two-hour sessions of lectures, video presentations and mock patient interviews which were observed by peers and supervisors, was considered to be helpful by 88 per cent of students. At University College London, as at many other medical schools, we start communication skills teaching in the second pre-clinical year, before students have any contact with patients. This is followed by further teaching in the first clinical year, using such methods as mock interviews and videotaping.

The second-year course initially consisted of four hours of lectures, and four hours of small-group sessions where students were asked to rate videotaped consultations between GPs and patients and learn listening skills. They were then asked to do a written project, which required them to read the literature on some aspect of communication skills. Students complained that they found this boring and could not see the relevance of the small-group teaching. In the academic year 1996–97 we initiated a new scheme in which we arranged with a local GP for the students to visit an elderly person at home as part of the course. The students now have, as well as the lectures, a two-hour small-group session in which they rate GP–patient consultations, do some listening skills exercises and are prepared for their visits to the patients. They are required to write up this visit with reference to the communication skills literature and come back for a further two-hour session, in which they do a short presentation of their 'case' and their experiences of the visit are discussed. As this is a new scheme we have only preliminary findings to report and we must be tentative in what conclusions we draw.

So far the results have been promising. Students report that actual contact with a patient made the literature more relevant, and they felt able to test out what they had learned in the lectures, such as watching for non-verbal cues and practising listening, in a setting that was less threatening than a hospital ward or clinic would be. A small group who have been followed into the third year report that they feel the course has helped prepare them for interactions with the patients they are now meeting in the clinical settings. However, as Bacon *et al.* (1997) and many other studies suggest, we have not tested the students' skills in any way, we have only assessed their opinions of the helpfulness of the course. Other activities, such as those carried out by Tamburrino *et al.* (1990) who looked at students' interviewing styles with patients after a communication skills course, found that the students' interviewing skills had improved on a number of measures and the students themselves reported preferring an 'understanding' style of interviewing rather than a pacifying and reassuring 'paternalistic' style of interviewing. Other studies, such as Usherwood (1993), looked at consultation behaviours as outcome measures for assessing communication skills and found that students were more likely to ask open-ended questions, more likely to listen to patients and showed more empathy with patients. Another study by Maguire *et al.* (1986) followed a sub-sample of their participants for four to six years and found that they had maintained their skills. These studies would appear to show that communication skills can be taught.

However, despite exhortations from the GMC in 1980 and 1988, as recently as 1992 Frederikson and Bull (1992) found in a survey of all medical schools in Britain that, of the 88 per cent who responded, only 25 per cent had had any formal assessment of communication skills training, suggesting to the authors that communication skills training was still being treated as a minor subject of low significance. There is some anecdotal evidence to suggest that, while some progress has been made, change is slow in coming in this area (Sandgrove 1997). Hopefully, the recommendations in *Tomorrow's Doctors* will accelerate this progress. However, I feel a word of caution must be inserted here. We must also be sure that what we are teaching are good communications skills and not just better 'bedside manners'.

Teamworking skills

Part of every curriculum must be an active learning of teamworking skills. This will prepare students for working in multidisciplinary teams in clinical settings. Teamworking encompasses responsibility and gives students a feeling of belonging and accountability (Irvine 1998). It also gives an understanding and appreciation of the roles and skills of other health professionals. In more subtle ways, it will teach students to be more open about 'not knowing' and about making mistakes. Teamworking also reveals macho attitudes, complacency and arrogance in team members, and in teamworking skills sessions students can learn to modify and unlearn some of these attitudes. A further value of teamworking skills training hopefully will be that tomorrow's doctors will come to regard patients as active partners in their decisions on care and treatment, a situation that will lead to less dissatisfaction and fewer mistakes and complaints.

Conclusion

When I was first approached to write this chapter, I was asked if I could do a piece on educating doctors for mistakes. This seemed to me to be a topic for an entire book. However, on reflection, I realized that many of the recommendations on undergraduate medical education in the GMC document *Tomorrow's Doctors* were, implicitly if not explicitly, laying foundations for educating for mistakes.

Although the recommendations for tomorrow's doctors are neither perfect nor infallible (there is no mention of pastoral care, or of the macho culture that exists in some areas of medicine), they do give this author some hope that things are changing and that we are at last on the road to educating for mistakes.

References

Anderson, J.R. (1990) *Cognitive Psychology and Its Implications*. New York: Freeman.

Bacon, C., Mullins, D. and Tarbox, A. (1987) Evaluation of an interviewing skills course for second year medical students, *Journal of Medical Education*, 62, 995–7.

Cape, J.D. (1996) Psychological treatment of emotional problems by general practitioners, *British Journal of Medical Psychology*, 69: 85–99.

Consumer Association (1989) You and your GP, *Which?*, October: 481–5.

Cushing, A. (1996) Communication skills, *Medical Education*, 30: 316–18.

Dalmans, H.J.M., Snellen-Balendong, H., Wolfhagen, I.H.A.P. and van der Vleuten, C.P.M. (1997) Seven principles of effective case design for a problem-based curriculum, *Medical Teacher*, 19(3): 185–9.

Dickson, D., Hargie, O. and Morrow, N. (1989) *Communication Skills Training for Health Professionals*. London: Chapman & Hall.

Evans, B., Kiellerup, F., Stanley, R., Burrows, G. and Sweet, B. (1987) A communications skills programme for increasing patient satisfaction with general practice consultations, *British Journal of Medical Psychology*, 60: 373–8.

Evans, B.J., Stanley, R.O., Mestrovic, R. and Rose, L. (1991) Effects of communication skills training on students' diagnostic efficiency, *Medical Education*, 25: 517–26.

Frederikson, L. and Bull, P. (1992) An appraisal of the current status of communication skills training in British medical schools, *Social Science and Medicine*, 34: 515–22.

Freeman, B., Negrete, V.F., Davis, M. and Korsch, B.M. (1971) Gaps in doctor–patient communication: Doctor–patient interaction analysis, *Pediatric Research*, 18: 298–311.

General Medical Council (1993) *Tomorrow's Doctors*. London: GMC.

Godden, D.R. and Baddeley, A.D. (1975) Context dependent memory in two natural environments, *British Journal of Psychology*, 66: 325–31.

Goudge (1998) *The Guardian*, 28 January.

Irvine, D. (1998) *The Guardian*, 28 January.

Johnson, J., Rice, V., Fuller, S. and Endress, M. (1978) Sensory information, instruction in a coping strategy and recovery from surgery, *Nursing Research and Health*, 1: 4–17.

Laurance, J. (1997) A trip to the doctor can make you sick, *The Independent*, 20 May.

Ley, P. (1988) *Communicating with Patients: Improving Communication, Satisfaction and Compliance*. London: Croom Helm.

Maguire, P., Fairbairn, S. and Fletcher, C. (1986) Consultation skills of young doctors, *British Medical Journal*, 292: 1201–4.

Sandgrove, J. (1997) Speech Therapy, *The Guardian*, 22 April.

Tamburrino, M., Lynch, D. and Nagel, R. (1990) Assessment of a brief interviewing course using the Helping Relationship Inventory: an interviewing assessment. *Medical Teacher*, 12: 273–7.

Usherwood, T. (1993) Subjective and behavioural evaluation of the teaching of patient interview skills, *Medical Education*, 27: 41–7.

Williams, C., Milton, J., Strickland, P. *et al.* (1997) Impact of medical school teaching on preregistration house officers' confidence in assessing and managing common psychological morbidity: Three centre study, *British Medical Journal*, 315: 917–18.

Part four | Views from the coalface

13 | Reflecting on medical mishaps

Raymond Hoffenberg

In Britain in medieval days quackery and charlatanism were rampant and the public had few ways of distinguishing between authentic and non-authentic medical practitioners. Scientific knowledge was so limited at the time that the distinction was in any event somewhat arbitrary. In 1421 the House of Commons sent a petition to King Henry V expressing concern that medicine was being practised by those who were 'unconnyng an unapproved' causing 'grete harm and slaughtre of many men' and asking for the practice of medicine to be restricted to those who had been formally and properly trained. Nothing seems to have been done about it until 1518, when Henry VIII agreed to the formation of the Royal College of Physicians of London, the objective of which was to establish and monitor standards of clinical practice within and for a radius of seven miles around the City of London.

Similar attempts to monitor the performance of medical practitioners were evident throughout Europe as various colleges and guilds were formed to ensure that those who had specialized knowledge and skills which they offered as a service to the public provided high standards of care. Despite all the steps that were taken, there were inevitably some doctors who failed to meet these standards and mistakes occurred; regrettably, this is still true today, and it is likely to remain true. Doctors are no different from other individuals. Their ranks will always include some bad apples, but the number is almost certainly small. Nevertheless, their presence is cause for discomfort and ways must be found of dealing with them.

We all know that medical mishaps happen and we have a rough idea of their frequency. What is less clear is how they are dealt with, and it is this aspect that has been of special interest to Marilynn Rosenthal, Linda Mulcahy and Sally Lloyd-Bostock. The consequences of medical mishaps are potentially serious, resulting possibly in profound and permanent physical or mental damage or even death. For this reason, if for no other, their causes need to be examined in detail and every means of reducing their incidence should be explored. The weakness of the professional bodies concerned with the setting and maintenance of standards has been in the follow-up – what they do when they find that standards have been infringed, particularly when an individual doctor does so repeatedly. In recent years, largely as a result of public pressure, there has been rather more effort by the main medical institutions concerned with these matters to improve their systems of appraisal but, as this book makes clear, there is room for further improvement.

My personal interest in the field of monitoring performance goes back a long time. As a teacher of clinical medicine at both undergraduate and postgraduate levels for about 35 years I had naturally to be concerned with standards of clinical competence and I spent a large part of my time instructing and examining students and young doctors on bedside medicine. For about 13 years I was head of a large department of (internal) medicine in the University of Birmingham where over 20 years ago we instituted a system of internal clinical audit of our own performance, based on open review and criticism of medical records chosen randomly from a list of recently discharged patients. The responsible physician was asked to explain and justify any apparent diversion from standard practice in the use of investigations and treatment.

Since it is not easy to define or quantify the end-points I cannot claim that this internal audit led to a clearly demonstrable improvement in clinical practice but, because we insisted on a written statement in the records about what was said to the patient and relatives, there was little doubt that communication, at least, improved. In the course of discussion it often emerged that the management of a specific problem was not universally agreed within the group or indeed by the medical community at large. This highlights one of the problems of assessing medical practice. There is often a difference of opinion about the 'best' way of investigating or treating a specific disorder and variance in clinical practice is more often explained by uncertainty than by ignorance or perverse obstinacy on the part of the doctor. Allowance must be made for this when mishaps are investigated. To what extent has the doctor deviated from accepted standards, and does the degree of deviation constitute negligence or irresponsibility on his part?

I was privileged to be President of the Royal College of Physicians of London from 1983 to 1989, and during this time we discussed ways in which we might identify those few physicians whose clinical performance was thought to be unsatisfactory. In a report on medical audit produced in 1989 we suggested that all hospitals should introduce a system of medical audit for their physicians, based roughly on the Birmingham model. The existence of such a system would be noted by the visiting teams who assessed their suitability as training institutions for young doctors. The primary objective of such audit schemes was educational; it was not intended to be punitive, and it was not aimed at the identification of 'bad apples'. A second report, published by the College in 1993, suggested that some form of audit was now in place at almost all hospitals in the UK and had been widely accepted by the profession. With the backing of the Department of Health all medical colleges and faculties have adopted systems for regular audit of clinical performance.

Several other initiatives have boosted attempts to enhance clinical competence. In 1993 the Conference of Medical Royal Colleges and their Faculties agreed to institute programmes of Continuing Medical Education (CME) for all physicians and these appear to be working well, except that participation in the scheme is far from complete; the rate of non-compliance reported by colleges ranges from 20 to 30 per cent of practising doctors. Through an initiative by the Chief Medical Officer the training of junior doctors has also been placed on a more formal footing, with dedicated time allocated for study and recognized educational programmes.

These new efforts to enhance clinical performance should help to reduce the prevalence of medical mishaps, but the big question remains: how does one deal with doctors who do not meet prescribed standards of competence or efficiency? The GMC has recently introduced a scheme for dealing with poorly performing doctors which covers clinical incompetence short of actual negligence. The emphasis, quite rightly, is on improving ways of identifying them and ensuring that they are retrained to an acceptable standard. Executives of health authorities have suspended doctors employed by them who are thought to be of unsatisfactory standard. Two cardiac surgeons, whose operative results in children were found through the national audit to be extremely poor, have recently been investigated by the GMC; one was struck off the medical register, the other suspended from further operations on children for a period of three years. Audits of outcome are especially informative in surgery because there are distinct and measurable complications such as rates of mortality, readmission, haemorrhage or infection. An interesting aspect of this case is that the chief executive of the hospital, himself a doctor, was also struck off the register for having allowed operations to go ahead despite having received reports about their incompetence.

One of the hallmarks of a profession is its prerogative to be self-regulating. There are good reasons for maintaining this position, especially when it comes to professional competence, as it is not easy for someone unfamiliar with the niceties and vagaries of practice to judge whether a doctor is competent or not. Indeed, it is not always easy for someone within the profession to do so. Criticism of such internal monitoring correctly identifies the tendency within a profession like medicine to 'protect' colleagues and to cover up for them when they stray; the relationship is too cosy. Some *esprit de corps* within a profession is to be expected, and indeed welcomed, but the potential damage arising from medical error or mishap is so great that an external disciplinary committee is needed when there are serious allegations of professional misconduct. Doctors who are aware of a colleague's unsuitability to practise through 'sickness' (the common euphemism for alcoholism) or simple incompetence must be encouraged to inform, and systems must be set up to deal with such information in a sensitive and confidential way, perhaps through an internal mechanism to start with, bearing in mind the need for continued coexistence and interdependence between practising doctors.

We should enthusiastically encourage educational initiatives of the sort outlined above, and persuasion may be the best way to start, but we need to be tougher in our handling of those who do not attend CME or audit meetings and devise schemes for achieving global compliance. The GMC has powers to discipline those who are habitually negligent or flagrantly incompetent. Lesser transgressions are more difficult to handle. What I personally would like to see is a professional ambience in which doctors take pride in their own standards of practice, recognize their own limitations and accept the need constantly to hone their skills and knowledge to ensure that patients receive the care that justifies the trust they place in the profession. They need to judge their colleagues by the same high criteria of performance and take action when they detect inadequacy. Only in this way will they fulfil the requirements of true professionalism.

Donald Irvine

Introduction

This book on medical mishaps is most timely. Patients want doctors who are well-trained, competent, kind, considerate and respectful of their views and wishes. They seek a less dependent relationship with their doctors and greater involvement in decisions about their care; and they want to know that they will be protected from poor practice. In short, they want doctors they can trust, on their terms.

In recent years the public has been asking the medical profession, with increasing insistence, how patients can be assured that the doctor they will see next week at the surgery or the hospital is really up to date and on top of the job. This change in expectation has come about partly because people have become much better informed about medicine and medical practice, partly because medicine has been substantially demystified, and partly because some recent high profile medical and NHS institutional failures have led to a requirement by government that doctors become more accountable for their clinical practice (Secretary of State for Health 1997). So, the spotlight falls as never before on the continuing competence and performance of hospital consultants and principals in general practice.

Doctors' reactions to these changing expectations vary widely. For example, some have enthusiastically adopted the ethos and methods of quality improvement and quality assurance while others remain sceptical. The practical application of the concept of clinical effectiveness is still very patchy. Some doctors welcome the evolving doctor–patient relationship with its emphasis on a more evenly balanced patient–professional dynamic rather than on paternalism. Others see assertive patients as difficult and demanding, adding unreasonably to what is already exacting, often technically complex and invariably stressful clinical practice. Across a broad spectrum of the profession there is a general anxiety that we may be drifting towards a more confrontational and litigious climate in Britain in which defensive medicine becomes part of everyday practice. Nevertheless, particularly in the immediate aftermath of the tragedy of paediatric heart surgery at Bristol, there is now a general realization within the profession that British medicine must be 'changed utterly' (Smith 1998; Horton 1998).

In this chapter I have attempted to summarize the General Medical Council's (GMC's) response to the challenge of the dysfunctional doctor. From this it will be clear that the GMC is itself undergoing major change for, especially in the last five years, it has recognized that, to maintain public confidence in the system of medical regulation, it must become proactive and far more assertive in changing the approach of doctors to their professionalism. In particular it must energetically foster and maintain good medical practice, and protect patients more effectively from poor practice.

Medical regulation today

In Britain the GMC is the fulcrum of our system of professional self-regulation. Established by Act of Parliament in 1858, the GMC is the statutory authority which administers the Medical Act 1983. The GMC has four main functions:

- To keep a register of those doctors it has licensed as competent to practise in the UK.
- To set general standards of medical practice.
- To determine the nature of university-based basic medical education; to ensure implementation; and to coordinate all stages of medical education.
- To deal with dysfunctional doctors whose registration has been called into question.

The GMC, 104 strong, has a small majority of elected medical members. Other doctors are appointed by the universities and medical Royal Colleges. From 1997 one-quarter of the Council has – on the GMC's initiative – consisted of members of the public appointed by the Privy Council. This strengthened 'lay' membership helps the GMC by keeping patients' perspectives always at the forefront of its thinking.

The medical Royal Colleges and Faculties, which are charitable bodies quite independent of the GMC, set standards of practice and postgraduate education for their specialties. They work closely with the large number of specialist associations which are, increasingly, the source of detailed knowledge and expertise in the sub-specialities they represent. Then there are the training authorities – the Specialist Training Authority and the Joint Committee on Postgraduate Training for General Practice – which certificate doctors who become eligible for appointment as consultants or principals in general practice in the NHS. Specialist certification leads to specialist registration with the GMC.

Professional self-regulation is, however, only one of several elements in the complicated relationship between the medical profession and the State. For example, Parliament makes doctors working for the NHS accountable to NHS management. Most medical education is paid for by the State – which raises further issues of accountability; a web of interlocking legislation controls the many aspects of doctors' responsibilities for the public health; and now the government has brought forward potentially far-reaching proposals for achieving more consistent quality in the NHS (Secretary of State for Health 1997, 1998).

Doctors' changing professionalism

Professionalism in medicine rests on three pillars: expertise, ethics and service. Expertise derives from a body of knowledge and skills whose utility is constantly being invigorated by the results of research. Ethical behaviour for each doctor flows from a unique combination of ethical principles, values and standards. Service to patients embodies an attitude and commitment which puts patients first. Together they constitute 'the profession of medicine'. They are the basis of 'professional autonomy'.

Autonomy is fundamental to the concept of 'profession' (Freidson 1988). It gives individual doctors the freedom to exercise judgement in making clinical decisions and the profession collectively the authority to regulate itself. Because medicine has to be in harmony with the people and the society it serves, autonomy can never be absolute. The more the profession and its practitioners are perceived to be at one with the public's general values and expectations, and so can be trusted to act in the public's interest, the greater the degree of autonomy that Parliament will allow. Trust – or lack of it – is thus the fundamental element that determines the relationship between the medical profession and the public, and between individual doctors and their patients.

The GMC – and by implication the medical profession – has been criticized in recent years for not maintaining that trust by making sure that professional self-regulation works properly (e.g. Kennedy 1983; Rosenthal 1987; Smith 1989; Stacey 1992; Allsop and Mulcahy 1996). The main criticisms are:

- an unwillingness to demonstrate to the public that established doctors – general practitioners and consultants – are competent and perform well;
- the impression that the medical profession does not protect patients adequately from poor practice;
- dissatisfaction with the paternalistic – and at times arrogant – attitude of some doctors to patients, and more widespread concern about the willingness and ability of many doctors to communicate satisfactorily with their patients;

- the conservative nature of professional self-regulation, in particular its slowness to recognize, accept and adapt to the public's expectations;
- lack of openness and transparent accountability in the system and by individual doctors.

The GMC and doctors generally now recognise that they must respond to these criticisms. Medical regulation needs to be modernized. To be really effective in today's world medical regulation, be it by the profession or by contract or by whatever combination of these and other means, must start locally with every doctor and every clinical team (Irvine 1997a). The traditional but narrow view – that medical regulation is solely the responsibility of central institutions like the GMC and the Royal Colleges – misses this essential point. Doctors, other professional colleagues and managers all have a responsibility to work together to assure and demonstrate good practice, and to act promptly and decisively when things seem to be going wrong. Only in this way can the principles of good medical practice be embodied within the culture and practice of medicine in every clinical unit in every NHS Trust, every primary care group, every general practice and in the private sector.

Such a dynamic and inclusive concept of medical regulation, in which all have their own parts to play, should be positive and helpful, embracing the continuing education, personal professional development and performance of all doctors. All involved need to adopt the principles and methods of quality improvement and quality assurance and to be open about their processes and results.

Maintaining good medical practice

In 1996 in a series of lectures, I proposed the development and implementation of a modern, comprehensive and systematically applied strategy of professional regulation (Irvine 1997a) directed at the maintenance of good practice by established doctors. I suggested six core components (Irvine 1997b):

1 Clear ethical values and, wherever possible, explicit professional standards.
2 Effective local professional regulation, based on medical and clinical teams.
3 Regular publication of data recording doctors' involvement in continuing medical education, audit and practice assessment (already collected by some Royal Colleges and others).
4 Sound local arrangements for recognizing dysfunctional doctors early and for taking appropriate action.
5 Clear criteria and pathways for referral to the GMC when severely dysfunctional doctors refuse or fail to comply with local recommendations.
6 At all stages, practical help and support so that doctors who get into difficulties can be restored to full practice, wherever possible.

These ideas have now been developed and taken forward by the GMC. There are three main strands to the GMC's approach:

- clear values and standards wherever possible;
- local medical regulation based on effective quality assurance especially in clinical directorates and general practice;
- sound professional arrangements for dealing with concerns about particular doctors.

And, at the time of writing, a fourth strand is emerging. The GMC has proposed a strengthening of the specialist register – and a comparable register for general practice – to enable consultants and principals in general practice to confirm and demonstrate the quality of their professionalism to the outside world. The regular revalidation of specialist registration would reflect doctors' continuing professional development, the results of audit and performance at work. Talks on the best ways of taking this proposal forward have now begun.

It is helpful to look at these strands in a little more detail.

Values and standards

Clearly enunciated values and standards are the foundation of good medical practice. There are two main approaches – foundation statements about values and standards and statements of current best clinical practice expressed as clinical guidelines.

In 1995, the GMC published *Good Medical Practice* (General Medical Council 1995). Here, for the first time, it described the duties and responsibilities of doctors explicitly and set out the principles of good medical practice. A second edition has just been published (General Medical Council 1998a). Both the profession and the public have reacted positively, showing how helpful and indeed essential it is that the GMC indicates to individual doctors what they must be prepared to do, and to the public what it can expect of them. Importantly, these are the standards against which the GMC will judge the performance or conduct of doctors who are dysfunctional, and whose registration may be called into question.

The GMC is now well into a major programme of implementation. So, for example, the medical schools are being asked to show that the new doctors they produce have been taught how to practise in accordance with these basic principles. The Royal College of Anaesthetists and the Association of Anaesthetists have together published new guidance on good anaesthetic practice – *Good Practice: a Guide for Departments of Anaesthesia* – using the basic principles of *Good Medical Practice* as the foundation (Royal College of Anaesthetists 1998). Other colleges are likely to do the same ensuring that the principles are reinforced in specialist training and continuing professional development. Most recently, all NHS trusts, health authorities and health boards have had their attention drawn to the professional standards that the GMC would expect of registered doctors whom they employ or engage as contractors.

The second approach is the use of clinical guidelines, which are simply a format for displaying a set of explicit clinical standards. Clinical guidelines flow from the drive to secure clinical decision making which is demonstrably effective and therefore based on the best research evidence available. It is obviously in patients' interests that doctors apply best practice as consistently as possible. The Government intends to establish a National Institute for Clinical Excellence to take forward and coordinate the development of clinical guidelines within a National Service Framework (Secretary of State for Health 1997, 1998).

In using clinical guidelines clinicians feel, rightly, that they must retain the freedom to decide with their individual patients what is best in the circumstances, since all patients are different. The key thing is that, in the exercise of clinical judgement, they must always be prepared to justify their actions. Neither arbitrariness and whim at one end of the spectrum of clinical decision making, nor rigidity and unyielding diktat at the other, are compatible with true professionalism.

There are many aspects of care – listening, explaining, comforting, counselling, consoling – which both patients and doctors know are fundamental, yet which cannot usually be measured. The standards are implicit. While it is important to see that care is as clinically effective as possible, it is equally essential to ensure that the value of care is not diminished or relegated to a second order of priority simply because it is difficult to express numerically.

Local medical regulation

Within the last five years or so we have begun to see more clearly that there is a missing link in the system of medical regulation – a missing piece of the puzzle. Individual practitioners have always been held responsible for keeping themselves up to date. That is in the essence of being a professional; and the licensing and certificating bodies have their institutional role. In between are those loose, informal, often *ad hoc*, local networks and arrangements which, as Rosenthal (1995) has shown, vary so widely in their consistency and effectiveness. As they are, they do not constitute a coherently structured, functionally effective, recognizable part of the system (Irvine 1997a).

The concept of local medical regulation is now being given proper form and substance by the profession, with a clearly defined role (General Medical Council 1998b). At the same time, the Government (Secretary of State for Health 1998) is about to introduce 'clinical governance', to make sure that local NHS management takes responsibility for the quality of clinical care provided by its health professionals. In the booklet *Maintaining Good Medical Practice* (General Medical Council 1998b) the GMC gives guidance to the medical profession and NHS management on establishing quality assured medical practice throughout the NHS. Quality assured practice must become the fundamental underpinning of good, clinical governance.

Most doctors today work in medical and clinical teams. In such teams they can and should accept some collective responsibility for their own and their colleagues' standards of practice. Properly functioning clinical teams are, by definition, critically dependent on every member performing effectively. Poor performance by one member therefore should be a matter of practical concern to all.

Recent experience shows that more and more doctors are seeing the value of practising in this way. Well-developed, self-regulated medical and clinical teams are committed to seeking excellence through continuous quality improvement, to assuring their patients of good practice, and to acting decisively when confronted with poor practice.

Effective clinical teams have some common characteristics (Calman 1994; Irvine and Irvine 1996; Irvine 1997b; General Medical Council 1998b). For example, they develop their own ethos based on their particular synthesis of values, ethical principles and standards; they have respect for their patients; they are learning organizations which positively encourage and cultivate a sense of 'belonging'. They make sure that the development of knowledge, skills and attitudes of individuals is relevant to the team's objectives and purpose. Formative appraisal facilitates personal professional development; and such teams have good systems, audit their own work, make imaginative use of risk management procedures, and are prepared to test themselves against others by inviting regular external peer review. A sense of collective as well as personal responsibility for professional performance, a 'no-blame' culture, and above all a commitment to try and understand and look after each other, shine through as outstanding qualities of successful self-regulating teams.

It follows that if team-based self-regulation is effective, the wider, local and national professional framework for assuring good practice can be lighter and less intrusive. Equally, the results could contribute in future to the regular revalidation of individual doctors' specialist registration.

When things go wrong

Teams following the approach described above seem to be better prepared, because of their attitudes, the skills they possess and the methods they use, to recognize and confront dysfunctional practice when it first appears. It is in their interests to do so, to protect their patients from harm, to help the colleague in distress, and to avoid damage by association with a dysfunctional colleague. There is little doubt that a combination of understanding and firmness at this stage can do much to manage dysfunctional practice especially if combined with a willingness to help put things right. Confronting a problem early is the kindest thing to do. It is not surprising therefore that the clinical team is the starting point for the third strand in the GMC's strategy for maintaining good medical practice, namely the arrangements for dealing with concerns about dysfunctional doctors. Here, GMC policy and practice are undergoing radical change.

Historically, the GMC has responded to complaints where serious professional conduct has been alleged or where it has been told that a doctor's health may be placing patients at risk. The GMC saw its responsibilities as being limited to those cases referred to it that came within its jurisdiction. This began to change with the realization that the GMC's fitness-to-practise procedures would have to be strengthened. An additional capability for assessing doctors at work was needed in those cases where the evidence suggested a pattern of seriously deficient performance such that, if continued, there would be a threat to patients. It was this realization that led to the Medical (Professional Performance) Act 1995. The Act gives the GMC new powers to investigate a doctor's performance and, where it finds the standard of performance to be seriously deficient, to impose conditions on or to suspend a doctor's registration.

One consequence of this reorientation is the recognition that far more attention must be given to the very beginning of the process, when dysfunction first comes to light. Hence the importance of clinical teams, clinical governance and local medical regulation. In *Maintaining Good Medical Practice* (General Medical Council 1998b) the GMC describes the steps that need to be taken locally when dysfunctional practice is revealed, and indicates the criteria for referral to the GMC. A determined effort is now being made to ensure that the circle of local arrangements for professional regulation, around and immediately accessible to doctors and clinical teams, is properly developed and put on a really sound basis. The medical directors of NHS trusts and the directors of public health are among those locally who have a key part to play because of the particularly sensitive positions they hold; and the boundary between the GMC and NHS complaints and disciplinary procedures will have to be clarified. Within the next year, as clinical governance and local medical regulation are implemented, everyone should become aware of what to do and when, what criteria should prompt colleagues working together to refer for local action, and what criteria should indicate secondary referral to the GMC; or, if institutional failures are suspected, to the proposed Commission for Health Improvement (Secretary of State for Health 1998).

Reporting poor practice

The GMC has made the ethical responsibility of doctors clear. *Good Medical Practice* (General Medical Council 1998a) states that doctors must act where they believe that a colleague's conduct, performance or health is a threat to patients, if necessary by telling someone from the employing authority or from a regulating body. Doctors who wilfully ignore this responsibility place themselves at risk of GMC action.

We are giving careful thought as to how best to make the reporting of persistently poor or dangerous practice a well-signposted, professionally acceptable thing to do. Having clinical teams which understand and know when and how to carry out this responsibility will help.

GMC performance procedures

The GMC's performance procedures came into effect in July 1997. With this the GMC thus has a range of mechanisms – conduct, performance, health – for dealing with severely dysfunctional doctors. Protection of patients is the first priority. Rehabilitation of the doctor, wherever possible, is the other objective.

Seriously deficient performance has been defined as: 'A departure from good professional practice – whether or not it is covered by specific GMC guidance – sufficiently serious to call into question the doctor's registration' (Standing Committee A 1995: Coll. 8). A doctor's registration may be questioned by repeated or persistent failure to comply with the professional standards appropriate to the work being done by the doctor, particularly where this places patients or members of the public in jeopardy. This may include repeated or persistent failure to comply with the GMC's guidance in *Good Medical Practice* (General Medical Council 1998a).

If, on the basis of one or more complaints, there is a prima-facie case of seriously deficient performance, this will trigger an assessment of the doctor's practice. The assessment will be conducted by a team normally consisting of three assessors, two medical and one lay. The medical assessors will be from the same specialty as the doctor being assessed. Assessment will normally take place at the doctor's place of work. The initial overall appraisal of performance may be extended if necessary to cover the doctor's knowledge and skills in greater depth. The assessment, and the evidence of pattern of practice given to the GMC in the initial complaint(s), should give as accurate a picture as possible of the doctor's performance.

Rehabilitation

One of the interesting results of the GMC's involvement with sick doctors is the clear impression gained that the combination of firmness and discipline, determining what the doctor under care can do while pursuing an active programme of rehabilitation, seems to offer a constructive way of handling such problems. The numbers are small. Nevertheless, anecdotal experience suggests that doctors have become less wary of reporting sick colleagues. This is probably because it has become more widely known in the profession that the GMC will take active steps to see that the doctor receives proper care, as well as providing proper protection for patients.

Such has been the confidence engendered by this approach that the GMC proposes to extend it to doctors whose dysfunction reflects deficiencies in their clinical competence or performance. This intention has been well received by the profession, which is keen to do all it can for colleagues who appear to have fallen behind.

Our experience with poorly performing doctors who come through the GMC conduct procedures shows that they fall into several categories. For example, there are those who have become complacent, isolated or for other reasons lost their way as doctors. This group of doctors includes a high proportion who, once the problem is pointed out to them, motivate themselves to put things right. These are the doctors who are most likely to benefit from assistance, and to recover their fitness to practise.

Some have more serious deficiencies and may have to be placed in a protected environment, for example, under supervision in a hospital unit or in a teaching general practice. But here also there have been some good results where dysfunctional doctors – supported by skilled teachers and supervisors – have worked hard with a desire to succeed.

More intractable are those doctors in whom the root cause of their dysfunction is attitude – arrogance, idleness, or a stubborn refusal to accept or even acknowledge that a problem exists. These are the doctors whose management is most difficult. It is they who in future will have to be confronted by the Committee on Professional Performance with the reality of their situation. They will have the offer of help with rehabilitation. If they do not take it, or in any event show no acceptable improvement, they face the possibility of suspension from practice, if need be indefinitely.

Evaluation

The GMC is now committed to a policy of openness and, wherever possible, explicit accountability for its own work (Irvine 1997a). This policy will apply, from the outset, to the fitness-to-practise procedures dealing with dysfunctional doctors.

Within two years of introducing the performance procedures, the GMC intends to publish a preliminary account of cases so that the public and wider profession can see what seriously deficient performance means in practice (Irvine 1997b). Alongside this, there will be a more formal evaluation concerned with the overall effectiveness of the procedures – in particular, whether they meet their objectives, their acceptability to complainants, the public and the medical profession, and their impact on the doctor concerned.

The procedures cannot be seen in isolation. So the NHS, as by far the largest employer involved, may wish to support further studies, in parallel with the GMC evaluation, concerned, for example, with documenting the effect the performance procedures have on the rehabilitation of dysfunctional doctors working for them and on strengthening local, clinical governance.

Conclusion

The public and profession share a common interest in ensuring that doctors practising in Britain provide a good standard of practice and care. Where they do not, patients must be properly protected. The maintenance of good medical practice and sound local clinical governance are the keys to the way forward.

A strategy for the profession based on clear professional standards, quality assured hospital and general practice teams, a regularly revalidated specialist register which identifies doctors who are competent and capable, and effective local and national arrangements for dealing with dysfunctional doctors, should offer the public, patients, government, employers and the profession a robust, modern form of medical regulation. The primary responsibility for implementing, maintaining and ensuring good medical practice lies with individual doctors and the medical and clinical teams with which they work. It is the employer's responsibility to see that doctors work in an environment in which there is the time, data, tools and other facilities needed to make this possible.

Through this kind of approach I suggest that public trust and confidence in doctors can be restored, and the profession can hold its head high once again.

References

Allsop, J. and Mulcahy, L. (1996) *Regulating Medical Work: Formal and Informal Controls*. Buckingham: Open University Press.

Calman, K. (1994) The profession of medicine, *British Medical Journal*, 309: 1140–3.

Freidson, E. (1988) *The Profession of Medicine: A Study of the Sociology of Applied Knowledge*. Chicago: University of Chicago Press.

General Medical Council (1995) *Duties of a Doctor: Good Medical Practice*. London: GMC.

General Medical Council (1998a) *Good Medical Practice*, 2nd edn. London: GMC.

General Medical Council (1998b) *Maintaining Good Medical Practice*. London: GMC.

Horton, R. (1998) How should doctors respond to the GMC's judgements on Bristol? *Lancet*, 351: 1900–901.

Irvine, D.H. (1997a) The performance of doctors I: Professionalism and self regulation in a changing world, *British Medical Journal*, 314: 1540–42.

Irvine, D.H. (1997b) The performance of doctors II: Maintaining good practice, protecting patients from poor performance, *British Medical Journal*, 314: 1613–15.

Irvine, D.H. and Irvine, S. (1996) *The Practice of Quality*. Oxford: Radcliffe Medical Press.

Kennedy, I. (1983) *The Unmasking of Medicine*. London: Granada.

Rosenthal, M.M. (1987) *Dealing with Medical Malpractice: The British and Swedish Experience*. London: Tavistock.

Rosenthal, M.M. (1995) *The Incompetent Doctor: Behind Closed Doors*. Buckingham: Open University Press.

Royal College of Anaesthetists (1998) *Good Practice: a Guide for Departments of Anaesthesia*. London: Royal College of Anaesthetists.

Secretary of State for Health (1997) *The New NHS: Modern, Dependable*, Cmnd 3807. London: HMSO.

Secretary of State for Health (1998) *A First Class Service: Quality in the New NHS*. London: Department of Health.

Smith, R. (1989) Profile of the GMC: The day of judgement comes closer, *British Medical Journal*, 298: 1241–4.

Smith, R. (1998) All changed, changed utterly, *British Medical Journal*, 316: 1917–18.

Stacey, M. (1992) *Regulating British Medicine: The General Medical Council*. Chichester: Wiley.

Standing Committee A. Considering the Medical Performance Bill. *Hansard*, 9 May 1995, Coll. 8.

15 Medical mistakes: a view from the British Medical Association

Vivienne Nathanson

Acknowledging errors: history

For many years the tradition in medical practice in the UK was to assert that doctors did not make mistakes, unless and until a court of law had proven that a specific doctor had made a specific error. Historians tell us that the general ethos among practitioners in the UK was one in which doctors would not readily admit mistakes and were also neither enthusiastic nor skilled at communicating with patients nor at encouraging patients to exercise autonomy. Those same doctors were equally unlikely either to report errors by colleagues or to cooperate with investigations of allegations of mistakes by themselves or others. Indeed in 1803 Percival, an influential writer on ethics, advised that 'the balance of truthfulness yields to beneficence in critical situations' (Leake 1927: 112). The notion that patients might be damaged by their trust in the infallibility of the physician being undermined was thus reinforced by an influential ethical writer.

Much of this ethos formed the basic subject matter of the 1979 Reith Lectures, by Professor Ian Kennedy (Kennedy 1981). It was at least in part in response to this lecture series that attitudes within medicine in the UK have changed significantly, with physicians becoming major drivers of this attitudinal reform. While physicians are still not uniformly excellent in all regards, part of the development has been a general willingness to acknowledge that medicine, like all professions and occupations, has poor practitioners as well as those who work to the highest standards, and that the profession has a duty to itself and its patients to deal with those who practise poorly (Brearley 1996).

The British Medical Association as a driver of reform

The British Medical Association has been a major driver of this reform. The guidance it produces for doctors, from the Medical Ethics Committee in particular, has consistently encouraged doctors to raise their personal standards of practice and to help their colleagues to do the same. In particular, doctors have been encouraged to recognize their role in informing patients and enabling those patients to make an informed choice about their healthcare, even where that choice is to allow the doctor to make the treatment choice.

The BMA has published advice to doctors on medical ethics since it was first established in 1832. The first committee to advise on ethics, and on the teaching of this subject to physicians, was established in 1849. The current committee emerged from the Central Ethical Committee, founded in 1902, having been expanded and renamed the Medical Ethics Committee. For most of that time matters of concern to the profession or to individual practitioners were considered by a committee of doctors and advice was published as articles, guidance notes and a variety of increasingly philosophically based books.

Today the committee includes up to eight non-medically qualified members, drawn from disciplines including moral philosophy, law, nursing and theology. The essence of its work is to try to find a consensus on matters of concern. Because of the broad base of its membership it does not follow any particular school of philosophy. However, its last chairman has stated that he believes it should and increasingly has based its decisions on a Christian ethical perspective (Horner 1996).

The advice produced by the BMA is publicized to members through the *British Medical Journal*, the *BMA News Review* and articles written for other medical journals. This is supported by postgraduate lectures delivered by committee members and staff throughout the UK, making doctors aware of the advice the BMA makes available. Increasingly this advice is posted on the Internet on the BMA's Web page.[1] The Board of Medical Education also emphasizes in its work the importance of teaching in medical ethics throughout a medical career.

The nature of medical education

While medical education in the UK is, as in most countries, subject to complex rules and guidance, and is formalized through a series of structures (involving medical Royal Colleges, universities, the General Medical Council and others), much of the practice of medicine is learned through a form of apprenticeship.

The 'see one, do one, teach one' concept of learning practical techniques grew up in a time when such techniques were relatively simple and low-risk. Whether this is a sustainable model for such skill development is today being questioned. While this approach worked well when learning relatively simple techniques, such as establishing intravenous infusions, it cannot work for new surgical skills such as 'keyhole' surgery. While the majority of doctors have recognized this, and the need for more formalized training, a few have been prepared to practise such complex new techniques with little or no formal training, and disastrous consequences for patients.

The development by the medical Royal Colleges of 'log books' itemizing the procedures trainees ought to see and carry out with different levels of supervision is a practical attempt to make the 'see one, do one, teach one' concept work (Jones 1996). It is subject to proper, formal educational audit and review and pushes the apprenticeship concept into the modern world of appraisal-based learning. Most UK-trained doctors value the apprenticeship part of their training and education. At its best, they learn to put theoretical concepts into practice, being trained by those who are skilled and practised in the techniques and who understand the skill level of the trainee. At its worst, poorly skilled doctors learn the art and science of medicine by practising on real patients who are unlikely to be aware that they are being used as teaching material.

Those responsible for medical education constantly face new challenges. The market structure of the NHS today, for instance, is such that some elements of care provided historically in secondary care institutions are now increasingly being offered in primary care settings. But there has been little time and scant resources put into training those now providing some of this care (including a substantial amount of surgical interventions), and little or no research looking at outcomes for the patient rather than simply outputs for the service.

The important lessons of audit

Lessons learned from the Confidential Enquiries into Maternal Deaths in the UK and the reports of the National Confidential Enquiry into Perioperative Deaths (NCEPOD) have been the springboard for much change (NCEPOD 1996). These clearly show that elements of medical practice, which are often associated with the apprenticeship concept, need to change. However, it is a sad reflection on British medicine that many of the lessons learned from NCEPOD and from specific outcome audits carried out by directors of public health, demonstrate the obvious – that patients do better where they are assessed and managed by experienced clinicians.

Admitting errors

Many doctors are concerned about admitting their mistakes, or even admitting where there has been a problem for the patient to which no fault could attach. Much of the effort of ethicists and other advisers has been to encourage doctors to admit error without necessarily admitting liability (Richards *et al.* 1996). This protects the doctor's position in terms of the potential for litigation but, more importantly, recognizes the absolute imperative for patients to be informed about what is happening to them.

But underneath there is a reluctance to be honest about mistakes, a fear that the UK could follow the USA down the road to ever increasing litigation about medical mistakes. The cost implications of this to the NHS and to individual practitioners generate considerable concern. This fear has increased both because the UK has moved into a political situation where healthcare is based upon a market model, and where patient expectations are fuelled by patient's charters and other patients' rights concepts without an equivalent driver for the concept of patient responsibilities. Fears over litigation have, without doubt, encouraged an already conservative profession to change only reluctantly. But the overwhelming evidence from national and local audit programmes, and the introduction by the GMC of its performance review machinery (General Medical Council 1996), has produced an acceleration of the necessary change.

The Patient's Charter

The Patient's Charter in England makes no mention of responsibilities for patients. By way of contrast, its Scottish equivalent mentions the importance of patients informing clinics if they are unable to attend for an appointment – an attempt to alert patients to their responsibilities in terms of resource utilization.

Physicians' concerns about such charters of rights are essentially twofold. First, they are concerned that charters raise expectations which the service may not be able to meet, or which it can meet only patchily or by inappropriate concentration on specific clinical areas. Second, they perceive that the rights are about issues which are superficial, and clinically of little relevance. However, these promises mean that resources, including the time of clinicians, are concentrated on areas which have little importance in terms of a successful clinical outcome for the individual patient or for groups of patients. The distortion of resource use which they can cause can even adversely affect patient outcomes. This is particularly likely when resources are switched to 'dealing with' waiting lists, and the usual clinical judgement process is distorted (Marks 1995). Patients can therefore wait longer than before with potentially serious results.

The fallibility of medicine

There is also an understanding that one of the main problems of medical care has been its own success and the willingness of doctors and medical scientists to 'talk up' medicine and to pretend that it can or will shortly be able to cope effectively with all healthcare problems if only enough money is thrown into the pot. While there have been enormous, perhaps even extraordinary developments in therapeutics and in medical technology, we are still very ineffective at ill-health prevention, and have few truly effective interventions for many chronic and disabling diseases.

Similarly, patients hear so much of the ability of modern medicine to treat the previously untreatable, to save lives even *in extremis*, and so little of the potential for poor outcomes even with the best care, that they have an increasing expectation of a perfect result. This is clear not only with surgical and other interventions but also in parents' attitudes to pregnancy and childbirth – the expectation is of a perfect baby, and even minor imperfections are too often regarded as intolerable. There is a strong tendency to attempt to lay the blame on someone – even congenital abnormalities are regarded as someone's fault.

Medicine is not an exact science (Evans 1993). All patients react differently to their own underlying pathology and to the interventions offered by doctors and other carers. This is demonstrated by the variability of response to all medical techniques and therapeutic interventions. But to this must also be added the complicating factor that many treatments are based upon symptom control and do not deal with the underlying cause. The intent may be to allow the natural disease or healing processes to continue while managing the unpleasant or unacceptable symptoms. Equally, when a disease is neither self-limiting nor benign the only treatment may be palliative because that is the only option modern medicine offers. The variability of responses to treatment can be seen in audit results but is rarely explained to patients, although it can be argued that it should be part of the process of obtaining informed consent.

This is not to say that patients, including expectant mothers, should not have a right to expect the best possible standard of care, but they should also understand that through no one's fault, a perfect result to care is not always achieved. Just as the birth of an 'imperfect' baby may have no attributable fault, so a poor outcome from a medical intervention may simply be the chance outcome seen in a percentage of patients treated according to a particular regimen. The unachievable expectations of patients can, at their worst and most damaging, lead, for example, to a decreased interest from young doctors in obstetrics as a specialty and an increased number of Caesarean sections, as a form of defensive medical practice.

Moving to a resolution

There is a clear need for patients to understand the limitations of medical science, in terms both of the imperfection and dangers of individual treatments and of the areas of health for which relatively little effective care is available. Awareness on the part of patients, coupled with a real informed involvement in decision-making about their own medical management, will enable a better understanding of those mistakes which are inevitable.

Mistakes will always be made; this is inevitable in any system based upon the experience and knowledge of many individuals. But the cost to individuals (both patients and clinicians) can only be reduced if there is shared understanding of how errors occur, how best they can be avoided, how damage can be limited and how repairs and reparation can be made. An increased atmosphere of openness and sharing will clearly demystify medicine, but is likely in today's society to increase the trust and value placed in patient–physician relationships.

Note

1 The BMA's Web sites can be found at http://www.bma.org.uk and http://www.bmj.com.

References

Brearley, S. (1996) Seriously deficient professional performance, *British Medical Journal*, 312: 1180–1.

Evans, L. (1993) Medical accidents: no such thing?, *British Medical Journal*, 307: 1438–9.

General Medical Council (1996) *Performance Procedures – A Summary of Current Proposals*. London: GMC.

Horner, J.S. (1996) *Medical Ethics and Medical Practice*, volume based upon an MD thesis.

Jones, P.F. (1996) Errors by locums. Each locum should carry a logbook, *British Medical Journal*, 313: 116–17.

Kennedy, I. (1981) *The Unmasking of Medicine*. London: Allen & Unwin.

Leake, C.D. (1927) *Percival's Medical Ethics*. Baltimore, MD: Williams and Wilkins.

Marks, D.F. (1995) *NHS Reforms: The First Three Years*. London: Middlesex University Health Research Centre.

NCEPOD (1996) *The Report of the National Confidential Enquiry into Perioperative Deaths (NCEPOD) 1993/4*. London: NCEPOD.

Richards, P., Kennedy, I. and Woolf, H. (1996) Managing medical mishaps, *British Medical Journal*, 313: 243–4.

16 | The role of quality improvement

Edward Dickinson

Introduction

Healthcare is a complex system operating under pressure and facing increasing user and clinical effectiveness demands. This chapter considers medical mishaps from the perspective of quality improvement and proposes a role for clinical audit in reducing adverse clinical events. The underlying theme is that adverse events in healthcare may be closely related to inappropriate systems and work processes which are exposed by human failings, an issue also discussed by Vincent and Reason (Chapter 3). Quality improvement through clinical audit may have the potential to overcome these two challenges and this is explored in the following ways. First, the role and function of the UK's Royal College of Physicians (RCP) is described. Next, some of the present forces for change towards a quality improvement emphasis are analysed. This leads to a short discussion of the extent to which medical mishaps may be a 'system' problem. The following sections track the diffusion of quality improvement into the health service and the present status of clinical audit. Finally, the future role for quality improvement in preventing medical mishaps is considered.

Role and functions of professional organizations

The RCP is a professional organization with historic origins in promoting standards of medical care, being concerned with the quality of health and of healthcare. The main activities of the RCP are policy development, education and training, accreditation of hospital posts and the holding of professional examinations. In recent years the RCP has been increasingly interested in tackling variations in healthcare by producing reports which contain recommendations about how healthcare should be delivered for particular health problems or in particular health situations. For example, recent reports have tackled the use of medication by older people, cardiac rehabilitation and care for people with renal disease (Royal College of Physicians 1997a; 1997b; 1997c). The present trend is for the professional organizations to play a role in developing and promoting clinical effectiveness and quality improvement through national clinical guidelines and national clinical audit.

Forces at work

Presently, there are irresistible forces putting pressure on healthcare systems which have both created complexity and fuelled the demand to overcome complexity. Medical mishaps may be one of the unintended consequences of such an increasingly complex system of care. In relation to demographics, a longevity revolution is taking place and societies around the world are ageing (Kalache 1991). Ageing populations put particular pressures on health systems because of the complexity of illness among older people, the chronicity of their disease, and the interfaces they cross in care. From the technological viewpoint, many of the increasing costs of healthcare have been ascribed to the introduction of numerous new health technologies – one of the revolutions in healthcare (Relman 1988). This rise in the costs of care is coupled with a drift towards the 'dehumanization' of care (Wooton and Darkins 1997) in the context of a faster pace of healthcare delivery, seen, for example, in reductions in hospital stays (Nocon and Baldwin 1998). Healthcare has always been high on the political agenda and is of great social interest. Several factors have raised the profile of medical mishaps and the expectations of patients as regards clinical excellence – the steady rise of consumerism, perceptions that improvements in the complaints system are slow and the greater involvement of people and their healthcare. This emphasis has been reflected in the development of policy (Department of Health 1991; 1998). These forces, largely global in nature, are pushing health systems towards finding sustainable solutions to cost and quality challenges.

Medical mishaps: a 'system' symptom?

Many medical mishaps may be a 'system' problem. In other sectors, major accidents are often found to occur as a result of failure of complex systems and activities. These may be brought to light when problems accumulate and may become coupled with human error. Examples include air and civil engineering disasters such as the King's Cross fire (1987), the sinking of the *Herald of Free Enterprise* (1987), the Piper Alpha explosion (1988) and the Kegworth plane crash (1989). Medical care systems are also highly complex, with many interdependent activities. The need for interprofessional care, teamwork and the use of high technologies all place increasing pressures on health systems for coordination, communication, and effective systems of organization and management. A simple but pervasive example of a systems problem is the current inadequacy of medical records and decision support. If some medical mishaps are a system problem, quality improvement approaches might help in the link between the delivery of individual clinical interventions and the organizational context for healthcare. Certainly, the quality improvement revolution has firmly arrived in healthcare.

Diffusion of quality improvement to health services

A clear pathway of diffusion of quality improvement into the health service can be seen. The early history of quality improvement was of its development in industrial sectors, and the early principles have stood the test of time (Deming 1986). During the 1970s, quality improvement was adopted in the service sector as this expanded. Inevitably, this led to the diffusion of quality improvement to the public service sector (Speller 1991). In the early 1980s this was seen clearly in social services, and in the late 1980s travelled to the health service. In 1989 the first comprehensive attempts were made to introduce quality improvement into the UK NHS with the introduction of clinical audit (described in greater detail below). A marker of the development of quality improvement between the sectors can be seen in the appearance of relevant awards. For example, in the health sector the Golden Helix award is now available across Europe and the Ernest Codman award is awarded in the USA. However, total quality management, which has been widely embraced to tackle potential system failures in many industries, has not taken root in the NHS (Øvretveit 1998). This is probably because there were so many other new management initiatives taking place within the health service at the same time so that health service staff could be confused about the importance of various initiatives and or cynical about the latest management 'fads'.

Status of clinical audit

Audit was introduced into the NHS in 1989 (Department of Health 1989). This initiative was largely supported by the professional bodies as an educational activity (Royal College of Physicians 1989; 1994). *Medical audit* gradually evolved to become *clinical audit*, to indicate the involvement of the whole clinical team. Despite concerns about value for money, involvement and commitment, two main factors have promoted clinical audit to a central position – the link with clinical guidelines and the stance of the new Labour government. Early experiences in developing audit measures had led to the conclusion that there was a need for an evidential base for such audit measurements. Clinical guidelines provided a solution to this requirement, as by the early 1990s clinical guidelines were being produced at national, regional and local levels to increasing levels of sophistication. There is now a national clinical guidelines appraisal system (Cluzeau *et al.* 1998) and an expectation that national clinical guidelines will be used as standards for national clinical audit. Along the way, audit appears to have become the NHS's own 'home-grown' version of quality improvement with the new important linkage to clinical governance. Through a turbulent period of development, the successes of clinical audit began to appear along with emergent leaders. Junior doctors were found to support the aims of audit generally but in practice were frustrated in the activities that they undertook (Greenwood *et al.* 1998). In national surveys, great variation in the state of play of clinical audit was found (Walshe and Coles 1993). However, examples of successful clinical audit programmes and projects were uncovered and the principles upon which this success was based were articulated (Walshe and Spurgeon 1998). But how might clinical audit be able to tackle system problems?

The strengths of clinical audit

Clues to the potential of audit to solve long-standing system problems and overcome complexity exist in a trio of links – to the new strategy for the NHS, the foundation on clinical guidelines and the conceptual links with the principles of quality improvement. The principles of good quality improvement activities are well known and it appears that clinical audit now reflects a continuous quality improvement model (Berwick 1996). It is cyclical, internal, peer-based and focuses on change. It leads to enjoyable cycles of improvement with reward and recognition for improvements in care. In this way clinical audit empowers clinicians continuously to improve what they do rather than being berated for failure. This approach reflects the success of local projects (Øvretveit 1998), the current political emphasis on self-regulation and the proposed National Institute for Clinical Excellence (Department of Health 1998).

The weaknesses of clinical audit

The major weaknesses of clinical audit are a set of failed links which need to be remedied. The first of these is the organizational link. The greatest challenge that has been found in implementing the audit cycle has been to implement change. Often, the changes that are required mean changes in systems and changes in use of resources. Clinicians who uncover these problems during the course of clinical audit frequently do not have the power to make these changes. As historically there has been poor joint working between clinicians and managers, it is the interface between managerial/organizational and clinical aspects of care that has led to failures of clinical audit. However, a number of initiatives are now beginning to tackle this issue and make some headway with it. King's Fund initiatives (Promoting Action on Clinical Effectiveness) have had a similar perspective, with a special focus on the managerial aspects of healthcare delivery. Our own Action on Clinical Audit work at the RCP has brought together clinicians, managers and clinical audit professionals in order to solve together system problems in their clinical audit programmes. This has resulted in close teamwork according to action plans to tackle mainly strategic issues in clinical audit. The introduction of clinical governance offers a new way to achieve this linkage on a national basis.

Second is the education link. Health professionals may not be equipped with knowledge and skills in relation to quality improvement, the management of change or the challenges of working in complex systems. However, this is now slowly changing with the introduction of communication skills training, management training modules and other similar activities. There is now a strong emphasis on continued professional development which is regulated through the Royal Colleges and similar bodies. Increasingly we can expect to see the materials which they use for this merge with clinical guidelines so that the derivatives of research knowledge are used within both clinical audit and continued professional development.

The final failed link concerns research and development. The needs of clinical audit for clinical guidelines have resulted in a much clearer idea of where the gaps exist in research knowledge. There has been a particular pinpointing of gaps in knowledge about how to organize systems of care in order to achieve the best outcomes for people and avoid medical mishaps. The Medical Research Council and the Wellcome Foundation are now promoting health services research, and this is becoming a more popular topic within academic units. Greater experience and expertise are developing rapidly and we can expect to see a portfolio of research, particularly within the NHS research and development programme, which focuses more and more on the organization of systems of care and the implementation of knowledge.

Additional challenges for clinical audit

It is pertinent to highlight two remaining challenges for clinical audit if, as a quality improvement activity, it is to tackle systemic problems to prevent medical mishaps. These are both concerned with interfaces, boundaries and communication. The first is the challenge of working effectively across the different care disciplines in clinical teams. There is a growing realization that teams are people who do not just happen to work together but also require development (Hunter 1997). The second challenge relates to the changing face of healthcare – the challenge of working across the different sectors of care: primary care, secondary care and community care. These have been highlighted by the recent Better Services for Vulnerable People initiative (NHS Executive 1997).

Clinical audit, quality improvement, systems and medical mishaps

This chapter has considered the potential of clinical audit for quality improvement to tackle systemic problems and hence medical mishaps. In the context of complex and pressured healthcare systems, quality improvement offers a sustainable solution to maintain clinical standards. Although total quality management has not taken root in the NHS, clinical audit is emerging as an appropriate quality improvement activity. It matches the principles of good quality improvement programmes and offers the link to the evidence of research. However, there are key links which still need to be fostered in order to fulfil the potential of clinical audit. Quality improvement offers a positive and constructive approach to the avoidance of medical mishaps. To achieve this, cultural changes may also be needed, but it appears that these are already under way. Indeed, the new agenda appears to have the capability to foster partnership and collaboration across specialties, disciplines and sectors of care.

Acknowledgements

The Research Unit of the Royal College of Physicians is supported by grants from the Wolfson and Welton Foundations, by other charitable donations, and by grants from other sources and the Department of Health.

References

Berwick, D. (1996) Improving healthcare, *British Medical Journal*, 312: 605–18.
Cluzeau, F., Littlejohns, P., Grimshaw, J. and Feder, G. (1998) *Appraisal Instrument for Clinical Guidelines*. London: St George's Hospital Medical School.
Deming, W.E. (1986) *Out of the Crisis*. Cambridge, MA: MIT Press.
Department of Health (1989) *Working for Patients*. London: HMSO.
Department of Health (1991) *The Patient's Charter: Raising the Standard*. London: Department of Health.
Department of Health (1998) *The New NHS. Modern, Dependable*, Cm 3807. London: The Stationery Office.
Greenwood, J.P., Lindsay, S.J., Batin, P.D. and Robinson, M.B. (1998) Junior doctors and clinical audit, *Journal of the Royal College of Physicians*, 31: 648–51.
Hunter, A. (1997) Teamwork, in P.P. Mayer, E.D. Dickinson and M. Sandler (eds) *Quality Care for Elderly People*. London: Chapman & Hall.

Kalache, A. (1991) Ageing in developing countries, in M.S.J. Pathy (ed.) *Principles and Practice of Geriatric Medicine*. Chichester: Wiley.

NHS Executive (1997) Executive Letter (97)62.

Nocon, A. and Baldwin, S. (1998) *Trends in Rehabilitation Policy*. London: King's Fund.

Øvretveit, J. (1998) The history and future of quality in the UK National Health Service: A personal view from abroad, *Healthcare Quality*, 4: 3–14.

Relman, A.S. (1988) Assessment and accountability: The third revolution, *New England Journal of Medicine*, 319: 1220–8.

Royal College of Physicians (1989) *Medical Audit – A First Report*. London: RCP.

Royal College of Physicians (1994) *Clinical Audit – A Second Report*. London: RCP.

Royal College of Physicians (1997a) *Cardiac Rehabilitation: Guidelines and Audit Standards*. London: RCP.

Royal College of Physicians (1997b). *Medication for Older People*. London: RCP.

Royal College of Physicians (1997c) *Treatment of Adult Patients with Renal Failure. Recommended Standards and Audit Measures. Guidelines*. London: RCP.

Speller, S. (1991) Service quality – the missing link. The need for a conceptual model: a case study. MBA thesis, Middlesex University, London.

Walshe, K. and Coles, J. (1993) *Evaluating Audit: A Review of Initiatives*. London: CSAPE Research.

Walshe, K. and Spurgeon, P. (1998) *Clinical Audit Assessment Framework*. Birmingham: Health Services Management Centre.

Wooton, R. and Darkins, A. (1997) Telemedicine and the doctor–patient relationship, *Journal of the Royal College of Physicians*, 31: 598–9.

17 | Medical mishaps: a managerial perspective

Liam J. Donaldson

Introduction

The operation of a health service depends upon a complex interaction between the patient, the environment in which care is provided and the people, equipment and facilities that deliver the care. It is the aim of most hospitals, those who manage them and those who work within them, to deliver care in a way which is of high quality and free of risk. Most hospitals or other providers of health services will also be dealing with a large volume of work, often around the clock, seven days a week, throughout the year. In practice, therefore, it is inevitable that problems and incidents will and do occur. The purpose of this chapter is to describe the main types of medical mishaps which occur in the daily running of a healthcare organization, their nature and the issues which arise when dealing with them.

An operational definition

The term 'medical mishap' is used in this chapter but it is not wholly satisfactory. Indeed, there is no standard terminology to describe the field of study. Terms such as 'incident', 'untoward incident', 'medical accident', 'medical mishap', 'error', 'failure' and 'adverse event' are often attached to incidents or decisions which have had (or could have) adverse consequences for patients. In this chapter, to encompass such situations, I use the following working definition: a medical mishap is an actual or potential serious lapse in the standard of care provided to a patient or patients or harm caused to a patient or patients through the performance of a health service and/or healthcare professionals working within it.

Sources of information

The routine information systems of most health services do not systematically capture and analyse data on medical mishaps. An understanding of the scale and nature of the problem can be derived from studies which have been carried out in particular healthcare settings or across healthcare systems as well as through the analysis of those health data which throw light on aspects of standards of care. The following are potential sources of data:

- studies of doctors with problems;
- inquiries following serious incidents;
- analysis of complaints made by patients;
- peer review processes;
- court judgements and legal cases;
- organizational and behavioural research.

Studies of medical workforces

There have been relatively few studies of problem doctors. Examples are contained in the work of Donaldson (1994; 1996; 1997) as well as that of Lens and van der Wal (1995). They describe the kinds of problems which can arise in an individual doctor's practice, including incompetence, ill health, disruptive behaviour, misconduct and dishonesty. All these characteristics, when they occur, can lead to lapses in standards of care or dangers for patients. Such studies are infrequent, in part because of the difficulty of describing and reporting problems about which there are particular professional taboos. They are therefore limited as a source of data on the nature and frequency of medical mishaps but they do draw attention to important issues concerning the culture of medical practice. Factors such as an unwillingness to be disloyal, uncertainty about whether a problem is serious, or concern about being responsible for ending a colleague's career mean that serious problems with the standard of care in an institution can go unrecognized or may even be concealed (Donaldson 1997). This context is important in understanding how an environment can exist in a hospital where serious medical mishaps are difficult to eliminate.

Commissions of inquiry into serious incidents

Particularly serious mishaps will often lead to large-scale investigations or commissions of inquiry. Examining the reports of such inquiries can yield important and relevant data about the kinds of problems which occur in particular settings. An early example in the British National Health Service was a judicial inquiry carried out into alleged inhumane treatment of mentally handicapped patients in a hospital in Wales (Department of Health and Social Security 1969). Of course, it is seldom possible to generalize from the results of inquiries undertaken into an incident or events in one particular healthcare organization. Nevertheless, the public airing of what went wrong, why and the consequences will often generate a debate among policy-makers, healthcare managers and professionals. This in turn will lead to the examination of standards in care settings throughout the health service concerned as the recommendations of such an inquiry are implemented. However, internal investigations of serious incidents can often be less satisfactory in terms of their rigour, degree of openness, the acknowledgement of problems and the extent to which lessons are learned (Blain and Donaldson 1995).

Analysis of complaints by patients and carers

Most health systems operate complaints procedures. Complaints made by patients, their carers or their relatives should be a way of providing valuable insights into lapses in standards of care. Whether they do depends on how thoroughly complaints are investigated and how the resulting data are aggregated, analysed and considered. It is of relatively little value (as is common) for a health service simply to record the number of complaints which have been made by patients and monitor them over time. Absolute and relative numbers of complaints may simply reflect people's willingness to complain, or may indicate the extent to which the hospital encourages complaints as a way of improving the quality of its services. On the other hand, analysing complaints for their content and the way in which they are handled (Donaldson and Cavanagh 1992) can provide important insights into the standard of care provided.

Results of peer review activities

The operation of peer review processes such as medical or clinical audit (Department of Health and Social Security 1989) is a way in which doctors and other healthcare professionals working in groups examine the standard of care provided by their service and the extent to which it departs from best practice, with a view to making improvements. This important process of professional scrutiny of standards of care should also be a source of valuable data. However, in practice, there are difficulties. This type of peer review has traditionally been seen as a professionally-led, educationally-based activity which is not integrated with other quality improvement processes within a managed service. Thus, the idea that healthcare managers might have access to the diagnostic phase of this peer review activity – in which mistakes or shortfalls in standards of care are identified – would be seen as anathema by many doctors. Up until now, peer review activities undertaken by doctors have largely been a mechanism for identifying the scope for improvement within specific areas of practice rather than a way in which the organization (or a whole health service) can systematically describe mishaps and learn lessons from their occurrence. Peer review activities with a wider remit – such as the confidential enquiries in Britain into maternal or perioperative deaths (Department of Health 1994; NCEPOD 1996) – provide a better example of how mishaps can be quantified and described, and then lead to recommendations for improvement in standards of care (including preventive action).

Analysis of court proceedings: medical negligence cases and coroners' inquests

Court proceedings resulting from allegations of medical negligence, or from deaths which take place in care, throw light on the most serious and catastrophic lapses in standards of service. Although they represent only a very small proportion of all the medical mishaps which occur, they can often lead to searching examinations of the standards of care provided in the institution concerned or sometimes more widely in a health service. However, the tendency of much medical litigation to be settled out of court sometimes works against a proper review of standards being conducted.

Organizational research and information gaps

Increasingly, it is apparent that the techniques of behavioural and organizational research, discussed elsewhere in this book and used in other industries (for example, in preventing aeroplane crashes), could be of value to health services. It is clear that no single source of data can provide good-quality information on the occurrence of medical mishaps. Different sources of data taken together can shed light on the problem but they provide no basis for a proper system of surveillance. The management teams of most hospitals, therefore, will largely rely on reports of single incidents and their analysis as an entry to an exploration of mishaps in their organizations. It is important that this information gap is closed by more research, not just into the problem of medical mishaps, but also into the design of surveillance systems to provide the intelligence which is needed.

Nature of the problems which arise

Box 17.1 shows some hypothetical examples of the kind of serious medical mishaps which can arise.

Complex clinical judgements

In a situation of the kind described in case A, attention is likely to focus on a number of factors including: the individual clinical decision to release the schizophrenic patient and how that was made; whether there was adherence to procedures for the assessment of risk by the mental health services

---

Box 17.1   Some hypothetical illustrative case histories

Case A   A 32-year-old schizophrenic is discharged from an in-patient mental health service and one week later kills his father.

Case B   A junior hospital doctor administers the wrong dose of a drug intrathecally and renders a patient paraplegic.

Case C   A radiologist prone to manic depression is found to have regularly skimmed dozens of X-rays in an afternoon and made his diagnosis through these cursory examinations.

Case D   A woman who has three times suffered full-term fetal losses is found retrospectively to have had missed diabetes mellitus in each pregnancy.

---

concerned; as well as the extent to which there was effective collaboration and communication between all the agencies involved in the care of the patient.

If events described in case B led to the tragedy described, the questions which would almost certainly be raised would concern: the extent to which there should be individual practitioner accountability for delivery of a safe procedure; whether there was a proper degree of delegation of clinical responsibility and supervision to a junior doctor; whether appropriate training had been given; and whether protocols and procedures for drug administration (including safety checks) were in place in the clinical service.

Case C raises issues concerning the adequacy of quality control procedures, whether peer review mechanisms were effective, as well as ways of recognizing and dealing with ill-health problems in a senior member of the medical workforce. In case D, the likely focus of an investigation into the circumstances of the missed diabetic pregnancies would be on the medical management of the case at senior level and the coordination of the clinical team, especially the mechanisms for the sharing of clinical information.

The cases described in Box 17.1 all illustrate serious incidents which are clearly recognizable as such. The reporting of such incidents will usually lead to an investigation into the reasons for their occurrence, the factors which may have contributed and the ways in which a recurrence might be prevented.

Clinical competence and performance

An alternative way in which medical mishaps present is through concern about an individual practitioner's performance. In these cases the problems

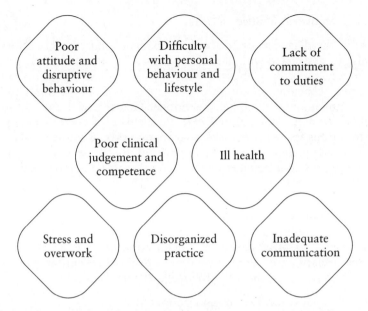

Figure 17.1   Categories of problems which can arise in a doctor's practice, leading to lapses in standards of care

are often not so clear-cut. They can come to light through concerns expressed by a doctor's clinical colleagues, by other hospital staff or through complaints made by patients. Initially there may be no single major incident, but reports may suggest a series of more minor mishaps over a longer period of time. Sometimes reports of concerns about a doctor are even vaguer, with colleagues having a general unease about a doctor's standards of practice. A wide variety of problems of this kind can occur (Figure 17.1). Those which will most obviously raise concerns are issues relating to a doctor's clinical judgement or competence. These have been classified (Leape *et al.* 1993) into errors in diagnosis, errors in treatment, errors in prevention and other types of error (such as poor communication or equipment failure).

While competence issues can arise in any doctor's practice they appear to be particularly associated with doctors in training who are placed in a clinical situation which is beyond their level of experience to deal with, and among older doctors who have not been able to keep up with changes in their field of practice. This latter problem, the deskilling of older doctors, is becoming more pronounced as rapid advances in medical technology and greater specialization within medical practice take place. Such a doctor can find himself or herself as the senior doctor on an out-of-hours on-call rota without the necessary skills to do the job well. This is a situation in which medical mishaps occur.

Attitude, behaviour, lifestyle, ill health

Errors in the diagnosis or treatment of patients and clinical performance can also be associated with ill health, with stress, or with lifestyle problems such as alcohol or drug abuse. Problems with conduct – poor attitude and disruptive behaviour, an abrupt or rude manner, a lack of commitment to duties – are amongst the other practitioner factors which can lead to poor standards of care (Donaldson 1994). Problems in a doctor's practice can lead to serious incidents perhaps after many years of mishaps which have not been adequately dealt with because of the sensitivities involved in confronting a senior member of the medical staff (Donaldson 1994).

Consequences and action

For a hospital or other healthcare organization, the regular occurrence of medical mishaps or a failure to prevent or deal with them can have serious consequences, among them the following (Donaldson 1997):

- dysfunctional clinical teams and poor staff morale;
- hospital developing poor reputation with referring or funding agencies;
- demonstrable reduction in standards of care;
- loss of public confidence in the hospital's services;
- hostile media stories;
- costly litigation.

The resulting poor staff morale and dysfunction among clinical team members can themselves further compromise standards of care. There may be adverse financial consequences in that the hospital is no longer favoured by funding or referring practitioners or agencies. Litigation, too, may be costly.

The ever present media spotlight

Anyone who has managed a hospital at a time when serious problems with medical care have surfaced will recognize the additional pressure which is created by media and public concern. In such circumstances, a problem can quickly become a crisis and the investigation and handling of the incident can run out of control. Healthcare managers often bemoan the media's failure to provide a balanced account of the facts. The media do fulfil an important role in uncovering problems and issues which the public would otherwise never be aware of. Moreover, the reality must be accepted: the media will often seek to develop a storyline which is antagonistic to the leadership of the healthcare organization and to the main protagonists (Donaldson and O'Brien 1995). This will cause further problems because reporting will suggest that the particular incident is but the tip of an iceberg of problems in the hospital. It may imply that similar incidents will happen again and the controversy will encourage a climate of seeking to find someone to blame and enforce accountability. More balanced reporting of events by the media can often be achieved by health-care managers being more open in the initial stages of dealing with an incident and setting out the context.

Cultures of blame and retribution

A culture of blame and seeking to identify individuals to be accountable for the mishaps which have occurred is not healthy. Whether engendered by a media witch-hunt or an employer seeking to act in a punitive way, a climate of fear and apprehension will be created within a hospital in which problems are exposed to hostile analysis. Over time, this is likely to lead to a situation in which problems are not reported or are actively concealed because staff fear retribution.

Doctors working in a hospital may become aware of problems with the standard of care provided within their own service or a colleagues' practice through, for example, clinical observation, peer review or complaints by patients or nursing staff. If they are to do something to help to resolve such a problem and ensure the quality of care in future, then such doctors must be able to share the information with the hospital's senior management. They are less likely to do so if the management style is always to investigate such matters in a way that establishes whether there are grounds for disciplinary action or termination of contracts of employment. Such an approach may be appropriate to some circumstances. So might referral of a problem to the national professional regulatory body (in Britain, the General Medical Council). However, if a punitive, legalistic approach is the norm, then problems will be driven underground. The desirable approach is that management of a hospital creates an environment where errors or lapses in standards of care are reported and investigated more neutrally. An emphasis would be placed on learning lessons for the future and seeking opportunities for remedying skill deficits which have been revealed by training and professional development.

When considering cases involving doctors with problems, the management of the hospital also needs to take particular care in striking an appropriate balance between protecting patients and fairness towards, and the welfare of, the employee. Action must therefore follow some guiding principles (Donaldson 1994), including fully establishing the facts and avoiding precipitate action (things are often not as they first appear); remaining non-judgemental and not being drawn into expressing preliminary opinions; and being aware of the possibility of being manipulated by those with personal agendas.

Individual practitioner errors versus systems failure

Most of the cases and problems used as examples of medical mishaps in this chapter would be viewed traditionally as being due to an individual's

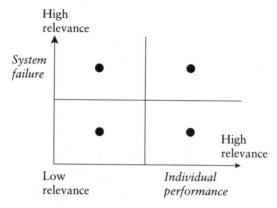

Figure 17.2 Determining accountability when there has been a serious lapse in the standards of medical care provided

behaviour. Thus, for example, case B (Box 17.1) may seem to be a situation resulting entirely from a young doctor making an error which had very serious consequences for a patient. However, analysed for its underlying causes, other factors such as the adequacy of training programmes for such doctors, mechanisms for competence assessment and supervision, protocols for drug administration, checking and fail-safe procedures to prevent the wrong drug dosage (or route of administration) being used would all appear to be relevant. These issues are all features of the organization, not the individual.

If mishaps are to be avoided in the future, accountability for mistakes and lapses in standards of care will have to be viewed as systems failures as well as poor performance on the part of an individual. This distinction is illustrated in Figure 17.2. This is not to say that doctors should not take personal accountability when things go wrong, but management must also take responsibility for problems in the organization which may have created an environment where a mishap is waiting to happen.

Good management of a hospital or other healthcare organization will seek to identify the processes and systems which are vulnerable to error and to strengthen them. It will also seek to create an organizational culture and a care environment in which serious lapses in standards of care are less likely.

Conclusions

Given the volume and complexity of patient care provided by a modern healthcare organization, some serious lapses in standards of care are inevitable. Although these may be small in proportion to the total work undertaken, they can have major repercussions for a patient, a family, the healthcare professionals involved and ultimately for the reputation of the hospital or other organization providing the care.

A well-led, well-managed healthcare organization will seek to minimize such incidents by preventing their occurrence and acting swiftly to limit their adverse consequences when they do occur. The present system is greatly hampered by having no good routinely available data to describe and monitor the occurrence of medical mishaps within a practice, a hospital or the healthcare system as a whole. Good information to enable surveillance is needed, and this requires research.

Many medical mishaps result in clearly defined serious incidents (such as death or harm to a patient). Others may result from problems over time with a doctor's performance (due, for example, to errors of clinical judgement or to misconduct) which may not always lead to a single major incident but to many less visible lapses in standards of care. This group of problems is often difficult to detect and deal with because of the great sensitivity in confronting a doctor with serious problems in his or her practice and the unwillingness of other staff to report them formally.

In the past, health services have tended to seek to identify individuals who are to blame for mishaps and to pursue action based upon personal accountability. However, most serious mishaps will also be caused by problems in the organization itself – systems failures. In the future, it is likely that this will become an important focus for analysis, research and preventive action.

Failing to prevent medical mishaps can have serious adverse consequences for a hospital – in terms of both financial costs and reputation. Public concern is easily aroused in these kinds of situations and the media will often seek to apportion blame. This can make situations much more difficult to handle and is an additional reason for taking an organization-wide view as a route to successful preventive action.

The barriers to organizational change are thus formidable and go beyond the confines of the health service. Societies seem to expect to receive health services which are entirely free of error. Poor quality in some aspects of care – for example, delay or minor discourtesy – is tolerated but failure to diagnose or to treat to a high standard is not. Indeed, media coverage of such incidents reinforces the impression of the public by portraying such occurrences as scandals rather than addressing the complexity of the issues concerned.

At an institutional level, the stumbling blocks to beneficial change in the way medical mishaps are prevented or dealt with include: a lack of experience or confidence of senior management in dealing with such matters; a lack of clear precedents as a basis for management training programmes; and an absence of multidisciplinary teamwork on a wide enough scale to prevent professional isolation.

References

Blain, P. and Donaldson, L.J. (1995) The reporting of inpatient suicides: Identifying the problem, *Public Health*, 109: 293–301.

Department of Health (1994) *Report on Confidential Enquiries into Maternal Deaths in the United Kingdom 1988–1990*. London: HMSO.

Department of Health and Social Security (1969) *Report of the Committee of Inquiry into Allegations of Ill-treatment of Patients and Other Irregularities at the Eley Hospital, Cardiff,* Cmnd 3975. London: HMSO.

Department of Health and Social Security (1989) *Medical Audit,* Working Paper 6. London: HMSO.

Donaldson, L.J. (1994) Doctors with problems in an NHS workforce, *British Medical Journal,* 308: 1277–82.

Donaldson, L.J. (1996) Facing up to the problem of the poorly performing doctor, *Student BMJ,* 4: 276–7.

Donaldson, L.J. (1997) Doctors with problems in a hospital workforce, in P. Lens and G. van der Wal (eds) *Problem Doctors: A Conspiracy of Silence.* Amsterdam: IOS Press.

Donaldson, L.J. and Cavanagh, J. (1992) Clinical complaints and their handling: A time for change? *Quality in Health Care,* 1: 21–5.

Donaldson, L.J. and O'Brien, S.J. (1995) Press coverage of the Cleveland Child Sexual Abuse Enquiry: A source of public enlightenment?, *Journal of Public Health Medicine,* 17: 70–6.

Leape, L., Lawthers, A.G., Brennan, T.A. and Johnson, W.G. (1993) Preventing medical injury, *Quality Review Bulletin,* 19: 144–9.

Lens, P. and van der Wal, G. (1995) An investigation into the malfunctioning of specialists in Dutch hospitals, *International Journal of Risk and Safety in Medicine,* 7: 191–201.

NCEPOD (1996) *The Report of the National Confidential Enquiry into Perioperative Deaths (NCEPOD) 1993/4.* London: NCEPOD.

18 Managing risk and claims: pieces of the puzzle

Susan Polywka and E. Jane Chapman

When we consider the 'pieces of the puzzle' that go to make up a medical mishap, much emphasis must rightly be placed on identifying the varying and complex causes. In this way we hope to inform our strategy for prevention wherever possible. Risks are inherent in the practice of medicine, but risk and claims managers hope to identify the risks more clearly, and to minimize those which are unacceptable. As Vincent and Reason (Chapter 3) and other contributors to this collection have said, an analysis of clinical outcomes should help us to target some of the systemic problems suffered by clinical teams, so that we can move beyond remedial or disciplinary measures directed at individuals, and implement process and system improvements.

However, in focusing upon the management of clinical risk to reduce the incidence of medical mishaps, we should not overlook the importance of how we respond to those medical mishaps which do – and always will – occur. The way in which we attempt to resolve the mishap, and its consequences, is of course important because of our continuing professional, ethical and moral duty to deliver fair treatment to any user of the service. At the very least, no one who has suffered a medical mishap should feel that this has been further compounded by the way in which 'the system' has responded.

Our mode and method of response should be far more than an exercise in 'damage limitation'. What happens after the mishap – the way in which we react; the information which we learn and the way in which we react to it – is, of course, fundamental to any ongoing programme of risk management and the provision of care. Only data provided by a detailed analysis of 'mishaps' and 'near-mishaps' can yield the information required to ensure that we may reliably target our efforts for future prevention.

A mode of response which is immediately defensive and adversarial, apart from failing openly to address the patient's concerns, does not readily yield this required information. Such an approach is directed to attempting to justify what happened, rather than to identifying what might have been done differently, and therefore what might be done to prevent the same problem recurring. Only by adopting a mode of response which attempts openly to address all of the patient's concerns (including an attempt to identify the concerns which may underlie the issues overtly in dispute), informed by an objective, detailed investigation and review of all the surrounding circumstances, can we hope to learn the lessons for application in future procedure and practice.

The mode of response should not just be directed towards achieving a quicker, cheaper and more accessible resolution for the patient – although all of that is important enough. It should also be directed towards achieving a better resolution in itself, delivering a better outcome, in terms of *both* the remedy afforded the patient (which should be comprehensive, addressing – if not necessarily meeting – all of his or her concerns, interests and needs), *and* the constructive feedback derived for future application, to the benefit of future patients.

Arguably, to ensure effective application of the lessons learned – and to ensure clinicians' compliance with any changes in practice proposed in the light of these – *how* we learn the lesson is as important as the fact *that* we have identified the lesson learned. Effective influence upon doctors and other healthcare professionals to change their clinical practice is not easily exerted. A study by Allery *et al.* (1997) found that nearly all changes in doctors' clinical behaviour are due to a combination of factors, including education (in about one-third of cases), as well as organizational factors and contact with other healthcare professionals (which together accounted for nearly half of all the reasons given for change). Clinical audit and guidelines were infrequently mentioned as a reason for change, and indeed clinical audit has been found to be one of the least effective change strategies in continuing medical education (Davis *et al.* 1992).

If this is so, then surely we must ensure that the whole clinical team is involved in first recognizing where there is a need for change, in thinking through the ramifications of its implementation and in determining how best it may be effected. All of these require the involvement of key clinicians in identifying and following up medical mishaps which occur, and their participation in the objective investigation, analysis and interpretation of all the surrounding circumstances.

Recognizing Rosenthal's identification of a medical profession whose members are all surrounded by uncertainty every day and see themselves as vulnerable to accidents, it is not difficult to understand a tacit norm of non-criticism, a conspiracy of tolerance (see Rosenthal, Chapter 10). So while the mode of response should not be directed to requiring clinicians to justify their clinical practice, it would probably be unrealistic – and not necessarily constructive – to require them to criticize their own or others' practice. Rather the process should be aimed, with the benefit of hindsight, at identifying what might be done better next time. This obviously need not necessarily imply that the care delivered fell below acceptable standards, although where it has, this may then be identified sooner, as may be any breach requiring disciplinary, retraining or other action.

A less adversarial, more inquisitorial, model of dispute resolution should facilitate a clearer appreciation of the underlying issues. In addressing the needs and interests of all parties – the patient, his or her advisers, the clinicians and the hospital – beyond the confrontational positions which may be struck, there should be a better chance not only of resolving the dispute but also of preventing any recurrence of similar circumstances which might produce further dispute in the future. Very often, demonstrable attempts to achieve the latter can constitute an important element in achieving the former, as where part of the patient's need is to be reassured that no other patient will suffer in the same way. And the very process of implementing change in response to an 'adverse' incident can highlight to the whole clinical team any potential for conflict inherent in the previous working practice at the time of the mishap.

If our procedure for resolving disputes arising out of medical mishaps can be aimed at uncovering the underlying interests and needs of each party, this should give us the information we need *both* to target remedial and future preventive action, *and* to provide a fully comprehensive response to the injured party (in terms of explanation and, where justified, compensation at an appropriate level). Let us explore this a little further, by reference to the case study below.

Case study

A 27-year-old woman in her first pregnancy was admitted for induction two weeks after her estimated date for delivery, and delivered of a live infant female by forceps (for prolonged second stage). In repairing the episiotomy performed in preparation for instrumental delivery, she was advised by the doctor (an acting senior registrar) that 'you have quite a few stitches and will need laxatives'. He did not follow her up on the postnatal ward, but midwives on that ward discounted any need for laxatives, although she continued to complain of a very sore perineum and passing flatus via her vagina within 24 hours of delivery. As she explained:

I didn't really know what to expect after having a baby.

She recounts:

I got the impression I was regarded as another first-time mother unprepared for the discomfort of childbirth, rather than as someone with a problem which needed to be investigated.

After discharge home, and having continued to complain of a very sore perineum to her community midwife, she was readmitted on day 5, passing flatus and faeces *per vaginum*, running a temperature, feeling very ill and requiring painkillers. On examination, the episiotomy site was found to be broken down, with an obvious anal-rectal fistula. Following immediate referral to a bowel specialist, a defunctioning colostomy was performed. On further examination under anaesthetic, a large and unsutured tear was observed, running from the vagina to the anal sphincter.

The patient underwent secondary repair of the unsutured tear some two weeks later. Some three months thereafter, following encouraging results from physiology studies conducted, closure of the loop colostomy and sphincter was performed successfully. While the patient's physiological prognosis was then generally very good, she did suffer continuing problems with control over passing flatus, affecting diet. Her physical relationship with her partner had been adversely affected, and she, perhaps not unnaturally, felt that:

> I have been robbed of a very precious time with my son which I will never have again.

When should the organization have been alerted to the mother's dissatisfaction?

How might we best achieve the most constructive resolution? Might the mother's concerns have been better appreciated if given the opportunity for expression within a 'birth afterthoughts' programme? Should not the midwives have investigated her physical symptoms as described on the post-natal ward? Might the mother's concerns, expressed on the post-natal ward, have been regarded more formally as a complaint, requiring more formal investigation and response? If not before, then should not her readmission at least have been reported as an 'incident' amounting to an unexpected outcome causing (in this case, actual) harm to the patient (whether in the short or long term)?

In the absence of any such mechanisms – each, in its way, constituting a 'risk management initiative' – we are dependent upon receipt of a solicitor's letter before action to alert us to the need for any concern. This, of course, may not arrive until many months or even years after the mishap, making the collection of factual evidence from key witnesses difficult. In this case, the incident of readmission was picked up within days by the (midwife) perinatal risk coordinator, through *ad hoc* review of the notes.

How should the organization respond?

Gather all the relevant factual information, obtaining statements from all parties. It is essential to obtain a clear chronology of admission, labour, delivery, post-natal follow-up, discharge, readmission, secondary repair, colostomy and sequelae – which may well, of course, identify issues beyond those initially complained of. In this case, a more detailed review of labour revealed additional dissatisfaction with the midwife's attitude to the administration of pain relief, and inadequate explanation of why Syntocinon was given at a certain stage. With regard to the colostomy, it also revealed dissatisfaction with the lack of clarity in communication between the bowel specialist's team and the patient (the patient having understood the physiology studies to reveal a risk of her being faecally incontinent for life, and not initially being told that subsequent admission would be planned for the reversal of the colostomy).

Identify the key clinical acts. In this case, identifying the key clinical acts involved focusing on the performance and repair of the episiotomy and follow-up (this mother had originally been discharged for GP follow-up), but looking back also to management of the labour, specifically the timing of the decision to intervene instrumentally, and reviewing the referral to a bowel surgeon on readmission.

Identify the clinical reasoning. Here we must bear in mind the legal test for negligence, being whether the clinical act (or omission), and the standard to which it was performed, would be accepted as proper by a responsible body of professional peers (the Bolam[1] test), also taking into account recent modifications to this test as a result of the House of Lords judgement in the case of Bolitho,[2] which held that any expert opinion advanced in support of the clinical practice must be 'logically supportable'.

In this case, the doctor stated that he had performed a post-repair vaginal and rectal examination, and that he had noted normal anal sphincter tone and intact anal mucosa.

Review the source of that clinical justification. Whether it be formal guidelines, protocol, or custom and practice, the source of clinical justification needs to be identified in order to determine whether there has been any violation of an accepted practice; and if so, whether that had been calculated as appropriate in the particular circumstances. In this case, the guidelines for performance and repair of episiotomy – to include a vaginal and rectal examination – did appear to have been followed. The error seemed to lie in the doctor's failure to identify (and therefore to suture) another large tear running from the vagina to the anal sphincter. This was compounded by the post-natal ward midwives' failure to investigate further, in response to the problems described by the mother.

Review the clinical systems and infrastructure. Reviewing clinical systems and infrastructure helps to identify the organizational and environmental conditions which might have impacted upon the clinical care given. In this case, the accoucheur would certainly have intended to follow up the mother on the post-natal ward, had he not been due to depart immediately on a period of study leave. We might question whether there were adequate arrangements in place for him to hand that over to a colleague of at least equivalent seniority.

Applying the lessons learned

Five key steps needed to be undertaken in this case in order to apply the lessons learned:

- Address the issues raised in reviewing management of the labour, including attitudes to the administration of pain relief, and how best to explain why and when Syntocinon would be given.
- Review the standards for performance and repair of an episiotomy, and the appropriate follow-up, to ensure consistent treatment of women who have had episiotomies repaired and whether they should be advised to use laxatives; and to ensure that we will at least identify through follow-up, if not at the time of primary repair, any missed tear. It is vital to work with midwives on the post-natal ward, to ensure that we can move beyond merely soothing and placatory noises, and recognize where further clinical assessment might be required.
- Review links with the community, to increase the chance of any missed tear at least being picked up early by the community midwife or GP, if not before.
- Review discharge arrangements, to consider the criteria by which post-natal check-up should be booked with the hospital's perineal clinic, rather than with the GP.
- Review links with the bowel specialist's team, to ensure that the highest levels of communication are sustained with the patient.

Clinical assessment of the 'key clinical act' in this case – failure of assessment prior to the perineal repair and failure in post-repair assessment and follow-up – adjudged this to have fallen below the appropriate standard of care which could rightly be supported by any responsible body of professional peers. Furthermore, it was felt that a causal link could be substantiated between that failure of primary repair, and the damage subsequently suffered by the mother (the colostomy and its sequelae). As such, early monetary settlement was sought and obtained. But, importantly, this was achieved in the context of constructive negotiations already under way to address the other issues raised. Not only did this provide remedies beyond purely pecuniary compensation – to the great satisfaction of the patient and at lesser cost to the hospital trust – it did so in a way which has ensured that the lessons to be learned from one woman's experience are firmly embedded for the future.

In this case, and at her specific request as part of the settlement reached through mediation of this dispute, the mother's statement has been, and continues to be, used as a training tool for midwives and obstetricians in the unit.

Concluding remarks

Where a dispute arises without there having been any advance notice that a 'medical mishap' has occurred – or indeed where there has been no identifiable 'medical mishap' (as where the dispute centres around disappointed expectations) – it is arguably all the more important to communicate a comprehensive explanation which addresses all the patient's concerns. It is also crucial to understand how and why expectations were disappointed; whether the chance of meeting them might be increased in the future; or whether better explanation may be offered prospectively, to shape more realistic expectations in future patients.

Even if a comprehensive response may in some situations constitute a complete refutation of any allegations made, the patient should still be able to feel that full consideration has been given to all of his or her concerns. Where there is any foundation for allegations of clinical negligence, it may still be, as illustrated in the case study above, that the patient's interests and needs are best addressed through a remedy which is not exclusively focused upon an award of monetary damages. Models of 'alternative' dispute resolution, such as mediation, have certainly been shown to yield more flexible outcomes. And if this may be patently attractive to a claimant, then consider that a defendant too might welcome the opportunity to resolve a case which has been 'stuck' for the want of such issues being adequately addressed.

Ultimately, if we are to reduce the incidence of medical mishaps, then all clinical services must adopt prospective, proactive risk management strategies. But, as we know, if we are not prepared to learn the lessons of history, we shall be doomed to repeat its mistakes. Our mode of response to those mishaps which do occur could equip us to learn and apply those lessons to best effect.

Notes

1 *Bolam* v *Friern Hospital Management Committee* [1957] 1 WLR 583.
2 *Bolitho* v *City & Hackney Health Authority*. Judgement given 13 November 1997. Bolitho (Administratrix of the Estate of Bolitho (Deceased)) v City and Hackney Health Authority [1997] 3 Weekly Law Reports, 1151.

References

Allery, L.A., Owen, P. and Robling, M. (1997) Why general practitioners and consultants change their clinical practice: A critical incident study, *British Medical Journal*, 314: 870–4.
Davis, D.A., Thomson, M.A., Oxman, A.D. and Haynes, R.B. (1992) Evidence for the effectiveness of CME: A review of 50 randomized controlled trials, *Journal of the American Medical Association*, 268: 1111–17.

19 | The patient's perspective

Arnold Simanowitz

Unlike in most countries, particularly the USA, the approach of patients in the UK towards medical mishaps has not been driven entirely by litigation or compensation. That is largely to do with the influence of Action for Victims of Medical Accidents, a charity established in 1982 as a result of the public reaction to a television play which portrayed the suffering of a real-life victim. The main aim of AVMA is not just to secure compensation for any patient negligently harmed during medical treatment but, as its first press release stated, to bring medical accidents on to the agenda. What patients found quite unacceptable was the complacency of healthcarers towards victims and the problem of medical accidents itself. Accordingly, AVMA's approach when consulted by someone who believed that there had been a mishap during medical care is to help identify what had gone wrong and to seek some form of accountability, including an apology.

AVMA's experience over the following 14 years, during which it was approached by more than 20,000 patients, confirmed that, more than anything else, what concerned patients who believed that they had suffered a medical accident was the issue of information and accountability. They wanted to know what had happened and why it had happened; they wanted an assurance that a similar accident would not happen to other patients; and they wanted to know that whoever was responsible would be appropriately held to account. Many of those who approached AVMA were also clearly in need of compensation to restore some quality to a life which had been shattered, and that obviously was not an aspect that could be ignored, but it was rarely the thought uppermost in their minds.

Ironically, however, it was in the compensation area that it was easiest to make an immediate impact. For years the doctors' defence organizations had been able to ensure that few malpractice cases were won, whether justified or not. Few, if any, patients' lawyers had the expertise to match that of the defendants' lawyers. AVMA believed that if plaintiffs' lawyers were trained, the lot of at least a proportion of victims would vastly improve.

But it was also immediately apparent that increasing the amount of successful litigation would concentrate the minds of healthcarers and government on the whole issue of medical accidents. In the USA the increasing rate of litigation and the specialization and effectiveness of malpractice lawyers elicited a reaction which was, until fairly recently, solely geared to resisting the claims and reducing the amount of the awards so as to reduce the cost to government, healthcarers and insurers.

That reaction took the form of vilifying malpractice lawyers and dreaming up ever more complex and fanciful schemes, such as unrealistic caps on the amount of damages, to prevent patients securing compensation or at least confining the size of the awards. This occurred whether or not the claim was justified or large sums were required to provide the victim with the necessary support to sustain some quality of life.

In the UK, however, the increase in successful litigation – which certainly put pressure on the government and healthcare providers – was coupled with a campaign, based on the accumulated experience of thousands of patients, for a change in the way victims of medical accidents were dealt with. Indeed, the point which was emphasized repeatedly by all those dealing with complaints on behalf of patients, was that if complaints, whether about conduct which resulted in damage or not, were handled in such a way as to meet the patients' requirements, litigation, and the consequent cost, would be substantially reduced.

The result of this dual approach was twofold. In the first place, the extreme polarization that developed in the USA between patients and doctors – leading, for example, to jokes of the 'support a lawyer, become a doctor' kind – did not occur. Of course doctors, particularly at grassroots level, did become extremely resentful about the hike in their payments to their defence organizations, and there were dark mutterings about defensive medicine. When a number of doctors gathered together to discuss medical accidents, and they believed themselves to be unobserved by the general public, jokes of the above kind were told and drew ecstatic applause.

But in the main, healthcare professionals did begin to consider the implications of medical accidents and review how they might deal with complaints in a more satisfactory manner. At this point, two new players came on the scene, approaching the problem from entirely different angles. On the one hand, the government was keen to reduce the cost of litigation and the payment of damages across the board by the NHS as well as to make some attempt to satisfy the patients' lobby, represented in the main by AVMA. On the other, risk managers saw an opening where they could help hospital trusts, now responsible for their hospitals' finances, to avoid the kinds of accidents that were costing them so dear.

The government appointed a committee under the chairmanship of Professor Wilson to review complaints procedures and come up with something better, more satisfactory to patients and doctors alike – perhaps an impossible demand. The risk managers, in so far as clinical negligence was concerned, concentrated much more on the need to deal with claims in such a way as to minimize the cost to NHS trusts and did not become involved in process issues.

Both these developments are considered by victims of medical accidents and their representatives as positive moves, but neither is seen as having effected a fundamental change in the way the victims of medical accidents are viewed. There are three reasons for this. First, the new complaints procedure, notwithstanding the excellent work done by Professor Wilson and his team, is not proving to be the user-friendly system which was needed to satisfy patients. That is because it is not run or controlled independently of the NHS (the fact that the procedure does not deal with private medicine at all is probably an even more fundamental defect). All those involved with complaints on behalf of patients are finding that in many respects the new system is actually worse than the old (see, for example, Society of CHC Staff 1996; NHS Trust Federation 1997).

Second, while risk management has begun to have an effect in reducing accidents, as well as improving the way some claims are dealt with, it is a process which is dominated by financial implications and approached from the vantage point, quite understandably, of the trust rather than the patient. Finally, the role of the media must not be underestimated. For some years after the establishment of AVMA the media had great sympathy for the plight of victims, and invariably their coverage showed patients' suffering and highlighted the bad behaviour of healthcare professionals and hospitals. That was while reports of medical accidents were something of a novelty. More recently, however, as in so many aspects of life today, the financial implications have become all important, so that coverage has concentrated on the 'greed' and 'unreasonableness' of those who sue the NHS for large sums, on the poor doctors and trusts who have become the victims and on the damage that is being caused to the NHS.

As a result, while it cannot be denied that there has been a considerable improvement in the situation for victims, the four major defects which have always existed and have caused so much hardship have still not been addressed.

The first defect relates to the prevention of accidents. That is the single most important aspect of the plight of patients, as prevention would obviously have a greater effect in improving the situation for patients than anything else. While risk management, clinical audit and the collection of statistics by the two new government bodies, the Clinical Negligence Scheme for Trusts and the NHS Litigation Authority, all purport to be aimed at reducing avoidable accidents, they all approach the problem from the vantage point of the trusts, semi-autonomous bodies competing with each other for patients and money. Only those with absolute faith in the market will believe that such a set-up, with all the secrecy it involves, can achieve the kind of prevention which patients are seeking to make life safer for them in hospitals.

The second major defect is that patients do not have the information on which they can decide where they are likely to get the best treatment and be least at risk. Again, none of the aforementioned procedures has any intention of allowing that information to be disclosed.

The third problem is that when something goes wrong there is still an onus on patients to seek information in a situation where they may not even be aware that a mishap has occurred. There is no obligation on a doctor, or indeed on the trust, to seek out and inform patients of the position and to offer and give them, and their families, all the necessary financial, emotional and medical support which their maltreatment has caused them to require. Finally, there is no accountability to an independent body, which most victims want above all else and which, in fact, would address many of the other problems.

AVMA has been calling for a number of years for an inspectorate which would deal with all these issues. Such an inspectorate would be a statutory body with a board comprising a substantial lay membership with knowledge of the issues. It would be proactive – with inspectors who could investigate wherever medical care is provided, and anyone who provides it, whether in response to a complaint, as a matter of routine or on their own initiative. It would also be reactive – investigating specific matters reported to it by patients or healthcare providers themselves.

The original proposal for the inspectorate included a provision for that body also to deal with compensation claims in place of the courts. This would have been by inquisition rather than by the adversarial procedure, which causes problems in terms of cost, delay and souring of the doctor–patient relationship (see Mulcahy, Chapter 11). It may be, however, that initially the inspectorate should concern itself simply with standards and accountability. Interfering with the legal process might be premature because, for all its defects, it does provide patients with some redress. While healthcare providers continue to act in the defensive way they do, the forensic skills of specialist lawyers are essential. The inspectorate could have a major influence in changing these attitudes, and once this was achieved other methods for providing compensation could be considered.

The proposal for an inspectorate was at first treated with hostility by the government and health providers. However, it is gradually receiving support from those who recognize that it could be of benefit to patients and providers alike. Indeed, the government now proposes to monitor, ensure and improve clinical quality (NHS Executive, 1998). It was suggested that this would be through a statutory body which would exist at arm's length from government, with patient representatives on its governing body. These proposals recognize the need for something approaching an inspectorate.

Concluding remarks

Notwithstanding the advances that have been made in the situation of victims of medical accidents, much remains to be done before patients will be sufficiently reassured that their grievances are being honestly addressed and that an atmosphere has been created which will help to reduce unnecessary litigation and enable the whole issue of mishaps to be dealt with in a sensible way.

Healthcare providers must be educated to accept that when something goes wrong they have a professional duty, as part of the caring process, to seek out and explain to patients and their families exactly what their understanding is of what has happened and why (see Polywka and Chapman, Chapter 18).

Some form of independent body must be established which will be able to investigate any incident, as well as take steps to ensure that the safety of patients is paramount. Once accountability has been satisfactorily addressed, a better procedure must be found for compensating those patients who have had something go wrong. These steps are achievable and will lead not only to a better situation for patients and healthcare providers, but also to the saving of considerable costs to the NHS.

References

NHS Executive (1998) A first class service: Quality in the new NHS. Leeds: NHSE.

NHS Trust Federation (1997) *Working Hard to Please*. London: NHS Trust Federation.

Society of CHC Staff (1996) *Are You Being Heard? A Six Month Review of the New NHS Complaints Procedures*. Birmingham: Society of CHC Staff.

20 | Community health councils: helping patients through the complaints procedure

Gary Fereday

Helping patients through the NHS complaints procedure is only one aspect of the remit of community health councils (CHCs). Yet it is an integral part of their work and it is often through the complaints process that people first become aware of their local CHC. In recent years there has been an increasing interest in patient evaluations of the quality of care, but complaints and claims remain two of the few user-instigated modes of calling medical professionals to account. As Nicol suggests elsewhere in this collection (see Chapter 21) they should be valued as providing evidence of medical mishaps which might not otherwise be available.

CHCs have an important part to play in this process. Operating with only a handful of paid staff for each CHC (two or three full-time equivalents, in Wales often even less) and with members offering their time for no remuneration, CHCs have provided an extremely low-cost health service 'watchdog' since 1974. However, their development has been chequered and CHCs are not without their critics. But as the statutory representative of their communities, CHCs have proved resilient and are one of the few bodies within the NHS that are still recognizable following the reforms of the NHS during the 1980s and 1990s.

Community health councils as the local voice of patients

Founded in 1974 following a series of scandals involving long-stay hospitals, CHCs were seen as a link between the NHS and the community that they served, separating the management of service provision from the representation of patient and community interests. 'Consumerism' was a rising force and the need to give voluntary groups a voice within CHCs was acknowledged by allowing voluntary bodies to elect representatives. At the same time it was considered important that there was more local authority input into the NHS; hence local authority representatives also made up the membership of the newly created CHCs (Hogg 1996).

There are 207 CHCs in England and Wales (16 health councils in Scotland and four health and social services councils in Northern Ireland perform similar functions to CHCs). Each CHC has around 16 to 30 members. Half are local authority nominees, while a third are elected by the local voluntary sector and a sixth appointed by the Secretary of State for Health (or the Secretary of State for Wales in the case of Welsh CHCs). CHCs are funded from a national budget held by the National Health Service Executive (NHSE), but are independent of the NHS management structure, each other and the Association of Community Health Councils for England and Wales (ACHCEW).

Health authorities are required to consult formally with CHCs on substantial variations in service provision, provide information required by the CHC in carrying out its public duties and arrange a meeting between the authority and the CHC members once a year.

The main roles performed by CHCs include:

- monitoring local service delivery (CHCs are able to inspect NHS premises, but not premises of general practitioners, dental surgeries and other non-NHS facilities, unless it has been written into the service provider's contract);
- representing the public and providing their communities' views during consultative exercises;
- offering advice and assistance to individuals (this usually includes offering advice and assistance when individuals wish to complain, although this is not an explicit statutory requirement).

ACHCEW: the national forum for CHCs

ACHCEW was set up in 1977 under provisions of the NHS (Reorganisation) Act 1977 to provide a forum for member CHCs, to provide information and advisory services to CHCs and to represent the user of health services at a national level. CHCs are not obliged to be members of ACHCEW but the overwhelming majority are. CHCs pay an annual subscription based on their own annual budgets and ACHCEW's Annual General Meeting decides national CHC policy. ACHCEW's statutory duties are to advise CHCs with respect to the performance of their functions, assist CHCs in the performance of their functions and represent those interests in the health service which CHCs are bound to represent.

Each year ACHCEW publishes ten newsletters, *Community Health Council News*, and ten briefing papers, *Health Perspectives*, which examine emerging themes and issues within the health service. Also published are occasional papers, *Health News Briefings*, which are often based on surveys of member CHCs. ACHCEW also hosts seminars and conferences and provides a wide range of training courses for CHC members.

CHCs and medical mishaps

CHCs deal regularly with patients (or relatives of patients) who have suffered medical mishaps. These mishaps can range from relatively minor problems that can be corrected to errors that cause the death of patients.

Recent years have witnessed a rise in medical audit and the development of clinical protocols. CHCs broadly welcome their development as a step towards the reduction of medical mishaps. However, some concerns have been raised about the wariness with which doctors approach the issue of involving users in the audit process and the secrecy surrounding both the audit process and the information gathered (Joule 1992). CHCs would like to see this secrecy removed and an increase in genuine involvement of consumers in the audit process and the setting up of protocols.

Despite increased use of clinical protocols, things still go wrong and patients or relatives of patients turn to their local CHC for help. However, while CHCs are able to advise on the NHS complaints procedure, they are not able to offer legal advice to those who wish to pursue their case through the courts in order to seek financial compensation. If complainants wish to pursue a legal action, the CHC will often refer them to AVMA, an organization able to offer assistance to people who are seeking compensation (see Simanowitz, Chapter 19).

The complaints procedure guidelines state that 'the complaints procedure should cease if the complainant explicitly indicates an intention to take legal action in respect of the complaint' (NHS Executive 1996: 16). However, complainants are entitled to take legal action if they so wish and no one should be excluded from the complaints procedure because they may consider seeking legal redress. Similarly, the complaints system must not be seen as a means of excluding people who intend to sue.

CHCs and the National Health Service complaints system

CHCs have a unique contribution to make in the debate about complaints in the NHS. ACHCEW estimates that in 1995 the total number of complaints handled by CHCs was in the region of 20,000 (ACHCEW 1996a). Extrapolation of complaints data for 1995 found that women are more likely to complain than men (either about their own treatment or the treatment of someone they are representing). Complainants are also more likely to be over 55 years of age, although this could be accounted for by the comparatively high levels of contact with the health service among this age group. There is a relatively high level of non-white complainants seen by CHCs, possibly as a result of initiatives by some CHCs to make contact with black and minority ethnic groups.

Most complaints relate to hospital care, despite the fact that the majority of contacts with the NHS occur within the community. Inappropriate care and diagnosis are the two most common causes for complaint both in the hospital and community services and in family health services (ACHCEW 1996a). While not all CHCs follow the same procedure in helping complainants, it is a role that is now seen by most as being part of their work, with some CHCs employing a dedicated complaints officer.

A new NHS complaints procedure was introduced in April 1996 (see Allsop and Mulcahy, Chapter 9). CHCs generally saw the old system as being complex (for both patients and staff) and failing to meet the needs of complainants. In the wake of the reforms ACHCEW surveyed its member CHCs to see if an early assessment of the new system could be made (ACHCEW 1997). The survey revealed that there is no clear consensus as to whether CHCs regard the new system as better or worse than the old one. However, two major findings are of particular relevance to medical mishaps. First, the survey found that the new procedures set up barriers to complaining which mean that vital information about possible medical mishaps is being lost. Second, the need for fair and impartial investigation of complaints is not being taken seriously by purchasers and providers, with the result that service users' regulatory impact is being undermined.

It is at the 'local resolution' stage in the new procedure that many CHCs see problems. Local resolution requires complainants to return to the place where the incident they complained about took place. Many feel that patients are deterred from making a complaint when they realize that they will have to face the very person about whom they are complaining. This is particularly problematic in primary care where the relationship between the patient and practitioner is often quite personal, and some patients fear being 'struck off' their GP's list if they complain (ACHCEW 1997).

CHCs would like the local resolution procedures of primary care practitioners to be monitored. At present there is no requirement for such practitioners to provide the NHSE with detailed quarterly reports on complaints. Without proper monitoring and evaluation, CHCs cannot be sure whether local resolution is working or whether patients are being deterred from taking their complaint on to the next stage.

Some CHCs have also expressed their concern that convenors are appointed by the relevant trust or health authority. This has led some to question the independence of the convenor who has to make a decision about whether to set up an independent review as the next stage if local resolution is unsuccessful. CHCs have become aware of complainants on more than one occasion being asked to go back again to local resolution. An underlying fear is that this is because independent reviews are costly and time-consuming exercises (ACHCEW 1997).

Moving the complaints procedure on:
The Patients' Agenda

In November 1996 ACHCEW launched its alternative to the Patient's Charter (Department of Health 1995). *The Patients' Agenda* (ACHCEW 1996b) sets out a whole series of rights not included in the Patient's Charter. Drawn up in consultation with CHCs and other bodies, it highlights areas where, at present, patients' rights are poor or non-existent. It deals with many areas of NHS care, including the complaints procedure.

The Patients' Agenda calls for a right for patients who are unhappy with the initial response to their complaint to put it to a genuinely independent panel (ACHCEW 1996b). This would avoid the need for a convenor (appointed by the trust or health authority) to decide whether to convene such a panel. ACHCEW believes that this independent panel would mean that not only would complainants be more reassured of a fair hearing, but also the number of referrals to the NHS Ombudsman would be cut.

The Patients' Agenda also calls for a right for patients to make a complaint about any aspect of care or treatment without the constraint of an imposed time limit (ACHCEW 1996b). The new complaints procedure requires the complaint to be made within six months of the event or within six months of the problem being discovered. ACHCEW believes that these time restraints are unhelpful as some patients may be too ill to complain or may be recovering from a traumatic event. Indeed many patients spend a considerable period reaching a decision to complain only to find that they have left it too late (ACHCEW 1996b).

NHS complaints: the future

Despite medical audit and clinical protocols, medical mishaps inevitably will continue to happen. When things go wrong people need to be sure that their concerns and complaints will be taken seriously and dealt with properly. Furthermore, people must also be allowed to take legal action if they feel that is necessary.

ACHCEW believes that the main needs of patients who make complaints are:

- to be told the truth about what happened;
- to understand why it happened;
- to know what action is to be taken to ensure it will not happen to others.

To ensure that complainants' needs are met, any complaints system must have the full confidence of those needing to use it. For full and proper assessment of the complaints system it must be properly monitored. CHCs and their national body, ACHCEW, will be suggesting improvements while continuing in their role of advising the public when things go wrong in the NHS.

References

ACHCEW (1996a) *Health News Briefing: An Analysis of the Complaints Work of CHCs*. London: Association of Community Health Councils for England and Wales.

ACHCEW (1996b) *The Patients' Agenda*. London: Association of Community Health Councils for England and Wales.

ACHCEW (1997) *Annual Report 1996/97*. London: Association of Community Health Councils for England and Wales.

Department of Health (1995) *The Patient's Charter and You*. London: Department of Health.

Hogg, C. (1996) *The Public and the NHS*. London: Association of Community Health Councils for England and Wales.

Joule, N. (1992) *User Involvement in Medical Audit*. London: Greater London Association of Community Health Councils.

NHS Executive (1996) *Complaints. Listening . . . Acting . . . Improving; Guidance on Implementation of the NHS Complaints Procedure*. Leeds: NHSE.

21 | The right to redress: complaints and principles of grievance procedures

Nicholas Nicol

Introduction

Everyone has a right to make a complaint or legal claim. If a person is wronged by someone else and suffers as a result, then he or she should be able to obtain some form of redress. This is the most basic principle of legal systems everywhere and applies to patients as much as anyone else. Indeed, some may argue that there is an even greater imperative in an area such as health, where a 'loss' can be devastating and the knowledge gap between patient and doctor considerable.

The legal system in England has grown over many centuries with the right to redress through the courts at its heart. The award of damages compensates the individual who has been wronged. It also provides an incentive for others not to commit similar wrongs, although the aim is to compensate, not to punish (Galanter 1983). In addition, recent years have witnessed increasing attention being given to providing redress outside the legal system, which is seen as inaccessible, expensive and limited (see, for example, Citizen's Charter Complaints Task Force 1993; Lord Chancellor's Department 1996).

There are three overlapping forces which have led to the growth of these grievance procedures and interest in them – consumer activism, management efficiency drives and the development of 'administrative' law. The principles which should govern any good grievance procedure have been forged by a combination of all three, but it is the law which provides the framework. This framework consists of the principles developed by the courts in administrative law, but based on fundamental notions of what is fair, just and equitable. They aim to provide minimum guarantees of fair treatment for those who come into contact with state and state-related organizations. If those principles are breached in grievance procedures which exist outside the courts, so that fair treatment is denied, the courts can provide a remedy through a process known as judicial review. This chapter looks at those principles.

Existing procedures

A number of procedures already exist outside the courts for taking up grievances against providers of medical services. If an NHS patient has a complaint about primary or secondary care, he or she may complain to the service provider and, if not satisfied with the response, to a convenor of an independent review panel. After that, if still dissatisfied, he or she may also go to an ombudsman called the Health Service Commissioner (HSC), if the complaint reveals a failure to provide a service, failure of that service or injustice or hardship in consequence of maladministration. Complaints about professional conduct may be made to the General Medical Council for doctors or the United Kingdom Central Council for nurses. Alternatively, complaints that general practitioners have not fulfilled the terms of their contract with the NHS can be referred by health authorities to medical services committees, which in turn are overseen by the Council on Tribunals.

The main aims are to provide redress where appropriate and to establish rules and principles. However, grievance procedures may have additional or different aims. For example, one of the objectives of the NHS complaints procedure is to provide feedback to management to improve service quality, while the professional disciplinary procedures were set up to maintain professional standards. Complaints are often seen by medical staff as threats or nuisances. However, quite apart from the justification that everyone should have the right of redress, they also play a role, through their contribution to quality and risk management, which it is in the interests of both users and providers of medical services to promote (Drummond and Morgan 1988; Kadzome and Coals 1992).

Process and outcomes

When people have grievances and consider pursuing a complaint, it is the outcome which concerns them – what redress there will be. This applies across the whole spectrum of complainants, from those just wanting an apology or an explanation of what happened to those who want substantial monetary compensation. This even applies to those who do not pursue a complaint: the most common reason given by potential complainants for not complaining is that it would make no difference – that is, the outcome is not worth the expenditure of effort it would take to achieve it (NHS Executive 1994). However, the principles of administrative law referred to above are actually mostly concerned with process. The idea behind the emphasis on procedures is that more just outcomes will flow from a procedure which is itself fair.

That is not to say that law and good practice are not concerned with outcomes at all. English law has developed the concept of unreasonableness or irrationality. This tests whether a decision should not be allowed to stand on the basis that it is so unreasonable that no reasonable person or authority could have reached it.[1] Obviously, this concept is vague and may be difficult to apply, but it is aimed at decisions which common sense would regard as absurd or perverse. The test is a very narrow one because the courts have always been wary of treading on areas they regard as being the province of those whose job it is to run public services such as the NHS.

Whether an outcome satisfies the test of reasonableness can depend on what kind of redress is provided to a complainant. Complaints procedures have advantages over courts, such as flexibility and relative informality, which should be reflected in the available remedies. These can include 'an apology, an explanation, remedial action, a commitment to review policies and processes to avoid the same thing happening again, compensation in kind and financial compensation' (National Consumer Council 1996).

There is also a point at which outcomes and the procedure by which they are reached interact and overlap. A common complaint against grievance procedures is that they take too long. Delay is a perennial problem and probably the largest single cause of work for the UK's various ombudsmen, such as the HSC. Justice delayed is not always justice denied, but if the delay is excessive then it will be. A good complaints procedure will have realistic targets for the time in which each stage is to be completed.

Natural justice

The thinking behind the principles of administrative law is fairly simple. The best decisions are made rationally. They can only be rational if they are based on a fair and impartial assessment of the evidence. These ideas have led the courts to develop the principles of natural justice. It is expected that all grievance procedures should, as far as is practical and efficient, comply with these standards. There are two main strands to the principles of natural justice, that a person may not be a judge in his or her own cause and that a person's defence must be fairly heard (Wade and Forsyth 1994). The first of these two principles essentially means that whoever hears and decides on a grievance should be as impartial as possible (see Donaldson and Cavanagh 1992). In many smaller organizations it will be difficult to find someone who can hear a grievance who is also distant from the cause of that grievance. This is, for instance, the case in many practice-based complaints procedures in general practitioners' surgeries, although research suggests that complaints about GPs are increasingly being handled by practice managers (Mulcahy *et al.* 1996). One of the dilemmas posed by the Wilson Report on NHS complaints systems was the need to balance impartiality with informal and conciliatory resolution of complaints at service level (NHS Executive 1994). These problems can be ameliorated by incorporating an appeal stage, like the new system of independent review panels, at which point someone who is not only impartial but also seen to be independent can be brought in.

The second principle of natural justice is that decisions should not be reached without hearing what the people concerned have to say. The Wilson Committee reiterates the importance of this principle by the emphasis it puts on staff being able to respond to complaints (NHS Executive 1994). Without giving the relevant people this opportunity, it would normally be impossible for decision-makers to claim that their decision was made from all the available evidence. If not based on all the evidence, the decision will be seen as irrational. Again, this concept seems to be common sense, but without a grievance procedure there is no route by which potential complainants can have their say.

Even the existence of a grievance procedure does not guarantee that a complainant will be heard. To ensure that happens, the procedure must also be accessible. This in turn depends on the attitude of those who run the procedure and on the quality and quantity of information available to the complainant. In practice, many people do not use grievance procedures because they do not know about them or find them intimidating (Mulcahy and Tritter 1994). Front-line staff have also been observed to set up unnecessary barriers such as by being rude, demanding that complaints be put in writing before they will be accepted and using jargon rather than plain language. It follows from this that accessibility requires any grievance procedure to be adequately publicized and for staff to be properly trained in how to respond to and deal with complainants.

A grievance procedure may also not be accessible to some complainants without help, such as those whose first language is not English or who have learning difficulties. A complainant cannot be said to have been heard if he or she cannot understand how to complain. A good grievance procedure will provide for friends, family, advocates such as community health councils and solicitors and interpreters to play their part.

The principles examined so far all look to the form of a grievance procedure. However, form can never entirely provide for proper substance. Attitude is equally important. Form for form's sake is not acceptable – for example, the right to be heard equally involves the right to be listened to so that a sham hearing will not comply with the principles of natural justice. The problem in practice is that complaints are seen in a negative light. The most common reaction to a complaint is still defensive, often based on the belief that the complainant 'wants blood' or that an adverse finding means that someone will be punished (Allsop 1994; Lloyd-Bostock and Mulcahy 1994; Mulcahy 1996). In fact, it is more common for a complainant to want nothing more than an apology or explanation and to prevent the same thing happening to someone else. Many complaints result from flawed policies and procedures rather than individual fault. Essentially, complaints should not be viewed as examples of wrong-doing but as opportunities to identify what can be done to improve things; as chances to repair rather than as witch-hunts.

Handling complaints

Some people still regard a complaint as akin to or the first step towards litigation. In fact, a complaint handled well is litigation avoided (NHS Executive 1994). A defensive reaction can turn a complainant looking for modest redress in the form of a mere apology into a litigant going to court where the only available remedy is financial compensation. This means that grievances should be dealt with at the earliest opportunity, before they become more serious and the position of those involved becomes entrenched. Normally, this will mean that the complaint will be dealt with at the same point of contact as that from which it arose (as is encouraged by the current NHS complaints procedure). Of course sometimes by its very nature this will not be possible, for instance where the relationship between the parties has broken down and cannot be repaired without the intervention of a third party. Also, some potential complainants will simply find it too intimidating to take their grievance back to its apparent cause. However, a good grievance procedure will first provide that there is an informal stage where those immediately involved in the complaint try to sort it out 'on the spot'.

On the other hand, the informal stage should be followed by a more formal stage and an appeals procedure. Although complaints are best dealt with at the informal stage, it is not appropriate for all. Complaints which are strait-jacketed into the wrong procedure will only frustrate those involved. This would only lead back to the problem of entrenched positions and deteriorating relationships. For example, sometimes the issues arising from a grievance can only be settled by an authoritative declaration of principle, which is of course what a court does. Complaints should proceed as quickly as possible to the point where they can be satisfactorily dealt with and that will sometimes mean the later stages of a grievance procedure, such as the appellate stage or referral to outside agencies such as an ombudsman or the courts. Further, complainants should always be kept informed that the option of such later stages exists.

Conclusion

The principles of a grievance procedure can be simply stated as access, simplicity and speed, fairness, attitude, information and redress (Citizen's Charter Complaints Task Force 1995). Perhaps the principal motivation for anyone in public service to try to make these principles work in practice is that the service is there for the user and the user should get the best possible service. Where a user has suffered a medical mishap, he or she has a right to an explanation and other remedies. But even where any complaint is unsubstantiated after investigation, the user has a right to be taken seriously and to a fair hearing. A good grievance procedure can make equally good sense for the NHS. It can identify problems and so provide an opportunity to improve the service. It can preserve relationships and avoid the escalation of disputes. The principles of administrative law are grounded in the same imperatives and it makes sense for all involved to try to make them work.

Note

1 *Associated Provincial Picture Houses Ltd* v *Wednesbury Corporation* [1948] 1 KB 23.

References

Allsop, J. (1994) Two sides to every story: Complainants' and doctors' perspectives in disputes about medical care in a general practice setting, *Law and Policy*. 16(2): 149–84.

Citizen's Charter Complaints Task Force (1993) *Effective Complaint Handling: Principles and Checklist*. London: HMSO.

Citizen's Charter Complaints Task Force (1995) *Putting Things Right: Main Report*. London: HMSO.

Donaldson, L. and Cavanagh, J. (1992) Clinical complaints and their handling: A time for change?, *Quality in Health Care*, 1(1): 21–5.

Drummond, M. and Morgan, J. (1988) *Learning from Complaints. Members Information Pamphlet No. 6*. Birmingham: National Association of Health Authorities.

Galanter, M. (1983) The radiating effects of the courts, in K. Boyum and L. Mather (eds) *Empirical Theories about Courts*. New York: Longman.

Kadzome, A. and Coals, J. (1992) Complaints against doctors in an accident and emergency department: A ten year analysis, *Archives of Emergency Medicine*, 9: 134–42.

Lloyd-Bostock, S. and Mulcahy, L. (1994) The social psychology of making and responding to hospital complaints: An account model of complaint processes, *Law and Policy*, 16(2): 123–47.

Lord Chancellor's Department (1996) *Access to Justice*. London: HMSO.

Mulcahy, L. (1996) From fear to fraternity: Doctors' construction of accounts of complaints, *Journal of Social Welfare and Family Law*, 18(4): 397–418.

Mulcahy, L. and Tritter, J. (1994) Hidden depths, *Health Services Journal*, July, 24–6.

Mulcahy, L., Allsop, J. and Shirley, C. (1996) *Different Voices: A Study of Complaints to Family Health Service Authorities*, Social Science Research Papers

Series. London: School of Education, Politics and Social Sciences, South Bank University.

National Consumer Council (1996) *Putting It Right for Consumers*. London: National Consumer Council.

NHS Executive (1994) *Being Heard: The Report of the Review Committee on NHS Complaints Procedures* (Chair: Professor Alan Wilson). London: HMSO.

Wade, W. and Forsyth, C. (1994) *Administrative Law*, 7th ed. Oxford: Clarendon Press.

22 | The price of deceit: the reflections of an advocate

Jean Robinson

In the benevolent self-evaluation by the liar of the lies he might tell, certain kinds of disadvantage and harm are almost always overlooked – the harm that lying does to the liars themselves and the harm done to the general level of trust and social cooperation. Both are cumulative: both are hard to reverse.

(Bok 1978: 24)

'I did not think a doctor would lie, Mrs Robinson'. Bewildered and distressed people used the same phrase over and over again when they sat in our tiny attic office at the Patients Association (PA) in Gray's Inn Road, London. I had become chair of the PA in 1973, taking over from its founder, Helen Hodgson, and was coping with up to 100 complaints and enquiries a week, with one superb paid officer and a few volunteers. In those days there were no community health councils and no other source of independent advice for patients.

People who came to the PA were remarkably humble and forgiving, even in the face of appalling disasters. They virtually never mentioned suing, and were intimidated by the mere thought of approaching a lawyer. In any case, there were few solicitors with experience of medical negligence – except those who worked for the doctors' defence societies – and patients had no idea how to locate them. They just tried desperately to find out the truth. As one bereaved husband, whose wife had died in childbirth after an anaesthetic accident, remarked: 'I do not want money. I just want peace of mind'.

All of us who did the work were radicalized by it. What impressed me was not just the extent of medical disasters, but also the profound additional damage inflicted when patients and the bereaved failed to get answers and were met with a stone wall of silence or outright lies. Families were stuck like flies in amber, reliving and repeatedly describing the incidents they wanted someone to believe. I still remember their voices, and the phrases they used. 'She died in the ward while they were dishing up shepherd's pie around her', said a mother who repeatedly described her child's death. In a paper on morbid grief, a psychiatrist wrote of helping bereaved relatives who were critical of medical care by helping them to write to the doctors concerned, though the letters were never sent (Dawson 1981). We helped people to write letters which were sent.

There is an added dimension to suffering when a death or injury is seen as not only avoidable but also apparently inflicted by the carelessness of those who are expected to care. The special needs of people so affected are seldom recognized or acknowledged. Few people in the health service wanted to listen to them or help them. At best they were an embarrassment, at worst a threat. The problem was trivialized and held at bay by much talk of 'frivolous complaints'. Like the henpecked husband accused of frivolity in a TV sitcom, I can only say that in 30 years of complaints work 'I never saw a single frivol'.

Although we may criticize the behaviour of doctors, the ethical standards of NHS administrators have hardly been discussed. They are under no threat of being struck off a professional register, like the doctor, nurse or midwife. It was the officials who built and maintained the stone wall which sheltered the truly incompetent. A common response in their letters was that something could not have happened because it is contrary to their usual practice. Later, their sophistication increased as they tried to forestall HSC investigations by constructing a web of pseudo-apologies such as assertions that they were sorry if the patient *felt* that they had cause for dissatisfaction (Association for Improvements in the Maternity Services 1992; Donaldson and Cavanagh 1992). It was such responses which eventually drove complainants into the arms of lawyers (Robinson 1987). The culture of the institution was as defensive as the culture of the medical profession.

What we, and other consumer organizations, saw was simply a cross-section of ordinary people, who usually went out of their way to praise aspects of their care which had been good. Remarkably few were in any way difficult to deal with, though some were increasingly affected by anger and frustration, and a few became so embittered and enmeshed in their pursuit of justice they eventually thought of little else. We tried repeatedly to pursue the NHS complaints procedure so that complainants could get some measure of emotional resolution, begin to grieve and then move on in their lives, but the success rate was pitiful. Complainants felt that if they could 'make sure it didn't happen to someone else' they would have achieved something.

At the PA I was able to construct a crude mental map of general practitioner quality based not just on the number but also on the type of complaints which occurred. There was no doubt that the passivity of patients contributed to poor-quality care, but we also had a system which exacerbated the power imbalance. In theory patients could change doctors, but in fact many were captive. Because patients had to register with one GP, and stayed with him or her, they had no means of comparison. If their doctor never measured blood pressure or did a vaginal examination, they thought that was the norm. Across the Channel French patients, who could go to any doctor and claim reimbursement from the state, had opportunities to shop around, compare and learn.

Recent reforms of the NHS complaints procedure

Under the new NHS complaints procedure, the patient's right to obtain a tribunal hearing (Medical Service Committee) for a GP complaint, when dissatisfied with service-level handling of the grievance, has now disappeared. Under the previous system complainants had a right to see the doctor's reply, to be present at the entire proceedings and hear the replies to questions, and to a formal report and finding at the end. It was the only piece of real power patients ever had over doctors in the NHS, although they were ill informed as to how to use it. Medical defence societies asked the Wilson Committee for the removal of this right, and they succeeded. Now the formal separation of complaints from any disciplinary procedures, so that patients and relatives have no rights or involvement, means that accountability to them has been lost. Yet in serious and fatal cases complainants see accountability as an essential component of justice, and failure to get it will prevent them from getting on with their lives. Complainants are seldom vindictive, but sometimes disciplinary action is appropriate.

With the new post-Wilson complaints procedure, the government is gambling that a more conciliatory complaints procedure – which often amounts to 'conciliation' whether the complainant wants it or not – will encourage less defensiveness, more honesty and better remedial action on complaints. I am not yet convinced. The problem is that there is no independent investigation of the facts before the conciliator moves in, so that underlying causes can be identified. The defensive culture is still in place, and crucial documents are still altered or disappear. Simply soothing and smoothing complainants without dealing with their underlying need for unbiased information, justice and accountability is not the answer.

One of my main concerns is that for GP complaints, with responsibility now handed over to the doctors to investigate complaints about themselves, the health authority can no longer collect data on frequency or severity of complaints – an essential part of monitoring quality and reducing medical injuries. Nor will underlying causes of errors be identified and remedied. In a medical magazine one GP smugly described how he had satisfied patients by apologizing for poor care given by locums. He showed no concern as to what the locum might now be doing elsewhere.

My complaints work at the PA demonstrated that when, occasionally, there was an open and constructive response, the improvement in the complainant's experience could be dramatic. I saw one widow who looked a different woman after a senior cardiologist frankly apologized and showed he had taken action to prevent a repetition of the serious mistake, made by one of his juniors, which had contributed to her husband's premature death. He enclosed a copy of the memo which he had sent to everyone in that department. She told me she had had her first night of sleep for months.

Pursuit of complaints through the courts

When some complainants, by now embittered and despairing, finally turned to the law, they went to their local high street solicitor who had no expertise in the field, and their efforts almost invariably ended in failure. Many articles have appeared in the medical and lay press about the 'dreadful' increase in medical negligence litigation, but none of them mentions that the increase came from a base line so low as to represent a national scandal. In the end complainants felt legal action was the only way to have their voice heard and protect others. Above all, the bereaved wanted some recognition of the worth of the life of the person who had been lost.

It was not until Action for Victims of Medical Accidents was founded in 1982 that expert legal advice gradually became more widely available to complainants. AVMA was created in response to a desperate need from patients who primarily wanted not money, but justice. It was the failure of the complaints system, and the failure of professionals to respond to reasonable requests for the truth, an apology if warranted and action to prevent further disasters, which led to the demand for lawyers' services. Even now, many litigants want their 'day in court' more than money, and are distressed to find they are unlikely to get it.

Doctors' responses to complaints and claims

Many complainants only suspected that they had had negligent care because of changes in staff behaviour. They were avoided, treated coldly, kept at arm's length – or worse. One young woman, only a few hours after a stillbirth, was shocked when a senior midwife marched into her room and said: 'You had better keep quiet. You could ruin that young doctor's career' (Beech 1997).

In those days, patients who dared to complain were often said by consultants to be 'impertinent' – a term which tells us more about those who use it than those of whom it is used. The words have changed, but pejorative labelling of complainants is still common. Complainants have been said to be 'neurotic', 'uncooperative', 'non-compliant', 'dirty' or 'difficult'. The current favourite is 'manipulative'. Dissatisfaction with care was likely to become a 'personality disorder'. If the patient was not blamed, the behaviour of the relative or friends was criticized. I was surprised at how often complainants were said to have 'defaulted' from clinic appointments – appointments which they insisted they had never been sent. It also became fashionable for administrators glibly to dismiss bereaved complainants, without investigation, as suffering the 'typical guilt syndrome of bereavement'. Where is the law that says only patients with perfect relatives are at risk of medical injury?

Now that patients can obtain their notes under the Access to Health Records Act, the allegations (sometimes defamatory) are less likely to appear so overtly in the notes, but circulate widely in the hospital and community network. Since the allegations are not directly relayed to the complainants, they are unable to challenge them, but nevertheless they affect the attitudes of those investigating a complaint.

It is often said that it is chiefly fear of litigation and complaints which prevents doctors and other healthcare professionals from being open and truthful. In my experience that is only a partial explanation. It is not the legal process or the courts, but any examination of the doctor's competence and threat to his reputation that must be resisted. They are not only his stock in trade, but by now are the core of his being. The threat is deep, and devastating. The essential emotional need to safeguard that core will cause some doctors to defend their practice even against overwhelming evidence that they need help or extra training.

After medical service committees, I would tell patients that however calm he or she seemed, the doctor would certainly be affected, but they saw only the cool professional exterior. But if the doctor was upset, was it just because of having to cope with a complaint or was it genuine remorse for providing unsatisfactory care? There was a moral difference, and it mattered. The BMA has gained effective publicity on the extreme stress suffered by doctors who are sued or complained about. However, they speak only about how awful it is to be the subject of a complaint and the doctor's need for protection, not the question of guilt and regret when a genuine error has been made.

When dealing with stillbirth cases at the Association for Improvement in the Maternity Service, I am struck by how much parents have been helped when staff have shown their own distress at the loss of a baby. 'I could tell they really cared'. 'The young doctor had tears in her eyes'. I was shocked to see in a study of obstetric complaints that a lawyer had advised the hospital that a registrar should not be present at a meeting with bereaved parents because 'his being upset might be interpreted as a sign of guilt' (Symon 1987). Such a human reaction would in fact be more likely to promote healing in the bereaved parents and probably discourage litigation.

However, a five-year study by public health physicians of hospital clinical complaints in one region found that doctors carrying out peer review supported only one-fifth of complaints about misapplication of clinical skills and a quarter of those alleging failures in investigation or treatment, whereas three-quarters of complaints about communication were substantiated. The authors concluded, not surprisingly, that doctors were more likely to uphold complaints about communication faults in their colleagues than those about errors in clinical judgement, perhaps because they were less threatening. Complaints were regarded by some doctors as an affront to their professional standing (Donaldson and Cavanagh 1992). I believe that it is this attitude, rather than litigation risk, which prevents complainants' needs being met.

The defensive culture was both expressed and reinforced by the code of conduct of the General Medical Council: 'The Council . . . regards as capable of amounting to serious professional misconduct ... [the] depreciation by a doctor of the professional skill, knowledge, qualifications or services of another doctor or doctors' (General Medical Council 1981: 15). There was no doubt of its influence. I found that doctors and medical students who were hazy on other aspects of the code could quote that phrase. I do not know of any case where a doctor was struck off for 'disparaging' another doctor, but the profession believed it could happen, and that was enough. By 1987 the GMC allowed that a doctor could 'in good faith' express a different opinion from another doctor, but he must 'always be able to justify such an action as being in the patient's best medical interests' and the doctor now had a duty to inform an appropriate body about a doctor 'whose behaviour may have raised a question of serious professional misconduct' (General Medical Council 1987: 17).

When I became a lay member of the GMC, I tried to move a resolution to get the 'disparagement' paragraph deleted, and eventually the GMC decided to put more emphasis on 'allowing' doctors to make critical comments:

> Honest comment is entirely acceptable ... provided that it is carefully considered and can be justified, that it is offered in good faith, and that it is intended to promote the best interest of patients ... However, gratuitous and unsustainable comment which ... sets out to undermine trust in a professional colleague's knowledge or skill is unethical.
> (General Medical Council 1992: 22)

This was greeted with howls of derision when I read it out at meetings of consumer groups. Hedged about with ifs and buts, it was not surprising that doctors were chary of acting on dangerous colleagues. Not until 1991 did the Council eventually progress to:

> It is any doctor's duty, where the circumstances so warrant, to inform an appropriate person or body about a colleague whose professional conduct or fitness to practise may be called in question or whose professional performance appears to be in some way deficient.
> (General Medical Council 1991)

But the price paid by the medical whistleblower may be high.

Even if serious cases were reported to it, the GMC could only discipline those of whom serious professional misconduct could be proved 'beyond reasonable doubt' to a panel consisting mostly of doctors who often thought 'There but for the grace of God ...'. In the USA it was thought that one of the factors leading to failures of state medical boards to protect the public was the substantial burden of proof that called for 'clear and convincing evidence' rather than the 'preponderance of evidence'. Wisconsin decided that 'preponderance of evidence' would be enough. Both California and Oregon can compel a doctor to take a clinical competence examination if there is reasonable cause to believe his or her skill level is inadequate (Kusserow *et al.* 1987).

The GMC now has the additional powers it asked Parliament for to investigate doctors whose performance my be 'seriously difficult'. They will be offered retraining and may be suspended or persuaded to retire. The complainant will have no choice, and no appeal against the screener's decision to send the case into the private performance system, where he has no rights, rather than the public hearing he could have attended at the Professional Conduct Committee. There is no formal competence examination at the end of retraining; it will depend on assessment. I saw some 'seriously deficient' doctors when I sat on the Professional Conduct Committee. Many of them were not retrainable.

The procedure for seriously incompetent doctors parallels the private, protective procedures used by the GMC's Health Committee for sick doctors. It may be that this discreet procedure – which protects the reputations not only of individual doctors but also of the profession itself – may encourage worried colleagues to take action. We shall have to see. Although cases are already entering the system, there is still no decision as to what, if anything, patients will be told before they give consent to an incompetent surgeon retraining on them.

Systemic approaches to medical mishaps

After three years as PA chair, I left to do research and get a wider picture of healthcare. There were too many bodies to pull out of the water, and I needed to find out what was pushing them in upstream. Blaming individual doctors, nurses and midwives was not the answer. Why were they incompetent, or why did the system not allow them to work well? It was not just the defects of the NHS, since errors in medical care were common under other systems, and have been well documented in the United States. As Leape (1994: 14) wrote: 'Prevention of medical injury requires finding ways to prevent errors as well as developing mechanisms to protect patients from injuries when errors inevitably occur'. I buried myself in journals and textbooks, but contact with complainants and healthcare professionals has taught me more.

The first part of the problem was what we did to doctors in training. I was often asked to speak to groups of medical students. First-year clinical students were always delightful – eager, bright, open-minded, keenly interested in ethical issues. Then I progressed to third-year clinical students and found I was talking to a different species. Issues such as communication with patients, consent, and complaints received more guarded, defensive and even hostile responses. These students were already constructing their professional protective carapace. Yet after meetings at prestigious London medical schools I was quietly approached by small groups of students who asked how they could retain their empathy and idealism, because they could feel it being leached away. I would suggest finding supportive colleagues, and keeping a diary of incidents which impressed or distressed them, since with increasing familiarity they would become less noticeable.

The moral damage of medical training is not necessarily permanent. Training for general practitioners has improved immeasurably, and on many courses for trainees and trainers once again I found warmth and interest in ethical questions and individual patient care. The encouragement of mutual support among the members of the group was the crucial element. But hospital doctors were missing out. It is a midwifery, not a medical, textbook that stresses how much those who provide care need nurturing and cherishing themselves (Flint 1986).

Junior doctors at three US medical schools filled in anonymous questionnaires about errors they had made. Nearly half reported making a mistake in the past year, and most of them had had significant adverse effects on patients. The doctors had felt remorseful, angry at themselves, guilty and inadequate. Most had made some change in practice in response to their mistakes, but women were significantly more likely to make constructive changes than men. If overwork was seen as the cause of the mistake, doctors were less likely to make constructive changes. One doctor wanted more discussion with seniors so that some of the unsaid horrors experienced could be discussed and dealt with. When mistakes were discussed at conferences the tough issues were not addressed. This remark has a familiar ring and I often heard similar comments at hospital perinatal death meetings in the UK (Wu *et al.* 1991).

What was clear from the study (which I would like to see repeated here) was that young doctors needed both a sensitive response to their distress and encouragement to accept responsibility. Too often they receive neither. I suspect it is the searing experience of those early years – long hours, too much responsibility, too little support and insensitive or even humiliating teaching – which lays the foundation for self-protection and mutual defensiveness later on.

Kieran O'Driscoll, a Dublin obstetrician, instigated a policy of active management of labour, which has been widely criticized by consumer groups and some other obstetricians. I fully support the critics, but I applaud the policy he describes that junior doctors at his hospital were not involved in the decision-making process:

> Residents are cast in the role of graduate student. Most young doctors are only too relieved when this situation is frankly acknowledged because no intelligent young man or woman would wish to be placed in a false position where it is necessary to pretend a level of expertise which he/she knows he/she does not possess.
>
> (O'Driscoll and Foley 1983: 3)

I regularly review the confidential enquiries into maternal deaths and into stillbirths and infant deaths. They make depressing reading, especially as common avoidable causes keep recurring. Since judgements of how many deaths were avoidable were made from official records, and no information is sought from patients and relatives, there is likely to be an underestimate of substandard care. The latest reports once again point out that avoidable tragedies are caused by junior hospital doctors doing work beyond their level of knowledge and experience (Department of Health 1996; CESDI 1997). One of the excellent Welsh studies showed that stillbirths rose not only with holidays and weekends, but also with the arrival of a new set of house officers every six months (Perinatal Survey Unit 1996).

Junior doctors provide 'cheap' labour, but no one has fully quantified the extra costs, in terms of either money or risk. A study (Dowling and Barrett 1991) from Bristol University found worrying gaps in the direct (and indirect) medical supervision of newly qualified doctors in areas in which, because of their availability on wards, they may often take the lead medical role. The NHS was operating a system of 'junior doctor abuse'. The authors made a cogent case for a new model of clinical training and for management of wards.

I found some older doctors at the GMC complacent about the situation. 'I did it when I was young' they burbled. But in their young days an appendicectomy patient stayed in hospital for a week and a hysterectomy two weeks (Rosenthal 1987). Medical care is now more intense. With shorter hospital stays, there is a rapid turnover of very sick people who require complex investigation and coordination of monitoring and treatment. So often the tragic outcomes which appear in complaints enquiries are caused not by one terrible mistake, but by the cumulative effect of small errors – medical, nursing, organizational and administrative. As the House of Commons Select Committee which monitors the HSC work has noticed, it is only the occasional junior doctor or nurse who is disciplined. What the Committee does not say is that they were often working in a system where they were set up to fall.

The risks to patients arise not just because juniors lack experience and knowledge, but also because they are brainwashed by the macho medical ethos. They have to prove that they can cope, can take responsibility and can 'hack it'. Small wonder that young doctors strive to acquire a misleading veneer of confidence to reassure not only the patients but also themselves. Getting the consultant out of bed once too often could affect your future career. The consultant may say 'Call me if there is a problem', but some are much more callable than others. The clinical standards of one consultant were so distrusted by junior medical staff that they were reluctant to approach him when a problem arose (Donaldson 1994). As I soon found when I sat on the disciplinary panel of the Overseas Committee at the GMC, doctors from other cultures found reading the runes particularly difficult.

The culture has also decreed that once a doctor has been trained, he or she is competent unless proved otherwise, and that the clinician will naturally update knowledge and skills as required by a process of osmosis, without extra formal training or reaccreditation being required. The latest Confidential Enquiry into Stillbirths, produced by a consortium of the Royal Colleges themselves, at last admits that formal training and accreditation are needed for obstetricians, paediatricians, pathologists and midwives in basic skills such as resuscitation and interpreting fetal heart monitors (CESDI 1997). Despite mounting evidence, it has taken years for the professions, and the Royal Colleges, to admit to the problem and begin to take action. Even in our threadbare health service, new technology still seeps in, without training costs being considered and education being organized. The covering up of complaints, and the failure to sue them constructively, has prevented primary causes being addressed more quickly.

Conclusion

My plea for openness and honesty is as much for doctors to be honest with themselves and each other as with us, their patients. It is not just individual care but medicine as a whole which would benefit. In one of the most thought-provoking medical books ever written, American paediatrician William Silverman described his discovery that the most dramatic epidemic of infant blindness was being repressed in the collective consciousness of medicine because it was too painful to recall. Thousands of premature babies had lost their sight through excessive exposure to oxygen. The culture, habits and thought patterns which had caused the original problem were unchanged. It is not only individual but also collective mistakes which are suppressed.

When Silverman met grown-up victims and their families he found they had been puzzled by the conspiracy of silence. They were angry with doctors not for the original mistakes but because, after the diagnosis, doctors had become cold, distant and unsupportive (Silverman 1980: 111).

We have no hope of getting satisfactory resolution for complainants, justice for the dead and injured, or reduction of avoidable errors, until healthcare professionals can cope emotionally with their own mistakes and the mistakes of their colleagues. If they are to do this, the culture of medicine must change, as perhaps must public expectations as well. We should have more, not less, confidence in a doctor who admits to uncertainty and doubt and openly admits to having made a mistake.

References

Association for Improvements in the Maternity Services (1992) *Childbirth Care – Users' Views*, Submission to the House of Commons Health Committee 1991. Iver: AIMS.

Beech, B. (1997) Personal communication.

Bok, S. (1978) *Lying: Moral Choice in Public and Private Life*. New York: Pantheon Books.

CESDI (1997) *Confidential Enquiry into Stillbirths and Deaths in Infancy, Fourth Annual Report 1995*. London: Maternal and Child Health Research Consortium.

Department of Health (1996) *Report on Confidential Enquiries into Maternal Deaths in the United Kingdom 1991–3*. London: HMSO.

Donaldson, L. (1994) Doctors with problems in an NHS workforce, *British Medical Journal*, 308: 1277–81.

Donaldson, L. and Cavanagh, J. (1992) Clinical complaints and their handling: A time for change?, *Quality in Health Care*, 1: 21–5.

Dowling, S. and Barrett, S. (1991) *Doctors in the Making. The Experience of the Pre-registration Year*. Bristol: Department of Epidemiology and Public Health Medicine, University of Bristol.

Flint, C. (1986) *Sensitive Midwifery*. London: Heinemann.

General Medical Council (1981) *Professional Conduct and Discipline: Fitness to Practice*. London: GMC.

General Medical Council (1987) *Professional Conduct and Discipline: Fitness to Practice*. London: GMC.

General Medical Council (1991) *Professional Conduct and Discipline: Fitness to Practice*. London: GMC.

General Medical Council (1992) *Professional Conduct and Discipline: Fitness to Practice*. London: GMC.

Kusserow, R., Handley, E. and Yessian, M. (1987) An overview of state medical discipline, *Journal of the American Medical Association*, 257: 820–4.

Leape, L. (1994) The preventability of medical injury, in M.S. Bogner (ed.) *Human Error in Medicine*, Hillsdale, NJ: Lawrence Erlbaum.

O'Driscoll, K. and Foley, M. (1983) Correlation of decrease in perinatal mortality and increase in caesarean section rates, *Obstetrics and Gynecology*, 61: 1–5.

O'Shea, R. (1981) Psychophysics discovers Piaget – comments on Fraymas and Dawson, *Perception and Psychophysics*, 1981, vol. 30, no. 4: 397–8.

Perinatal Survey Unit (1996) *All Wales Perinatal Survey and Confidential Enquiry into Stillbirths and Deaths in Infancy, Annual Report 1995*. Cardiff: University of Wales College of Medicine.

Robinson, J. (1987) How to get sued: The step by step guide to increase litigation against your trust, *British Journal of Midwifery*, 5: 641.

Robinson, J. (1989) *A Patient Voice at the GMC*. London: Health Rights.

Rosenthal, M. (1987) *Dealing with Medical Malpractice: The British and Swedish Experience*. London: Tavistock.

Silverman, W. (1980) *Retrolental Fibroplasia: A Modern Parable*. New York: Grune and Stratton.

Symon, A. (1987) Improving communication: Apologies and explanations, *British Journal of Midwifery*, 5: 594–6.

Wu, A., Folkman, S., McPhee, S. and Lo, B. (1991) Do house officers learn from their mistakes? *Journal of the American Medical Association*, 265: 2089–94.

Index

Page numbers in *italic* refer to figures, *n* refers to chapter notes.

THE INCOMPETENT DOCTOR
BEHIND CLOSED DOORS

Marilynn M. Rosenthal

Based on qualitative, ethnographic research carried out in England and Sweden, this book examines a neglected area of professional self-regulation. It explores the range of informal and quasi-formal mechanisms used by doctor colleagues, health care managers and professional organizations in attempts to cope with the 'problem' or 'incompetent' doctor. Focused on Consultant Surgeons and senior General Practitioners, extensive interviews reveal a repertoire of mechanisms that include, amongst others, the 'Frank Talk', 'Protective Support', the 'Veiled Threat', being 'Forced out of the Partnership', the attempted 'Golden Handshake' and, when all else fails, 'Stalemate and Marginalization'. Each chapter includes a number of specific cases as well as extensive quotations from those interviewed. How information is gathered and assessed, the relative success or failure of these mechanisms, the factors that determine their use or non-use, medical perceptions of mistakes and the changing attitudes of the public are examined.

The book includes a discussion of current changes in the National Health Service and their likely impact on these issues and quality assurance in medical care. Some comparisons with the informal processes in Sweden provide insight into the universality of the informal mechanisms. The book ends with a proposal for a total, integrated peer review system that recognizes and strengthens the informal mechanisms and links them to systematic clinical practice analysis and other efforts that enhance the medical profession's commitment to effective self-regulation.

> Professor Rosenthal has done her job extremely well. In an area in which there are few facts and figures, and those that exist are largely held in secrecy, she has produced a clear picture of what actually is going on and we should be grateful to her.
>
> Sir Raymond Hoffenberg

Contents
The issues: why they are important – Making mistakes: how doctors think about this – Friendly efforts: the informal mechanisms – Frustration mounts: requiring 'the skill of a politician and the tact of a diplomat' – Behind closed doors: how effective are the informal mechanisms? – Empirical research on medical mishaps and mistakes: challenges to professional norms – Coming changes: will they make a difference? – References and notes – Index.

192pp   0 335 19506 7   (Paperback)   0 335 19507 5   (Hardback)